# Sermons Delivered in Times of Persecution in Scotland

GREYFRIARS' CHURCHYARD, EDINBURGH.

*ntispiece.*

DELIVERED IN

# TIMES OF PERSECUTION IN SCOTLAND

BY

## SUFFERERS FOR THE ROYAL PREROGATIVES OF JESUS CHRIST

THE ORIGINAL PREFACE BY JOHN HOWIE.

COMMEMORATION SERMON ON THE MARTYR BI-CENTENARY;

AND

BIOGRAPHICAL NOTICES OF THE AUTHORS OF THE SERMONS

By the Rev. JAMES KERR, Greenock.

With Illustrations.

EDINBURGH:

JOHNSTONE, HUNTER, & COMPANY.

MDCCCLXXX.

𝔍𝔫 𝔐𝔢𝔪𝔬𝔯𝔶 of

THOSE EMINENT SERVANTS OF GOD IN SCOTLAND

WHO, TWO HUNDRED YEARS AGO,

WERE HONOURED BY HIM TO SUFFER

FOR

𝔗𝔥𝔢 𝔕𝔬𝔶𝔞𝔩 𝔓𝔯𝔢𝔯𝔬𝔤𝔞𝔱𝔦𝔟𝔢𝔰 𝔬𝔣 𝔱𝔥𝔢 𝔏𝔬𝔯𝔡 𝔍𝔢𝔰𝔲𝔰 𝔆𝔥𝔯𝔦𝔰𝔱

AND WHO

SECURED THOSE CIVIL AND RELIGIOUS LIBERTIES

PRESENTLY ENJOYED

THROUGHOUT THE BRITISH ISLES.

1880.


PASTOR S. BOAL.

Two hundred years ago, a great conflict was being waged in Scotland. The issues involved in the conflict comprehended all that is dearest to the hopes of humanity. The Civil and Religious liberties of the people then, and of succeeding generations, were at stake. In the course of the Second Reformation, which for eleven years went steadily forward, those liberties were achieved, and by various deeds, both National and Ecclesiastical, raised to a position from which it seemed impossible for any power soon to dislodge them.

At the beginning of that Reformation, the nation arose from the dust and burst from its neck the fetters of Papal and Prelatic superstition and tyranny. On the last day of February, 1638, within the Greyfriars Churchyard, Edinburgh, noblemen, barons, gentlemen, ministers, and commoners renewed Scotland's Covenant with God, and, with uplifted hand, swore to resist "all kind of Papistry," uphold the King "in the defence of Christ, His Evangel, and liberties of our country," and "be good examples to others of all godliness, soberness, and righteousness, and of every duty we owe to God and man." Towards the close of the same year, a General Assembly of the Church—the first Free Assembly for forty years—was convened in Glasgow. Undeterred by the threats of the Sovereign, that Assembly overthrew all the innovations which Prelacy had intruded upon the Church, and restored to the Church all the attainments reached during the First Reformation, and heroically asserted her liberties under her own and only Sovereign—King Jesus.

In 1643, the three Kingdoms subscribed the Solemn League and Covenant, pledging themselves to preserve

Popery and Prelacy, superstition and profaneness, and "whatsoever shall be found to be contrary to sound doctrine and the power of godliness;" to maintain the King's Majesty in the "defence of the true religion and liberties of the kingdoms;" and all, that "we and our posterity may, as brethren, live in faith and love, and the Lord may delight to dwell in the midst of us." This document, writes Hetherington of the Solemn League, is "the noblest, in its essential nature and principles, of all that are recorded among the international transactions of the world." In execution of one of the clauses of that Covenant, the Assembly of Divines at Westminster framed subordinate standards as a basis of Ecclesiastical union and uniformity. The Nation and the Church co-operated in the most amicable relations for the consolidation of the attainments secured by these different methods. In fidelity to Christ, the Head of the Church and the King of the Nations, and in loving friendship the one toward the other, both joined hands in the work of Reformation.

A day which promised to shine brightly and endure long, then dawned upon the British Isles. The thick darkness had been driven away at the approach of the Sun of Righteousness, who arose with healing in His wings. But bright hopes were doomed to bitter disappointment. The midst of the day had been but well nigh reached when murky clouds eclipsed its brightness and thunder began to roll. Bent upon his idol of absolute authority, the Stuart sovereign, breaking audaciously the most solemn vows, employed the nation's arms to reduce to the most abject subjection the defenders of the nation's constitution and liberties. Upon the anvil of the Covenanters, with blows repeated with force ever more brutal, was the hammer of royal tyranny made to fall. Unfurling their blue banner, with its inscription in gold—"For Christ's Crown and Covenant"—the

And chased them up to heaven."

It was in those "Killing Times" that the sermons tha follow were delivered. In various ways did their author suffer because they could not consent that Christ should be robbed of His crowns, and His crowns set upon the head o an earthly despot. Many of the sermons were delivered a conventicles, while scouts were stationed to give th congregations notice should the royal troops appear. Larg is the debt due to John Howie of Lochgoin, for collecting the manuscripts and notes of hearers, and transmitting th whole, in such excellent form, to succeeding generations He has been received to a better reward than earth could bestow, and has entered into the goodly fellowship of those martyrs and other worthies, whose deeds and memories he did so much to immortalize. The present edition is a reprint, in modern and more orderly form, with but very slight alterations—and these for the most part but verbal of the first edition, dated March 19th, 1779. The new matter consists of Biographical Notices of the Authors o the Sermons, and a Sermon on the Bi-Centenary of the Covenanting Struggle. The former contains but the merest record of the principal events in the lives of the several preachers; and the latter was first delivered in the Greyfriars Churchyard, Edinburgh, on the evening o the Sabbath nearest the two hundredth anniversary of the publication of the Sanquhar Declaration. A number o illustrations, also added, will doubtless enhance the interest attaching to the volume.

The suitableness of these sermons to the present day wil be recognised at once by every diligent reader, acquainted even casually, with the signs of the times. The grea leading doctrines of the Scriptures are expounded and enforced with singular clearness, fidelity, and zeal. The

3

merit of the righteousness ——— — ——

in, the absolute necessity for the Spirit of God to apply the redemption purchased, imputed righteousness received by faith the only method of a sinner's justification, the crown-rights of Immanuel—King of Zion and King of Kings, the Divine right of Presbyterianism as the Church's form of Government, and the anti-scriptural character of Prelacy and Popery—these were the doctrines that,

> "By Cameron thundered,
> Or by Renwick poured in gentle stream,"

were blessed, by the powerful demonstration of God the Spirit, to the maintenance of true religion in the souls of men, and that, putting life into dry bones and clothing them with power, enabled them to do battle for the Lord of Hosts. And the unflinching maintenance and vigorous defence of these doctrines are now urgently demanded, in order not only that the British nation may never again yield its neck to the iron yoke of the Papacy, but that the Evangelical churches may be delivered from the Rationalism and the Ritualism which, by their present persistent invasions, threaten to deprive them of the liberty wherewith Christ hath made them free. This volume is committed to the press with the earnest hope that it may be the means of diffusing the knowledge of the grand Scriptural doctrines of the Reformation, and of reviving the spirit of those eminent men who suffered for

> "Owning Christ Supreme,
> Head of His Church, and no more crime."

GREENOCK, *November, 1880.*

## WILLIAM GUTHRIE.

### SERMONS.

## MICHAEL BRUCE.

## JOHN WELWOOD.

---

# RICHARD CAMERON.

## LECTURES AND SERMONS.

## JOHN GUTHRIE.

### SERMON.

# ILLUSTRATIONS.

## THE PIETY, PRINCIPLES, AND PATRIOTISM OF
## SCOTLAND'S COVENANTED MARTYRS;
### WITH APPLICATION TO THE PRESENT TIMES.*

---

"Thou hadst a favour unto them,"—PSALMS XLIV. 3.
"Whose faith follow" (imitate).—HEBREWS XIII. 7.

THROUGHOUT the greater part of the forty-fourth Psalm we feel the beat of the pulse of the oppressed, we hear the cry of the martyr. In the opening verses, the inspired penman recalls some of the ancient glories of his country, the memories of which had been fast sinking into the azure of the past. He recites the deeds of an Omnipotent arm for Israel in the days of old. The Amorite and the Hittite and the Anakim had been driven out of the promised land, and over Jericho and Ai and Hebron there waved the banner of victorious Israel. From Dan to Beersheba, and from Jordan to the sea, the vine from Egypt had stretched, and the chosen people of the living God were planted in their place. Great was this work of conquest; mighty this revolution in Canaan! Did Joshua and Caleb and their hosts perform it by their own arm? Did their own swords cut the alien armies in sunder? No; for "they got not the land in possession by their own sword, neither did their own arm save them; but Thy right hand, and Thine arm, and the light of Thy countenance, because Thou hadst a favour unto them." God's sovereign goodness was the originating cause, and God's almighty arm the performing agent of all.

But, having thus raised a memorial to the goodness of God to his fathers, the Psalmist proceeds to lament the evils and tribula-

* A Sermon preached in Greyfriars' Churchyard, Edinburgh, on Sabbath, 20th June, 1880, on the Bi-centenary of the Covenanting struggle; and re-delivered, by request, on Sabbath, 11th July, in the Dock Park, Dumfries; and on Sabbath, 25th July, at Renwick's Monument, Glencairn.

B

shadow of death." "Our soul is bowed down to the dust." And in the midst of these sighs he turns his face to Him who had done so great things "in the times of old," and prays fervently that He would put forth His arm and build up the broken walls. "Thou art my King, O God, command deliverances for Jacob." "Awake, why sleepest Thou, O Lord; arise, cast us not off for ever." "Arise for our help, and redeem us for Thy mercies' sake."

These words are written for our instruction, and the application of them to these covenanted lands, and especially to Scotland, is evident. For "we have heard with our ears, O God, our fathers have told us, what work Thou didst in their days, in the times of old." Two hundred years ago, a great Reformation was accomplished in this land. Ancient forms of error and superstition, mighty like Anak's giant sons, were hurled from the place of their usurped dominion. Scotland rid herself of the bonds of idolatry, and placed upon her throne King Jesus—her own Sovereign by everlasting decree. A people who entered into covenant with God were planted in the land, and truth and liberty raised their heads in triumph. Did Scotland accomplish this great Reform in her own might? Is she entitled to attribute her deliverance to any arm of flesh? Nay; for "they got not the land in possession by their own sword, neither did their own arm save them; but Thy right hand, and Thine arm, and the light of Thy countenance, because Thou hadst a favour unto them." God's free favour and mighty power were the cause of all. And when we consider present defections from the lofty Scriptural attainments of the past, the general disregard of the claims of the King of Nations, the many and determined assaults upon the foundations of Christianity, and the low state of practical religion, every lover of Christ and of his country may well sorrow with the sorrowing Psalmist, and pray the prayers he prayed. "Wherefore hidest Thou Thy face; . . . for our soul is bowed down to the dust: . . . arise for our help, and redeem us for Thy mercies' sake."

A little before he pens our selection from the Hebrews, the sacred writer has been presenting a list of some of the Worthies

others. And we may well believe that when he calls upon the Hebrews to follow the faith of "those who have the rule over you," he had not forgotten the list of the heroes of the faith which he had been enumerating. Admiration of those eminent saints was not enough: the noblest eulogies upon their personal character and public deeds would be of little account. Something more was desired; something better was necessary. "Whose faith follow." Let admiration pass forth into imitation. Be like them in faith, in self-denial, in holiness, in constancy, in the high heroism of battling for God. If that list of faith's nobles were continued by some inspired hand till the present times, there would doubtless appear in it the names of those who, two centuries ago, "for Christ's royal truth and laws, and Scotland's Covenanted Reformation," jeoparded their lives in the high places of the field. By faith the Marquis of Argyle esteemed the reproach of Christ greater riches than all the honours of his high rank, for he had respect unto the recompense of the reward. By faith Richard Cameron and his compatriots nailed their Declaration to the Cross of Sanquhar, not fearing the wrath of the King, for they endured as seeing Him who is Invisible. By faith Margaret M'Lachlan and Margaret Wilson beheld with composure, as they were tied to the stake, the rising of the waters that were to engulf them, for they judged Him faithful that had promised. And what shall we more say, for time would fail us to tell of Donald Cargill, and of Hugh M'Kail, and of John Brown, and of David Hackston, and of James Renwick, who "through faith subdued kingdoms, waxed valiant in fight, turned to flight the armies of the aliens; they were stoned, were slain with the sword, being destitute, afflicted, tormented; of whom the world was not worthy."

But mere admiration of these heroes is not sufficient in the way of commemoration. The most eloquent eulogies upon their character and exploits will fail to form a sufficient tribute to their memory. It is not enough though our hearts were melted at the recital of their sufferings, and though we were moved to tears as we look upon the place where reposes their hallowed dust. Our aims in the

oulders of the men of this generation. It should be ours to
new our acquaintance with and redouble our efforts for the
tension of the knowledge of those everlasting doctrines for which
ey contended to the death. It should be ours to pray and
our to induce these covenanted nations to lift up the banner for
e supremacy of King Jesus, under which the martyred band
nt forward, and to unfurl every fold of it to the breeze. It
ould be ours to awaken the whole people to a sense of present
ngers and present duties that, with united hearts as with one
art, we might give Jehovah no rest till His Anointed and
ppointed King should be brought back again to Britain, and till
ry greater than ever should have her habitation in the land.
us would be the noblest tribute we could render to the memory
Scotland's Covenanted Martyrs; this a more appropriate and
sting memorial than forests of monumental pillars of marble; this
e finest chaplet we could wreathe around their tomb. Let our
miration of the martyrs include our adoption of their testimony;
our commemoration of their struggle include the unflinching
intenance by us of the Scriptural principles which made that
ruggle glorious. So shall we escape the withering curse of our
rd upon the pretended admirers of the martyrs of old :—"Woe
to you, Scribes and Pharisees, hypocrites! because ye build the
mbs of the Prophets, and garnish the sepulchres of the righteous,
d say, If we had been in the days of our fathers, we would not
ve been partakers with them in the blood of the Prophets.
herefore ye be witnesses unto yourselves, that ye are the
ildren of them which have killed the Prophets."

I. SCOTLAND'S COVENANTED MARTYRS WERE CHRISTIANS OF
   EMINENT PIETY. They were eminently pious because "Thou
   hadst a favour unto them." That piety we are to imitate.

When they look back to the Reformers and Martyrs, people in
neral direct their attention more particularly to the attitude
sumed by those men as public witnesses and national bene-

Cameron the undaunted opponent of tyranny than of Richard Cameron the man of prayer; of James Renwick the public heroic sufferer than James Renwick the saint. Yet, this is as if we should admire more. the streams than the fountain; as if we should concentrate our attention upon the light to the exclusion of the sun whence it emanates. The streams that irrigate the waste and make the desert blossom as the rose flow from the fountain; the light that dispels the darkness and floods the world with glory, comes from the great luminary of the day. The reformers and martyrs succeeded in beautifying the moral wilderness with righteousness and filling the nations with light, because of the purity of their soul and the heavenly light that shone in their understanding—that fountain of purity within being supplied from the river of water of life, clear as crystal, coming from the throne, and that light emanating from the uncreated Sun of Righteousness that had arisen upon them with healing in His wings. Yes, the reformers and martyrs were social regenerators because they were regenerate men; they were eminent sufferers because they were eminent Christians; they were illustrious reformers because they were illustrious saints. But for their piety, the Reformation and the subsequent valiant struggle in its defence never would have been accomplished.

The martyrs were Christians of great piety because they were Christians of strong faith. Their faith was the root of their piety, and by that faith they were unmoved. They had a personal interest in the Saviour of sinners; rested on Christ alone for Salvation, and believed in Him. They were not men of weak faith; they were men of mighty faith. Had their faith been weak, they would have failed before the difficulties that confronted them, they would have bowed their heads, like the willows, before the blasts that swept around them. They trusted God much, and God strengthened them mightily. He set their feet on a rock and established their goings. By faith they resisted every shock of their many and mighty adversaries, as the rock in the ocean breasts the giant billows and dashes them back in foam. They were pavilioned in the tent of the Lord of Hosts, and they feared not

a, there was exceeding peace and joy. Trusting in the Lord·
d compassed by the Angel of the Lord, they felt that their
arts were safe. Their foes might be successful in their assaults
on the outer defences—they might tear their bodies in pieces and·
ample them in the dust, but upon their souls no injury could be·
flicted. Impregnable was the citadel of their souls. They were
stled within the everlasting covenant; fortressed by Almighty
d.

> "He that doth in the secret place
> Of the Most High reside;
> Under the shade of Him that is
> The Almighty shall abide."

Within that fortress they had every comfort; they laid their
ads on a soft and downy pillow.

> "His feathers shall thee hide, thy trust
> Under His wings shall be;
> His faithfulness shall be a shield
> And buckler unto thee."

I do not say I am free of sin," said old Donald Cargill at the
affold, "but I am at peace with God through a slain Mediator.
bless the Lord that these thirty years and more I have been at
ace with God, and was never shaken loose of it; and now I am
sure of my interest in Christ and peace with God, as all within
is Bible and the Spirit of God can make me. And now this is
e sweetest and most glorious day that ever my eyes did see."
What do I see," said Margaret Wilson to her murderers, as
ey pointed her to the waters closing over Margaret M'Lachlan,
r companion in tribulation, "What do I see but Christ
ruggling there? Think ye that we are the sufferers? No, it is
hrist in us, for He sends none a warfare on their own charges."

> "Tyrants! could not misfortune teach
> That man had rights beyond your reach?
> Thought ye the torture and the stake
> Could that intrepid spirit break,

consecration to His service. Theirs was a love which cruel mockings could not damp; a love which the boot that made the white marrow swim in purple gore could not abate; a love which the swelling waters could not drown; a love which the scaffold could not expel; a love which, by the faggots and the fire, was fanned into a brighter flame. For, many waters cannot quench love, neither can the floods drown it. Though a man were to give all the substance of his house for love, it would utterly be contemned. The martyrs felt they were redeemed men; redeemed by the most glorious person in the universe—the mighty God; redeemed at an enormous price—not with corruptible things, as silver and gold, but with the precious blood of Christ, as of a Lamb without blemish and without spot; redeemed from the most degraded and most dreadful of all conditions—from sin and all its dread everlasting consequences; redeemed to the possession of an undefiled and unfading inheritance for ever; redeemed perfectly, for by one offering He hath perfected for ever all them that are sanctified; and redeemed wholly—soul, body, and spirit redeemed. A sense of being thus redeemed enabled the martyrs to stand forth in heaven's own majesty. How shall they make some return to Him who, by His unparalleled sufferings for them, has laid them under such an insolvent debt of gratitude? They will make a total surrender of themselves to Him who gave Himself wholly for them. They will consent, yea, they will count it all joy to be laid on the altar of sacrifice in love to Him who by the cords of His own everlasting love bound Himself on the cross of Calvary for them. What cared they for the shame of their sufferings? They are ready to be esteemed the offscouring of all things for the sake of Him who for them was exposed to shame and spitting, and became a curse. Calvary to Christ was more glorious than his throne to Cæsar, and the Grassmarket of Edinburgh was more glorious to the martyrs than the frowning castle or gorgeous palace to its Stuart owner. Jesus transformed the shame of His sufferings into glory, so that the offence of the cross has for ever ceased; and the shame around the scaffolds of the martyrs has been transformed likewise into pre-eminent

of execution. But the blasphemous sneer has been transfigured into glory, and Jehovah has encircled the names and memories of the sufferers with imperishable renown. Love, consuming love; consecration, entire consecration. "I am one of Christ's," said Margaret Wilson, as they tempted her to recant, "I am one of Christ's, let me go. I think my life little enough in the quarrel of owning my Lord and Master's sweet truth, for He hath freed me from everlasting wrath, and redeemed me." "I take God to witness," said James Guthrie as he stood upon the ladder, "that I would not exchange this scaffold with the palace or the mitre of the greatest prelate in Britain."

And what shall I more say of the elements of their eminent piety? What of their peace—that peace that passeth all understanding, and fortifies the heart and mind in Christ Jesus? "I go up this ladder," said M'Kail, "with as little fear as I go to my father's house. Every step is a degree nearer heaven." What of their hope—that hope that is as an anchor of the soul sure and steadfast, entering into that that is within the veil? "This is the day," said Richard Cameron on the morning of Ayrsmoss, "This is the day we shall get the crown." "Oh, how can I contain this!" said James Renwick, "to be within a few hours of glory." What of their joy—that joy that is unspeakable, and full of glory? "I hear the voice," said Marion Harvie as she came out of the Tolbooth for execution, "I hear the voice of my Beloved, saying unto me, 'Rise up, my love, my fair one, and come away?'" What of their meekness, their patience, their holiness, their brotherly love, their fidelity, their fortitude? All these fruits of the Spirit they bore plenteously. And, of their whole piety, Jesus was the Author and Finisher.

Doubtless the piety of the martyrs was rendered more sterling, and shone forth more brilliantly, by reason of the afflictions wherewith they were afflicted. Trees of righteousness, they were pruned that they might bring forth more fruit; jewels of gold they were put into the furnace—heated seven times—that the pearls of their graces might sparkle by the fiery trial. He who sat as the Refiner and Purifier brought out more clearly His own image upon them.

"And a seraph unfolded the door bright and shining,
All dazzling like gold of the seventh refining :
And the souls that had come out of great tribulation,
They mounted the chariots and steeds of salvation.

"On the arch of the rainbow the chariot is gliding,
Through the path of the thunder the horsemen are riding ;
Glide swiftly, bright spirits, the prize is before you,
A crown never fading, a kingdom of glory."

The piety of the martyrs was eminent, because it rested on right foundations—on the doctrines of the Book of Inspiration. It rested, not on the rubbish of self-righteousness, nor on the sand of self-will, but upon the everlasting rock of revealed truth. Those eminent saints believed in the great doctrines of election—sovereign, absolute; predestination; the total depravity of human nature by the fall ; the substitution of Christ in the room of sinners; regeneration by the Spirit alone; justification by faith alone in the righteousness of the Lord Jesus Christ; the perseverance of the saints; an eternal hell; and an eternal heaven. The martyrs' piety had its roots in the everlasting Covenant, and drew its inspiration from the everlasting God. The doctrine of sovereign grace—of God all in all in the plan, execution, and application of redemption, was the soil on which their piety flourished—the doctrine of Knox; of Luther; of Augustine; of Paul; of Him who came from the Father's bosom to reveal the Father's will, for, said He; "No man can come to Me except the Father which hath sent Me, draw him." By reason of their belief in these doctrines, the martyrs cast forth their roots as Lebanon and stood forth majestic as the cedars — because "Thou hadst a favour unto them."

"Whose faith follow." Whose piety imitate. Several Christian denominations contest with each other the honour of the ecclesiastical representation of the reformers and martyrs. They eagerly claim to be their faithful followers and the true representatives of the Church of the Reformation and the times of Persecution. Is the contention so strong to be regarded as the representatives, l adherents of their principles? Is there not reason to call upon hristians to be imitators of the martyrs in their faith in, and ve for Christ, in their self-denial, and entire consecration to the rvice of Christ? Why attempt to create a divorce between iitation of the martyrs as to the maintenance of their principles id imitation of the martyrs in their piety. The Lord's hand not shortened that it cannot save, nor His ear heavy that it innot hear. Ye are not straitened in God, ye are straitened in ourselves. Though our martyred fathers are no more, the God our fathers liveth. He is from everlasting to everlasting God. he Saviour of the martyrs is still a willing and Almighty Saviour; id, as an ambassador of the Lord of Hosts having the ministry of conciliation, we offer you that Saviour and all the benefits pur- iased by the sacrifice of Himself. Whosoever will, let him take the water of life freely. We offer you the salvation in which ie martyrs rejoiced; the Saviour whom they loved; the God in hom they gloried. If you would maintain the martyrs' principles, elieve in and love the martyrs' God. Oh, for a baptism of the Holy host upon all the people in these lands! Oh, that the God of Cameron nd Cargill and Renwick would cause His saving and enlighten ig influences to descend in rich abundance, that multitudes would iy, "I am the Lord's," and would "subscribe with their hand to he Lord, and surname themselves with the name of Israel." The trength of Britain this day is not in her armies nor her ironclads, ut in those who are the disciples of Christ. "Ye are the salt of he earth." "The holy seed is the substance thereof." Would that he number of these were greater! The work of national reforma- ion, at present loudly demanded, requires men of faith, self-denial, ioliness, piety—men in whose souls, as in the souls of reformers wo hundred years ago, runs deep and strong the current of verlasting life; men who are firmly rooted in the everlasting ovenant; men who draw their power from Jacob's mighty God. They that trust in the Lord shall be strong and do exploits." The Spirit of the Lord came upon Gideon and he blew a trumpet, nd all Abiezer was gathered after him." "Whose faith follow, onsidering the end of their conversation, Jesus Christ, the same esterday, and to-day, and for ever."

so because "Thou hadst a favour unto them." In these views
and sympathies let us imitate them.

The work to which the Scottish Reformers were called, was a
great work. Mountains of ecclesiastical and civil opposition to
the claims of Christ, the universal and only Monarch, had to be
levelled; and the people required to be lifted up from the depths of
ignorance and superstition. How are the reformers to bring down
these mountains, elevate these valleys, and prepare the way of
the Lord? How can they pull down the principalities and powers
and spiritual wickednesses in high places? How arouse the multitude from their deep sleep, and possess them with those liberties
to which they had been perfect strangers? Where are the weapons
for this mighty moral warfare? A perfect armour is provided:
it is the Word of the living God. This is the rod of strength;
this the hammer to break the rock; this the sharp two-edged
sword. By means of this the Reformers are destined to level the
mountains and elevate the valleys. And by means of it they
moved Scotland and brought it to the feet of King Jesus. Jehovah
ordained strength out of the mouth of babes and sucklings, that
He might still the enemy and the avenger. "For they got not the
land in possession by their own sword, neither did their own arm
save them; but Thy right hand, and Thine arm, and the light of
Thy countenance, because Thou hadst a favour unto them."

The great and leading doctrine then, and the doctrine that
underlay all the other doctrines for which the Reformers contended
and the martyrs died, was the Supremacy of the Scriptures as the
Word of God—the Scriptures, the whole Scriptures, and nothing
but the Scriptures. In all matters of faith and duty, the Word
of God was their court of appeal, and God, speaking in His Word,
was their sole Judge of appeal. The Word of God was to them the
supreme, and alone infallible standard. The question with them
was not, What saith popular taste? or, What saith convenience?
or, What saith tradition?—but, What saith the Word of God?
"I'll hear what God the Lord will speak." That Word of God
was above Protestant minister; above Papal priest; above

nfallible; above Assemblies, however learned and godly; above Jabinets, and Commons, and Lords; above Sovereigns and Emperors. In the re-erection in Scotland, two hundred years ago, rom its ruins of the Zion of the Holy One of Israel, this doctrine f the Supreme authority of the Scriptures was the foundation tone: adopted and applied, it elevated the Church and nation to noral majesty. It was the boast of the builders that they took heir pattern "not from Rome, not even from Geneva, but from he blessed Word of God."

In those Scriptures, the Reformers found a doctrine that was f special importance in the accomplishment of their Herculean abour. It was the doctrine of the Exclusive Headship of the Lord 'esus Christ over the Church. As they searched the Word, this recious truth was ever flashing before their eyes. Jesus Christ vas appointed King in the Church by the Father's everlasting lecree; He was anointed to be the Church's King; He laid down His life for the Church, so securing a right to reign over her; and vhen His work on earth was done, and He returned to the father, He was formally invested with this exclusive control. 'or the suffering of death, He was crowned with glory and honour. This royal prerogative of Headship over the Church, which lelongs exclusively to the enthroned Messiah, must not be usurped. To claim or exercise this prerogative is blasphemy, vhether it be by priest or presbyter, premier or potentate, or by ny other person or power whatever. The Church, having Christ for er own and only Lord, must call no man master. She possesses n independent jurisdiction under her King and Lawgiver, and in he exercise of that jurisdiction she is required and entitled to be ree. As Christ's spiritual kingdom, she must not submit that he prerogative of her King be invaded, nor permit any to wrest rom her the liberties with which her King has endowed her. In he First Reformation, this precious doctrine was vindicated loriously by the liberation of the Church from Papal domination; n the Second Reformation it was vindicated yet more gloriously y the liberation of the Church from prelatic domination. At the leginning of the Second Reformation and against the attempts of he reigning monarch to invade the prerogative of King Jesus and

able. Refusing to comply with the behests or be deterred by the threats of the King's Commissioner, the Assembly proceeded to annul all the acts of the corrupt assemblies by which Prelacy had been introduced; to set aside the infamous Five Articles of Perth; to abolish the Book of Canons, the Liturgy, and Book of Ordination; to condemn Diocesan Episcopacy, or Prelacy, passing an act that "all Episcopacy different from that of a pastor over a particular flock was abjured in this Kirk, and to be removed out of it;" to restore those constitutional rights and liberties by Sessions, Synods, and Assemblies, of which they had been deprived by Prelatic usurpation; and by other similar Scriptural measures to maintain the honour of King Jesus and the independence of His kingdom. It mattered not that upon that Assembly the royal countenance frowned while the light of God's countenance shone; for their noble work was not accomplished by their own arm, but by "Thy right hand, and Thine arm, and the light of Thy countenance, because Thou hadst a favour unto them." The words of Alexander Henderson, the able Moderator of that noble Assembly, when bringing the proceedings to a close, merit a lasting memorial:— "We have now cast down the walls of this modern Jericho; let him that re-buildeth them beware of the curse of Hiel the Bethelite." That Assembly of 1638 was, in short, the very Bannockburn of the Church's spiritual freedom.

It will be evident from this reference to the work of the Glasgow Assembly, that the Reformers maintained that the form of Church Government laid down in the Scriptures, and sanctioned by the Church's King, was Presbyterian. Their principle here was this:—The Presbyterian form of Church Government is the only form prescribed in the Bible, and therefore of Divine right and original. They did not suppose that several distinct and differing forms of government were to be found in this infallible standard, and that Christians were at liberty to select the form that would best suit their taste or convenience. If it were so, there would be some good reason to argue that the Head of the Church, who is also the Author of the Scriptures, did not know or did not care to reveal the form of government that might best promote the Church's highest interests. But the Reformers and Martyrs had not so

ciples of Presbyterianism, and nowhere could they find a warrant for Independency or Episcopacy. Hence, they valiantly contended for the former and resisted the latter to the utmost, realizing that the honour of their King and the rights of His subjects were involved in the struggle.

Moreover, the Reformers brought themselves into complete subjection to the Scriptures as to its directions affecting worship in the Church. Hence they removed all rites and ceremonies therein that were opposed to the prescriptions of the Word, or for which no Scriptural warrant could be produced. This was following out the Supremacy of the Scriptures and the Headship of Christ to one of their last and grandest conclusions. It was like the lopping off of the topmost boughs of papal superstition and ecclesiastical corruption. It was the erection of the headstone of the corner, and the ornamentation of the ecclesiastical structure. The Reformers of the First Reformation grasped this principle tenaciously and applied it with much thoroughness. John Knox enunciated this principle in such words as these:—"It becomes the Kirk of Jesus Christ to admit what He speaketh, and when He maketh end of speaking or lawgiving there to rest. All worshipping, honouring, or service invented by the brain of man in the worship of God without His own express commandment is idolatry." So said all the Reformers. By this principle Knox and his co-Reformers wiped away all the Christ-dishonouring ceremonies of the Church of Rome. And by the still more thorough application of it in the Second Reformation, when, by its unauthorized rites, Episcopacy still marred the Church's beauty, Henderson and his co-Reformers loosed the Church from these bands of her neck, and arrayed her in the beautiful garments her King had prescribed for her. The simplicity of the Church's worship is her special adornment. It would have been well had the English Reformers risen to the same high platform of principle, but they conceded to the Church a power to decree rites and ceremonies, and because of this, to a large extent, the English Church to-day is a productive recruiting ground for Rome. The Reformation in Scotland was a "root and branch Reformation." "It is not brick nor clay," said Rutherford, "nor Babel's cursed

Out of these enlarged views of doctrine and duty arose that catholicity of spirit and those broad sympathies which were such prominent characteristics of the Reformers and Martyrs. They mourned over the evils of the Church and land in their times. They longed for the salvation of souls, and laboured to bring men to the feet of Jesus. They concerned themselves with the public weal, and devoted themselves to the good of all. Intensely did they love the Church which their own Saviour had purchased, and their own King ruled. "If I forget thee, O Jerusalem, let my right hand forget her cunning; let the tongue cleave to the roof of my mouth, if I prefer not Jerusalem above my chief joy." Earnestly did they labour to secure union and uniformity in doctrine, discipline, worship, and government, among professing Christians. Their union aims embraced not the people of Scotland only, but those of the three kingdoms. "We do welcome," said Rutherford, "England and Ireland to our Well-Beloved." "Oh, when," said Renwick, "shall those be agreed on earth that are agreed in heaven. Methinks if the shedding of my blood would effect this, I would count it a small sacrifice for so great an object."

By these doctrines, then, the desolated temple of the Church of Christ was raised up in Scotland two hundred years ago. Zion "looked forth as the morning, fair as the moon, clear as the sun, and terrible as an army with banners."

> "How fair the daughter of Jerusalem then?
> How gloriously from Zion hill she looked,
> Clothed with the sun, and in her train the moon,
> And on her head a coronet of stars;
> And girdling round her waist, with heavenly grace,
> The bow of mercy bright, and in her hand
> Emmanuel's cross, her sceptre and her hope."

> "Walk about Zion and go round,
> The high towers thereof tell;
> Consider ye her palaces,
> And mark her bulwarks well."

But the Church of Christ was not to be left long in the peaceful possession of the rights and liberties which she had succeeded in achieving. The restoration of Charles Stuart in 1660 was the

mined tyrannical attempt was made to raze even to its foundations the Reformed Protestant Presbyterian Covenanted Church of Scotland. The vineyard of the Lord of Hosts was to be a vineyard of red wine. The king is resolved to reduce the Church to subjection to his absolute will—overturning her liberties and dethroning her King. The question in contention was this—Shall King Charles reign in the house of King Jesus; or shall King Jesus reign in His own house? The call to battle sounded: Who is on the Lord's side? Who? A devoted band of Covenanters fearlessly responded, "Thine are we, David; and on Thy side, thou Son of Jesse." King Charles, supported by the whole civil power, said, "I shall reign in Christ's house." "Nay," said the Covenanters, "thou shalt not, neither shall any arm of flesh; but King Jesus shall reign in His own house." And then

"Their blood about Jerusalem
Like water they did shed,
And there was none to bury them
When they were slain and dead.

"For these are they that Jacob have
Devoured cruelly,
And they his habitation
Have caused waste to lie."

By the standard that had been erected, God's faithful servants stood; stood with their faces to the foe; stood without flinching; stood to be hewn down even to the last man. They stood for the Supreme Authority of the Holy Scriptures; for the Exclusive Headship of the Lord Jesus over the Church; for the Church's independent spiritual jurisdiction and power; for the Divine right of Presbytery; for the purity of worship in the Church and the Church's freedom from all unauthorized rites and ceremonies. They stood for every pin of the tabernacle, for every item of truth to which they had attained. The bush burned with fire, but the bush was not consumed. The "course of the ship of glory was traced by the white sheen of sufferings left on the sea of time." The persecuted did hang their harps on the willows and wept, as they thought on Zion—tears now as they cease from their former joys. On one occasion, as their persecutors, hunting for them,

finding expression in the Old Testament prayer—"O Lord, Thy holy cities are a wilderness, Zion is a wilderness; Jerusalem is a desolation: behold, we beseech Thee, visit Zion in Thy mercy bring her out of the deep waters." Assuredly it was "Thy right hand and Thine arm and the light of Thy countenance" sustained and cheered them "because Thou hadst a favour unto them."

"Whose faith follow." Let us embrace those doctrines affecting the Church's existence, privileges, and prosperity, for which the martyrs suffered, and let us imitate their fidelity to the high attainments of a preceding period. The great Scriptural doctrines for which they were honoured to contend and which constituted the Church's glory, are still more or less lightly esteemed by even many professing Christians and ecclesiastical denominations. The past two hundred years have not witnessed so daring an assault as have the present times upon the infallible truth and supreme authority of the Scriptures—this daring assault too being made within churches reputedly orthodox, and by men who have subscribed the Westminster Standards, and have never repudiated that subscription. Many have discovered a new standard of theology and religion in this enlightened century. This new standard is nothing less than the "human" or "Christian consciousness"—a standard sufficiently elastic for a loose generation, and by which every man becomes a standard and law unto himself. A wave of Biblical criticism, very unlike the wave that came from Geneva in the days of Luther, has passed from the Continent to this land, and some men of theological standing are being whirled within its eddies. The theology of Naturalism and Rationalism is taking the place of the theology of Revelation—the only true theology. A blow at the inspiration and infallibity of the Scriptures is a blow at the foundation. Arising out of this, that central doctrine of the Gospel of Salvation—the substitution of Christ for sinners—is ignored or denied by not a few prominent leaders in some of the evangelical Churches, and Arminianism is making rapid strides to popularity. Dishonour is done to the royal prerogative of Christ as Zion's King by those Churches that appeal to or base their claim of rights upon the Revolution Settlement—a Settlement that proceeded upon Erastian principles,

c

dishonour is intensified by the appeal of the same Churches to the Act of Union, by which provision was made for the national support of that Prelacy against which the Covenanters fought, and fighting fell. The doctrine of Christ's Exclusive Headship over His own Church, and of the freedom of the Church, under her exclusive Head, requires to be vindicated and testified for against all modern departures therefrom. There is need to maintain and propagate the doctrine of the Divine right of the Presbyterian form of Church government, for at the present time only two of the Churches—and these among the smallest—hold this doctrine in all its Scriptural completeness. There is need to maintain the high scriptural doctrine concerning the modes of worship in the Church, that no rite or ceremony is to be introduced into the forms of worship for which an express prescription, direct or indirect, cannot be produced from God's Own Word. The additions to the Church's worship of forms of human invention, and called for in order to the gratification of mere religious fashion, constitute one of the saddest signs of the present time. "As though God had been defective," as Charnock writes with reference to such innovators, "in providing for His own honour in His institutions, and modelling His own service, but stood in need of our directions and the *caprichios* of our brains. In this they do not seem to climb above God, yet they set themselves on the throne of God, and would grasp one end of His sceptre in their own hands. They do not attempt to take the crown from God's head but discover a bold ambition to shuffle their hairy scalps under it, and wear part of it upon their own." By the unflinching maintenance and profession of these doctrines, then, we are to prove ourselves the legitimate descendants of Scotland's Covenanted Martyrs. This duty may draw down upon us reproach and shame, but, as the doctrines are Scriptural, the shame, like that of the martyrs, is transformed into glory. These doctrines are not now popular nor fashionable; still they are in advance of this age and prevailing ecclesiastical opinions, and they shall be popular and fashionable in the Church everywhere when "God shall help her, and that at the breaking of the morning." They shall have a resurrection with power, when Zion shall be set upon

wave upon the battlements of the Millennial Church of Jesus.
"O thou afflicted, tossed with the tempest, and not comforted;
behold, I will lay thy stones with fair colours, and thy foundations
with sapphires; I will make thy windows of agates, and thy gates
of carbuncles, and all thy borders of pleasant stones."

> "When Zion by the Mighty Lord,
> Built up again shall be,
> In glory then and majesty,
> To men appear shall He."

III.—Scotland's Covenanted Martyrs were Patriots of
Distinguished Loyalty. They were so because "Thou
hadst a favour unto them." Let us imitate their distinguished loyalty.

We meet to-day to commemorate those who refused to acknowledge or swear allegiance to the king that ruled them—to commemorate those who died as rebels at the hands of the State; and
the claim now put forward on their behalf is that they were
patriots of pre-eminent loyalty. How can this be? Ah! as the
scar upon the wounded soldier who had been fighting for the
liberties of his native land against a ruthless invader is pointed to
as a mark of honour, so this scar of "rebellion" upon those who
were slain in fighting the battles of the Lord of Hosts is a mark
of the noblest valour—a badge of everlasting fame. Were the
three Hebrews unpatriotic when they refused to bow before the
image set up by Nebuchadnezzar on the plain of Dura! Were
the Apostles unpatriotic though they did teach things contrary to
the decrees of Cæsar, saying there was "another King, one Jesus?"
Was Jesus unpatriotic though charged with being a mover of
sedition, and condemned to be crucified because His claims were
irreconcilable with the claims of Cæsar? Nay, verily. True
patriotism, Christian patriotism, may require of subjects the most
resolute opposition to the claims of their sovereign and the civil
constitutions and principles of administration under which they
live. True patriotism may even demand of the people the duty

onour had the Scottish martyrs of two centuries ago. They ould not and would not acknowledge the authority of a king who vas bent upon the complete subversion of the Christian constitu ion, which the nation had framed for itself; who claimed the ight to interfere with the Church in the exercise of her rights, ind make her the abject slave of his own absolute will; and who ised his authority by the rack, the gibbet, and the stake, to xtinguish every spark of liberty in his subjects, and compel hem to render obedience to his tyrannical demands. While nany were found to flatter their royal master and play the part of cowardly sycophants, the Covenanters could not see the best liberties of the land crushed out, nor the royal prerogatives of King Jesus blasphemed, and fearlessly they repudiated the authority and sought the dethronement of the royal tyrant. Patriots they, stern and unbending, when, patriotism forgotten, the many became the fawning minions of a lawless sovereign.

> "Their names shall nerve a patriot's hand,
> Upraised to save a sinking land;
> And piety shall learn to burn,
> With holier transports o'er their urn."

In the Scriptures the Reformers and Martyrs found the doctrine of the Headship of Christ over the nations. Christ was "King of kings, and Lord of lords;" He was the "Governor among the nations;" He was "Head over all things to the Church, which is His body;" He was exalted and made Head over all "princi palities, and power, and might, and dominion." And they found many exhortations addressed to kings and their nations to serve Christ and His Church; denunciations of the wrath of the King of nations if these exhortations should be despised, and promises of a time to come when nations should assemble to serve the Lord. In fact, these two doctrines—Christ's Headship over the Church, and His Headship over the Nations—were the two massive pillars upon which was built up the whole ecclesiastical and political structure of the Covenanted Reformation. These two doctrines our fathers comprehended under the phrase—the Supremacy of Christ; and

was, "Let King Jesus reign." They were quite as much under obligation to accept, apply, and contend for the one as for the other—for the Headship of Christ over the nation, and the duty of the nation to their King, as for the Headship of Christ over the Church, and the duty of the Church to her King. Both doctrines they found in the Word of God, and it was at their everlasting peril if they shut either of the doctrines out of their heart, or narrowed their profession so as to exclude them. Like honest, god-fearing men, they unhesitatingly embraced both, and boldly endeavoured to carry both out to all their legitimate issues. Our Covenanted fathers held a high view of magistracy. They did not believe that rulers were to be the mere representatives of the people, and that in their legislation they should consult only, and be guided by, the people's will. That notion of magistracy, a popular one just now, would bring it down to a low level indeed, and deprive the ruler of that independence and dignity that he ought to display in the fulfilment of his office. To the ruler, the voice of the people is not to be the voice of God. In his high station, the ruler is to be guided by the will of God, and he is to use the extensive influences with which his very office invests him, to lead the people he represents to the throne of the great Potentate whose subject the ruler himself is. Nor did our fathers for a moment imagine that any king of earth should entertain the slightest jealousy toward the King of kings. In their view, there was not the most remote approach to antagonism between the claims of the Governor among the nations, and the lawful claims and rights of any sovereign in the world. Nay, there was a grand harmony between the claims of both. The recognition of the claims of Christ by any king would cause his throne to rest on immovable foundations, and diffuse peace and prosperity throughout the nation he ruled. Such a king would not lower his royal dignity, but exalt it; he would not degrade his throne but encircle it with an amaranthine crown of glory. And the kingdom ruled, as wrote a God-serving king, by the spirit of "Inspiration," would be "as the light of the morning when the sun riseth, a morning without clouds, and as the tender grass springing out of the earth by clear shining after the rain."

They felt that these titles set forth, in part, Christ's royal prerogatives and claims, and that kings and their kingdoms should hear and obey. From those titles they justly drew such inferences as these :—That kings and nations, in their official and national character, should recognize by formal declarations the great Sovereign, King Jesus, that reigned over them; that they should frame their constitutions and enact their laws in obedience to that Sovereign, taking His Word as their great Statute Book; that those only should be chosen to rule in a Christian nation who were fearers of God, and resolved in their office of rule to honour Messiah, and that the avowed enemies of God and His Anointed should be excluded from the throne and from all legislative power; that kings should exert their high authority for the removal of all impediments to the progress of Christianity, and should contribute toward the extension of the Church of Christ in the world. While the State should reserve to itself its own independent civil jurisdiction and the Church her own independent spiritual jurisdiction, yet both powers should co-operate for their mutual benefit, and should strengthen one another's hands—the one in subjection to Christ's Headship over the Nations, and the other in subjection to Christ's Headship over the Church—for the establishment, by the willing recognition of the whole nation, individually and collectively, of the universal Mediatorial Supremacy of the Lord Jesus Christ. The Reformers and Martyrs were not Erastians, for they were ever struggling against the invasions of royalty upon the Church's liberties. Neither were they Voluntaries, for there was not one of them that ever broached the modern error that the "State has nothing to do with religion, and religion nothing to do with the State;" or, as Principal Cunningham defines it, that "the only relation that ought to subsist between Church and State —between the civil government and religion—is that of entire separation." If Voluntaryism be right, then all these titles of Christ mean nothing, and all the exhortations to kings and nations in Scripture with respect to Christ and His cause and Church are mere sounds. If Voluntaryism be right, then one of the principalities and powers of the earth is set loose from the dominion of the Mediator. Christ is not universal Monarch, but is shorn of

clear of the Charybdis of Voluntaryism. They laboured, indeed, to liberate religion from State patronage and control, but they never for a moment dreamt of liberating the State from the control of the enthroned Messiah, and of yielding up the nation to an Atheistic license. Had they not done the latter they would have been Erastians of the Erastians; for what is Voluntaryism but an Erastianism of the most Christless kind? Does not Voluntaryism claim to *control* religion *out* of all national action and offices? Does it not *compel* Christ to stand outside the National School—to stand outside the Halls of Legislature—to stand away from the Throne and Constitution? It will not grant Christ the universal right He claims to rule over all; nor Christianity the unlimited liberty it is infinitely worthy to receive. And is that not an Erastianism of the deepest dye? If Voluntaryism be right, then the whole Covenanted Reformation in one of its principal aspects was a grand mistake; for, that the king and the nation, as such, espoused it, was one of its central excellencies. Never did Scotland, never did these three nations behave themselves more princely than when they entered into covenants with the God of nations; than when, by those national deeds, they surrendered themselves to God. It was "the day of the Redeemer's strength, when the princes of the people assembled to give themselves willingly to the Prince of the kings of the earth." These lands were Hepzibah and Beulah, the Lord's Delight, and married to Him in an everlasting covenant. "God hath laid engagements on Scotland," said the Marquis of Argyle on the scaffold, "we are tied by covenants to religion and reformation; those who were then unborn are yet engaged, and it passeth the power of all the magistrates under heaven to absolve from the oath of God." When then the nation entered into those covenants, the step was a public, practical, national exhibition of the Headship of the Lord Jesus Christ over the nations. Of that covenanted nation then it might have been said, "Open ye the gates that the righteous nation that keepeth the truth may enter in."

Ere twelve years had passed, however, that storm burst that was to lay in ruins the whole structure of a Covenanted Reformation. Soon after the restoration of Charles to the throne, it became too

Reformation temple (would be broken ———

liament of Middleton and the Royalists—fit authors of a deed so
godless—initiated the crusade by the passing of the Act Rescissory
—rescinding the Covenants, and pronouncing unlawful and treasonable these and other national deeds in favour of the Reformation.
And, immediately thereafter, an absolute supremacy, both ecclesiastical and civil, was vested in the Sovereign. Before the baseless
supremacy of Charles Stuart, the everlasting supremacy of King
Jesus must go out in darkness! Against all who refuse to
acknowledge the former, there goes forth the decree of extermina-
tion. Never did a Persian ruler with his drunken Haman, nor a
lawless monarch of Babylon issue fouler decrees, or better act the
despot. Sharp, and Clavers, and Lagg, and Crichton lead, from
time to time, in the execution of the bloody behests of their royal
master. What will the Covenanters do now? Yield to the
supremacy of King Charles, and let the supremacy of King Jesus
go? Turn back now when the blast of the trumpet has been blown
for the battle? Never! They are overwhelmed with sorrow as
they contemplate this assault of tyrants upon the honour of their
God and the liberties of their land; but yield they cannot, yield
they will not. To the help of the Lord, to the help of the Lord
against the mighty! Like Israel when Joshua addressed them
reminding them of the difficulties of fidelity to their God, so said
they, "Nay, but we will serve the Lord." And

> "Diocletian's fiery sword
> Work'd busy as the lightning."

> "Their moans,
> The vales redoubled to the hills,
> And they to heaven."

The Covenanters had not learned the doctrine of the Divine
right of kings, or of passive obedience. They could not lay their
consciences at the feet of even the most exalted prince on earth.
Great interests were at stake, and faithless guardians of them
they could not be. The nation's rulers had thrown off and cast
out the Covenanted Constitution and Covenants, with the whole
work of Reformation, and with these this devoted band were
willing to go—to go even to prison and to death. With Christ

of their enemies, however high in royal favour. Where was liberty then? Where was patriotism? With the persecutors or with the persecuted? With the murderers or with the murdered? Liberty and patriotism beat high in the breasts of the outcast, the wanderers, the tortured, the slain : they were to be found there—there only—there in their heavenly beauty and strength.

> " They first on earth, while all the morning stars
> Looked on spectators from the heavenly skies,
> Proclaimed, Resistance is a right Divine ;
> And, to the beating of their hearts, in shouts,
> Answered the echoes of posterity."

Long did they bear, perhaps too long, with their persecutors before adopting aggressive measures of resistance. After twenty years of endurance, the time came when a bold stroke must be made for the overthrow of tyranny and the restoration of liberty. On the 22nd of June, 1680, about this very time two hundred years ago, Richard Cameron, in company with a number of fellow patriots, rode into the burgh of Sanquhar, and nailed up his famous Declaration to the Sanquhar Cross. James Stuart was declared to have forfeited the crown, and open war was proclaimed against him—

> " Men called it rash, perhaps it was a crime ;
> His deed flashed out God's will an hour before the time."

In a few years afterwards the bloody House of Stuart was hurled from the throne, and the sword of persecution was laid to rest in its scabbard. "The just shall be in everlasting remembrance ; but the memory of the wicked shall rot."

Although the Revolution Settlement possessed several excellencies, it was matter of lamentation that it left unrestored much of the Covenanted work of Reformation. It fell far short of conceding and "settling" all that the martyrs so nobly contended for. The Act Rescissory was allowed to remain untouched in the Statute Book, and the nation's Solemn Covenants were wholly ignored. That Revolution Settlement, moreover, proceeded upon the principle of political expediency—the will of the people, for it

the extent of establishing one form of church government in this kingdom and a different form in the sister kingdoms—this latter a form which the martyrs constantly resisted. It was Erastian, for by it the Standards of the Revolution Church were appointed for her before a single Assembly was called, and the meetings of her Assemblies were subsequently, in the Erastian spirit of that Settlement, interfered with and controlled. It was, in fine, a Settlement that did not take for its guide the supreme authority of the Bible; that did not conserve the Headship of Christ over the Church and Nation; that did not defend Presbyterianism as of Divine origin; and that in various other respects fell far below the platform of the Scriptural attainments of the Church and State in their purest times. The faithful followers of Cargill, Cameron, and Renwick were overwhelmed with sorrow when they beheld the crushing of the bright hopes they had entertained. Bitter, indeed, was their disappointment. Their martyred sires and they had marched under the banner for that whole Covenanted work—braving the wrath of their keenest foes, and how could they desert it now that peace had returned to bless and liberty was so plentiful in the land? They could not, they dare not; and the whole history of the Revolution Church since, as well as of the nation, justifies the position of separation from Church and State our Covenanting fathers then felt compelled to assume. "The Lord our God will we serve," said they, "and His voice will we obey."

A few years after the Revolution Settlement came the Act of Union between Scotland and England, one of the "fundamental and essential conditions" of which was that the Church of England should be left undisturbed, and that all the Acts for her establishment and for the preservation of her doctrine, worship, discipline, and government should "remain and be in full force for ever." Ah! the testimony uttered by every Scottish martyr on the scaffold, and the testimony on every martyr's monument now throughout the breadth of the land, cries out upon that Act as a surrender of a Reformation heritage and a dread act of apostacy from Scotland's covenanted King.

To that Revolution Settlement and Act of Union we trace

we love the nation less, but because we love Christ more. Our national constitution and national administration to a large extent ignore, and are in conflict with, the claims of the Lord's Anointed. There is still in the Constitution that Act of Uniformity which occasioned the ever memorable exodus of the Puritans from the Church of England—an Act which remains in all its tyrannical force, but is restrained meanwhile by an Act of Toleration. In the British Constitution there is an Erastianism by which the Church of England is as helpless for reform, without the aid of the Sovereign and Privy Council and Parliament, as is the Church of Rome without the interference of infallibility. Prelacy is in the Constitution, and the nation is bound to maintain it "inviolable for ever"—that Prelacy in all its unscriptural elements which the three nations bound themselves to extirpate. The Liturgy of the Church of England is in the Constitution—a Liturgy which affords protection for the apostles of the Oxford heresy, and contains the dogmas of the Papacy in their germ. And it is this Liturgy and Prelacy and Erastianism that are included in the popular clamour for the maintenance of the "Protestant Reformed Religion as by law established." The Prelatic Church of England receives about six millions annually from the national exchequer, while it enjoys revenues and property, granted by the nation, which represent a capitalized sum of about two hundred millions. The Papacy is in the Constitution, warmly fostered and richly endowed. From the national funds it draws in various ways, in the course of a year, one million of pounds. To such an extent does the British nation support that system which God in His Word has doomed to destruction by the breath of His mouth and the brightness of His coming. "And I saw one of his heads as it were wounded unto death, and his deadly wound was healed; and all the world wondered after the beast." The British Constitution and the British nation admit to the high office of legislators those who are the avowed enemies of the Lord and His Anointed—Secularists, whose State theory is blank Atheism; Roman Catholics, who are idolaters and profane the sacrifice of Christ at Calvary; Unitarians, who deny the Deity of our Lord; and Jews, who hold that Jesus was an impostor—all are eligible to rule this

by the exclusion from rule of the avowed enemies of God and the Christian religion. Now, it seems, these are as much entitled to rule, and as well qualified to rule aright, as the firmest believers in God and His Word ; and this is cried up as an evidence of the growing charity and greater enlightenment of this century !  " Grey hairs are here and there upon us, and we know it not."  In all these respects the British nation is doing dishonour to the King of nations.  " They have set up kings, but not by Me ; they made them princes, and I knew it not."

And, worse than all, an Ecclesiastical Supremacy is vested in the British Crown.  Over the Church of England, the Sovereign is Supreme Governor and Head ; the royal prerogative of Christ is invaded ; the Church's independent jurisdiction is blotted out. Queen Victoria is perhaps the noblest queen, and is certainly one of the noblest sovereigns that has ever swayed the British sceptre ; but still, never can we palliate the dishonour done the Church's exclusive Head, the Lord Jesus Christ, by this assumption of an ecclesiastical supremacy.  The guilt of this dishonour rests not so much upon the sovereign, who by solemn oath assumes this headship, as upon the nation which requires that coronation oath to be taken.  This claim of ecclesiastical supremacy is in all respects, except in the matter of persecution to enforce it, the same as it was in the time of the Stuarts, two centuries ago.  The headship of the present sovereign is in no essential respect different from what it was when Henry the Eighth, quarrelling with Rome, took it from the head of the Supreme Pontiff, and placed it upon his own.  Our fathers could not suffer any sovereign to bear the title, Head of the Church.  Whether written on the mitre of the priest or on the diadem of the sovereign, they denounced it as one of the names of blasphemy.  " This is the magistracy I have rejected," said Donald Cargill at his execution, " that which was invested with Christ's power.  And seeing this power taken from Christ, which is His glory, made the essential of the crown, it

---

* Since this was spoken, an avowed Atheist has been admitted to the House of Commons—the "narrow ledge of Theism" having been broken down by a Resolution of the House.  There are at present in the Commons, among others, fifty-seven Roman Catholics, nineteen Unitarians, and five Jews.

of the acknowledger from being a partaker of this sacrilegious robbing of God." "Own you the King," said his accusers to John Nisbet, "in all matters civil and ecclesiastical, and to be Head of the Church?" "I will acknowledge none," was the reply, "to be the Head of the Church but Christ." "I leave my testimony," said James Renwick, the last of the martyr throng, as he stood on the scaffold, "against all usurpations made on Christ's right, who is the Prince of the kings of the earth, who alone must bear the glory of ruling His own Kingdom, the Church." Were these martyrs with us to-day, they would exert every effort to have this dishonour to Christ removed, or at least their beloved Covenanted Scotland delivered from being "partaker in this sacrilegious robbing of God." This headship over the Church is, in the words of Blackstone, "an inherent prerogative of the crown." To the maintenance of this "inherent prerogative," every member of Parliament swears when he takes the oath of allegiance; and the oath of allegiance is, in the words of Macaulay, "the safe-guard of the crown." Thus it is that this usurpation on the rights of Christ is protected and maintained by all the power of the British Crown and nation. And scarce a voice lifted up throughout all Scotland in condemnation of the flagrant iniquity! While this iniquity, and the others already particularized, are not simply administrative but fundamental, not incidental but essential, not temporary but permanent! The millions quarrel about the respective policies of parties, while they forget these great moral questions that lie deeper far; and the parties devise and discuss methods for the removing of the eruptions on the surface, while they seem utterly oblivious of the fact that a powerful leprosy is doing its work at the core. "Shall I not visit for these things, saith the Lord? Shall not my soul be avenged on such a nation as this?"

Why speak ye not a word about bringing the King back? If thou altogether holdest thy peace at this time, then shall there enlargement and deliverance arise from another place, but thou and thy father's house shall be destroyed. The liberties of the land

"Their mountain stands strong. Britain shall never be moved." And they fold their hands and laugh at those who seek to arouse them to repel the increasing assaults. True, no kingdom on earth enjoys greater advantages; in none are the rights of man more faithfully guarded, while the powers of sovereign and subject are limited and established by laws that have been settled into their place through the lapse and experiences of generations. But still, never was there a time within the last two hundred years when a more determined assault upon these rights and privileges was made than at present. And that which creates most alarm is the indifference to these assaults of the Christian subjects who ought to be most zealous and valiant defenders of the precious heritage that has been entrusted them, procured at the expense of their fathers' blood. "The Gospel of the grace of God," said Martin Luther, "is like a flying summer shower, it drops here and there and then passes on." Let us beware lest these lands are receiving the latter drops of this shower of blessing, and lest already the shower is passing away. Other nations, as highly evangelized and as well established as we, have gone back in the roll of nations; ashes and dust hide their perished glories. Throughout lands once full of Bibles and privilege there now rises the minaret by the side of the mosque, from which goes forth ever the doleful proclamation, "There is no God but God, and Mahomet is His prophet."

In this hour of our peril, our whole efforts should be directed to the restoration of the work of the Covenanted Reformation; this is the hope and safety of the nation. It was by the grand Scriptural principles in the maintenance and application of which the Covenanting struggle was waged that the foundations of our civil and religious liberties were laid. If those liberties are to be conserved and transmitted in their entirety to coming generations those great principles must be believed in and applied. Who could persuade themselves that the superstructure will stand when the foundations are being removed? The superstructure of our liberties will crumble to the ground if we tamper with the doctrinal foundations on which those liberties rest. Therefore let us gird ourselves to keep in their place what of the foundations are still secure, and let us gird ourselves for the work of restoring those

sovereign Lord—this is the great and honourable work which the God we serve imperatively demands at our hands. If now an extensive movement should commence for the accomplishment of this noble object, the memory of the martyrs and their partiotic struggle for liberty would receive an appropriate commemoration, and this two hundredth year after their martyrdom would be memorable in the history of the land. Our hope for this is not so much in the rulers in the State or the leaders in the Church, though we know that the Lord of Hosts holds in His hand the hearts of all, and can turn them at His sovereign pleasure; but our hope is in the people. Usually in the past the people have been the most powerful factor in reformation. In the Reformations in the times of Luther, and Knox, and Henderson, the people awoke from their lethargies and rose up in new life to carry on the work to its completion. Be up then and doing, we beseech you, and, by the help of Almighty God, we may yet succeed in driving the battle to the gate. The restoring of the ruined temple of the Covenanted Reformation, and thereby the effecting of a Third Reformation for Scotland,—this is the work of the present hour, the work of every true patriot, of every lover of the Church, of every lover of Christ's crowns. "When Christ comes," said Richard Cameron, "to raise up His own work in Scotland, He will not want men enough to do it." May He come soon, then, to raise up His tabernacle that is fallen, and restore it from ruins, as in days of old! Awake! why sleepest Thou? Pluck Thy hand, even Thy right hand, out of Thy bosom. Gird Thy sword upon Thy thigh, Most Mighty, and ride forth for the sake of truth, and meekness, and righteousness. Take to Thee Thy power and reign. Reign over Scotland, and over Ireland, and over England. Reign over Europe, and over Asia, and over Africa, and over America. Take the throne of every heart, and the throne of every household, and the throne of every community, and the throne of every church, and the throne of every nation, and the thrones of all worlds; and let every knee bow and every tongue confess that Christ is Lord, to the glory of God the Father.

Behold! is now come to an end.

> "Thy saints take pleasure in her stones;
> Her very dust to them is dear;
> All heathen lands and kingly thrones
> On earth Thy glorious name shall fear."

And, when this sublime prophecy of Old Testament times shall have been fulfilled, there shall go up from the redeemed and emancipated millions of the broad earth, as the voice of many waters, and as the voice of mighty thunderings, the triumphant ascription,— "Alleluia! for the Lord God Omnipotent reigneth!"

# COLLECTION

OF

# LECTURES AND SERMONS,

Preached upon *Several* SUBJECTS, moftly in the
Time of the *Late* PERSECUTION.

Wherein a Faithful Doctrinal TESTIMONY is tranfmitted
to Pofterity for the DOCTRINE, WORSHIP, DISCI-
PLINE and GOVERNMENT of the Church of SCOT-
LAND againft Popery, Prelacy, Eraftianifm, &c.

By thefe FAITHFUL and EMINENT SERVANTS of
JESUS CHRIST; Meffrs. WILLIAM GUTHRIE,
MICHAEL BRUCE, JOHN WELLWOOD, RICHARD
CAMERON, DONALD CARGILL, ALEXANDER
PEDEN and ALEXANDER SHIELDS.

To which are added, fome Sacramental Difcourfes
by Mr JOHN LIVINGSTON and Mr JOHN WELCH,
and a SERMON on the BREACH of COVENANT,
by Mr JOHN GUTHRIE.

---

Carefully collected and Tranfcribed from feveral MANU-
SCRIPTS by J. H.; and now Publifhed at the defire
of the OWNERS of 'that CAUSE, which fome of the
Worthy AUTHORS Sealed with their Blood.

---

ISAIAH lii. 7. *How beautiful upon the mountains are the feet of
him that bringeth good tidings, that publifheth falvation.*

*G L A S G O W*:
*PRINTED AND SOLD BY J. BRYCE.*
M,DCC,LXXIX.

D

# ORIGINAL PREFACE

## BY

## JOHN HOWIE.

FROM Scripture and history thou wilt find that the Lord, in all ages of the world, has had a church more or less visible; and that it has been the inestimable privilege of that community to have an objective revelation of Himself, and the way of salvation infallibly made known unto them. But it has been the peculiar blessing of the New Testament Church only, to have a more glorious and refulgent display of Himself, and the method of man's redemption promulgated, and set forth in the everlasting gospel by the manifestation and ministration of His own Son: God, "who at sundry times and in divers manners, in times past spake to the fathers by the prophets, hath in these last days spoken to us by his own Son."

But, then, at the same time, it is as evident that the Church of Christ has undergone a variety of changes from first to last, for which in Scripture she is frequently compared to the moon. And although she be mostly represented there as in-suffering and wilderness condition, yet (not to mention her patriarchal, ceremonial, and Christian eras) she, in general, as a collective society or body of men, similar to the case of individuals therein, has passed through different vicissitudes of prosperity and adversity. For some times we find her looking forth as the blushes of the morning, "Fair as the moon, clear as the sun, and terrible as an army with banners." And then she is all joy singing this song, "My beloved hath a vineyard in a very fruitful hill," "Sing ye unto her, a vineyard of red wine:" "Arise and shine, for thy light is come; for the glory of the Lord hath arisen upon thee." Such seems to have been her case in the first, fourth, and sixteenth centuries, and never more remarkably than in our own Church in this land in the last century, when she might have been called Hephzi-bah, *i.e.*, "The Lord delighteth in her," and Beulah, "a land married unto the Lord."

Again, we find her on a sudden all eclipsed and reduced to the most mournful circumstances, sitting solitary upon the ground, expressing herself in the words of the lamenting prophet in her name, "Is it nothing unto you, all ye that pass by: behold, and see, if there be any sorrow like unto my sorrow. Zion spreadeth forth her hands, and there is none to comfort her." And this seems to have been her situation, not only under Rome-Pagan and Rome-Popish, but also more than once in our own land under

orest, who drives the woman to the wilderness, and ——
er at his pleasure, or from apostacy, corruption, and these little
oxes of errors that spoil the vine, or from a complication of all
hese together, like a violent torrent or cascade, bearing all down
efore it with great velocity (as was the case when the following
iscourses were delivered), at such a time her faithful watchmen,
n obedience to the command of the Church's Head, are obliged to
ift a standard, not only personally and judicially, but even doc-
rinally, in the gospel for the word of Christ's patience, and against
ll the sins and prevailing evils of the times, an example of which
hou hast here in the following sheets presented unto thy view.
'I have set watchmen upon thy walls, O Zion, who shall never
old their peace day nor night. Ye that make mention of the
Lord, keep not silence."

I suppose it would be quite superfluous to detain thee, reader,
now with any historical account of the lives of the authors of
hese discourses, as having so lately given a short narrative of the
most part of their lives elsewhere already.* Neither would it be
ltogether expedient at present to say much in commendation of
hese discourses themselves, or the remarkable providences by
which they have hitherto been preserved. It may therefore be
is necessary, in the first place, to notice, in a few particulars,
ome of the principal or cardinal truths contained in these dis-
ourses themselves in the way of contrast with some of those
loctrines, now taught and maintained ; and, secondly, to observe
a few things concerning the way and manner wherein they are
now published : and these things of course may probably not only
evidence their utility, but perhaps may be the best apology that
an be offered for their publication at present. And

First, these prefaces, lectures, and sermons, in general, are in
their scope plain and easy to be understood : they are not properly the productions of a large and well-furnished library. But
they are deduced from the Scriptures of truth as the Spirit of
God gave them utterance ; and notwithstanding their being mostly
delivered to a people labouring under the cross, and in the furnace
of persecution and affliction (the Church being in distress); yet
they quadrate so with our present situation, that one would think
that, in many places, they had been rather calculated for the
meridian of our present circumstances, than for those times wherein
they were delivered, as may be more obviously demonstrated from
these few particulars following.

1. In these discourses, a Trinity and Unity of persons in the

* "Scots Biography; or, The Lives of the Scots Worthies," to which I
now refer the reader.

and exhibited. But, alas! how many Arian and Socinian preachers are now to be found amongst us! But, perhaps, they will deny this charge because they have not the confidence with Arius, Servetus, Lælius, or Faustus Socinus, to assert Christ to be a mere man only. And yet the sum or substance of their doctrine upon this head, turns upon this hinge, that Christ died only to confirm His doctrine, ratify His miracles, and leave us a pattern of heroic virtue, patience and magnanimity in suffering affliction. Nay, some of these pedantic preachers*, when dispensing the most solemn ordinances, have got it by rote; "Remember that glorious Person, who, by His death, confirmed His doctrine," &c. It is true He did all this; but if He did no more, as they seem to put an *iffability* to it (when they say, *if* He died for our transgressions, and *if* He was bruised for our iniquities), then every martyr, or ring-leader of a sect is not only put on an equal level with our Lord and Saviour Jesus Christ (as in this sense they confirm their doctrine, and leave their followers an example of courage and constancy in suffering). But even Christ is stript of His Godhead, degraded from His offices, and deprived of the true merit and end of His sufferings. Consequently, He can be nothing more than a sort of a very good man now glorified. Thus the Christian religion becomes a mere farce, or chimerical notion, while its great Head and Author appears in the character of God, while He really is not; and that is ascribed unto Him which He actually did not. But let us hear and believe His own testimony: "I and my Father are one." "And I lay down my life for the sheep."

Again, there are others running into very strange and unprecedented notions concerning His incarnation, affecting to be wise above what is written, some asserting, "That His body was not made of the substance of the Virgin, but created in her by the Holy Ghost." Others will have the person of Christ to be only the word of God, or Logos (as He is called in the Greek), become the Son of God by a concurrence of the first person of the Trinity with the Virgin Mary, as two distinct parents, uniting the personal word unto human nature. A third sort seem to exchange what all orthodox divines call the eternal generation of Christ for a seeming temporal one, in what they call the pre-existent human soul of Christ, or super-angelic spirit, "which (say they) existed or subsisted, distinct from the divine nature, before His incarnation." By the first of these, He cannot be real man; by the

---

* I am not in this and what follows to be understood as if I meant all indiscriminately; for doubtless, there is a number who yet teach orthodox doctrine, and wish well to religion in the Church of Scotland.

super-angelic, and a third human, as we cannot otherwise possibly conceive how He could be possessed of human nature before His incarnation. Which hypotheses accumulated together, as they seem to be fabricated by whimsical brains, investigated by corrupt inventions, and partly founded upon the theory of animalcular generation; so they seem all very much to diminish the glory of Him who is the express image of His Father's person,* and " who thought it no robbery to be equal with God." " And God sent forth his Son made of a woman."

Now, all these someway or other seem to conspire to make Christ less than what He really is. But lo! another scene opens here by some of the same actors, wherein more is ascribed to Him than what He really did. For universal redemption comes on the stage under the mask of universal satisfaction or atonement, and a universal restoration or redemption of all things by Christ seems to peep out, and take air from behind the curtain; a time when there shall be neither sin, devils, nor damned spirits. Nay, hell itself (according to them, after an unknown age or long time, when sin hath worn out itself) must be for ever banished without the limits of God's empire, beyond the verge of creation.

2. We have, in these sermons, the depravity of man's nature by his original apostasy from God; his utter inability now, of himself, to do that which is spiritually good, the necessity of the Spirit, and the way of salvation in and through the death and righteousness of Christ, set forth and illustrated. But is it not awfully certain, that in many places in Scotland one may attend many sermons (if they may be properly so called), and yet be at a loss to know by them whether man be a fallen creature yet or not? while little else flows from the pulpit than some insipid scraps of morality—a few dislocated fragments of divine truth, or something worse. Did I say worse? Yes; for these someway or other have their authority from Scripture. But many of these catholican discourses, now taught, seem rather to be extracted from some heathen economy than divine revelation; when almost every sentence must either be deduced from, or confirmed by, some ancient or modern poet, naturalist, or moral philosopher.† The import of which (if it has any) must be, that man is now made in an imperfect state,

*" Who this is we must learn, for man He seems;
In all the lineaments of His face
The glimpses of His Father's glory shine."—Par. Reg.

† Such as Plato, Epictetus, Socrates, Seneca, Bolingbroke, Shaftesbury, Pope, Shakespeare, Hume, and Voltaire, with a large circle more of the same kidney.

Christ's righteousness, in order to obtain salvation; by which means free-will and the merit of the creature claim the ascendant, while the doctrine of original sin is either reprobated and treated as a figment, or imprisoned in the jail of silence, until in process of time it is got urned in the land of oblivion.*

3. In these discourses, thou wilt find man's corrupt nature delineated, the plagues of the heart ransacked, practical religion pointed out, and every vice and immorality detected, with an eternity of well or woe unto all who obey or obey not the gospel of Christ. But ah! here again is ground of sad complaint, that notwithstanding all the light we enjoy by preaching, teaching, and other means of instruction, there is but little experience in religion, or true practical knowledge amongst us. There are

* Although I neither have room nor abilities here to enter upon any dispute anent these points of free-will and original sin, yet I cannot help thinking as to the first of these, that if man had it in his own natural power to do that which is spiritually good, then he might at first hand curb every vice in its very first motion in the bud; so that there needed be no acts, so no habits, and consequently no sin at all. Nay more, it is agreeable unto the human mind, that whatever men's lives have been to desire to be happy at last; and if man by his own free-will could convert himself, though even in his last moments, then there needed none be damned at all, for it were absurdity upon the head of absurdity to suppose one to go into a state of eternal misery and woe when he had it in his own power to be for ever happy. Indeed Taylor, Nilson, and their disciples would have us believe that Adam was in such a state, and yet fell. But the case is quite different; for Adam's offence proceeded from a propensity in his nature to himself, for without this he could not have done it; and yet there was no propensity in his nature to sin. But hear the case with us: "Can the Ethiopian change his skin, or the leopard his spots? Then may ye also do good that are accustomed to evil." And says Christ Himself, "Without me ye can do nothing."

And as for original sin, I must think these Pelagian and Socinian gentlemen in this to be most inconsistent with their own scheme, even reason itself. For I suppose it will be granted by all, that reiterated acts of sin become habits, and habits of sin become incorporated with the nature of the sinner, else how could they be imputed acts of sin to the whole man? And according to philosophical reasoning, in the very nature of things everything—whether vegetable, insect, or animal—specifically brings forth things in their own kind and species, I should think it as impossible for one thus contaminated with the pollution of sin to propagate or bring forth one that is pure from it, as for one of these to bring forth one of another species, or to elicit pure water from a defiled fountain. Job seems to put an impossibility to it when he says, "Who can bring a clean thing out of an unclean?" No, not one. Which the Poet illustrates thus—

"What mortal power from things unclean
Can pure productions bring?
Who can command a vital stream
From an infected spring?"

world, or even of the public news in Church and State, nay, there are many who can speak well upon many controverted points in religion; yea, upon the most parts of the doctrines of Christianity; but ask them anent the plagues of the wicked heart, the various ups and downs of an exercised Christian, of the pangs of the new birth, saving faith, true and evangelical repentance; how these work and operate upon the soul, then they are over; all terminates in profound silence. These to them are trite old-fashioned and ungenteel subjects; and as for almost every kind of vice and immorality, were they ever more rampant and triumphant amongst the human species than now, as being not only encouraged and perpetuated in their very seminaries, by those shields that should defend the earth, and that with impunity, but also palliated, connived, and winked at by these patrons, creatures who must needs occupy the place of teachers, especially in respect of the vices of men of opulent circumstances in the world, unto whom a pecuniary fine (if anything is required), will serve a turn: and thus Church censure can be bought and sold, in imitation of the Pope's absolutions and indulgences, for a piece of money, more or less, according to the circumstances of the delinquent. O wretched deceit! *Proh nefas!* A striking picture of selfish, partial and disingenuous spirits. No wonder, since some of these mercenary creatures and their underlings are culpable themselves; and how can they either show a good example or inflict censure upon others. Whereby these words of divine inspiration are verified, " Put me into the priest's office that I may eat a piece of bread." "They have put no difference between the holy and the profane." "For the priests teach for hire, and the prophets divine for money."

Hence it is that men, beholding this with the chicane and divisions amongst the professors of religion, one hesitates whether to follow God or Baal; another turns sceptic; a third becomes nullifidian, and doubts of almost everything; while a fourth turns Deist and denies revealed religion altogether. Nay, some of this deistical or rather atheistical tribe, are arrived at such a pitch of audacity, that the reality of spirits good or bad, existing in a future state, is with them become a matter doubtful. Yea, that there is such a place as hell to punish wicked men, is by them in a wanton and sportive way debated, as a thing that has no other existence than in the brains of men of a morose temper, of a low and illiberal turn of mind and ungenerous sentiments. In opposition to these pernicious notions, it were too great a compliment to produce scripture unto men who will believe nothing contrary unto their own corrupt inventions; wandering stars to whom is reserved the blackness of darkness forever! men sunk below the level of heathenism. The very heathens had a

"This way unto Elysium leads, where such do dwell
As have liv'd virtuously. The other leads to hell:
Easy is the way that leads to hell." *

4. In these discourses are contained a doctrinal testimony for the royal prerogatives of Jesus Christ as King and Head of His own Church, with the moral and perpetual obligation of our solemn Covenants, national and solemn League. But how many places of solemn worship will ye go to, and how long must you attend there, ere you hear one of these two prime gems in Christ's crown, so much as mentioned, unless to be exposed? For although these truths have now of a long time been buried under the ashes of the Revolution Settlement and the incorporating Union; yet these sacred mounds of our former laudable national attainment were never more awfully attacked and impugned from the pulpit than of late, and that by men of no small repute in the Church of Scotland; some declaring openly that they will both pray and preach against them; others affirming that they have bad influence upon men's morals, and that they are the badges of pride, fiery zeal and bigotry; a third finds it a matter of thanksgiving to heaven (as they express it), that these Covenants, so much boasted of by some, are not binding upon us in this generation. O what sallies of blind zeal here! But let them remember, that these were vows to the Most High, and that breach of covenant is not only a brand upon the heathen, "Covenant breakers," &c., but even punishable in others, when made to heathen men. Shall he break the Covenant, and be delivered? Indeed it has been the canting objection of most of our modern anti-Covenanters, that we have no warrant for national or public covenanting under the New Testament.† But it would

* "Hac iter Elysium nobis; at læva malorum
Exercet pœnas, et ad impia Tartara mittit.
Facilis descensus Averni."—Vir. Æn. lib. IV.

† As it cannot rationally be thought that the limits of a Preface, much less a marginal part therein, can contain any copious vindication of our Covenants, I shall therefore only notice an objection or two made very lately against this duty by a minister of no small figure in the Church of Scotland.

Objection 1. Under the new Testament, we have no warrant for national covenanting. That under the old was purely ceremonial and abrogated (Heb. viii. 13). On which I observe,

1. That the Jewish and Christian Church is only one and the same Church under different administrations; so that which is morally binding under the old, can never be abrogated or antiquated under the New Testament dispensation.

2. In the moral law it is required, "That we avouch the Lord to be our

ry to be in covenant with God; and it was the distinguishing aracter of His Israel of old, that they were a people in covenant th Him; and it was their peculiar privilege and blessing, that

d, walk in his ways, keep his statutes and his commandments." Now, s was the sum or substance of national covenanting under the Old Testant, and the covenant engagements we came under in these lands are stantially the same, only with this alteration of circumstances: under Old Testament they were bound to the whole body of laws—moral, laical, and ceremonial—as then suited unto the Jewish Pedagogue. der the New Testament we are bound to the same moral law, which ver can be abolished by the circumstance of time, and to these institus substituted in place of the former Judaical and typical ceremonies, as culated unto the meridian of Gospel light and purity. To say that the supersedes or makes void the other, is to make the great Author of the ristian religion a liar, who says, "I came not to destroy, but to fulfil law."

And as for that text, Heb. viii. 13, brought in here to prove the abolition public covenanting under the New Testament, it is no ways pat or conuous to the present purpose; for both from the text and context, and exposition of all sound divines upon it, it is evident, that the two renants there are the different dispensations of the covenant of grace der the Old and New Testaments; that covenant under the Mosaical ministration being full of ceremonies, types, and shadows, waxed old and s ready to vanish away, when superseded by a more glorious display the dispensation of the Christian economy. Had this objector not itively declared that he would sustain no authority, Divine or human, hout the bounds of the New Testament, I could have adduced many timonies of these kinds pointing out this duty under the New Testament. hall therefore just notice one of unquestionable authority, where it is d of the Church of Macedonia, "Who first gave themselves to the Lord, l to us," that is, according to a sound annotator, "They made an entire l fresh surrender of themselves unto God, solemnly binding themselves cleave unto His truths, ordinances, and commandments." Otherwise, at had been more noticeable unto the apostle about them than other arches? Nor can these words properly signify collections, as this objector uld suppose; for, in that case, other churches collected also. But the ster objection yet follows.

Objection 2. That since the covenant of works, the Lord never made a renant with man; and it were absurd to say, that man as a party can er enter into covenant with Him. I observe,

1. I was just going before to say, that he would never deny private or rsonal covenanting, and from the lesser I would have argued to the eater in number. But here personal covenanting is cut down also; a ty which no sound divine ever yet denied, but inculcated, nay, David ouches his practice in this, "I have sworn, and I will perform it, that I ll keep thy righteous judgments."

2. If he meant by covenanting the covenant of grace properly, I shall t dispute the point. But I find that the Lord made a covenant of safety th Noah and his family (Gen. ix.); a covenant of property with Abraham ap. xv.); a covenant of royalty with David (2 Sam. vi.; Psal. lxxxix.); ovenant of priesthood with Phinehas (Numb. xxv.); and besides the public ation of the covenant of works, and the covenant of grace at Sinai, he

Lord, and swear by his name"—at the wanton and lavish expense of throwing away both precept, example, prophecy, and promise,

made a national covenant with Israel (chap. xix. to xxv.), of which covenant it is above twenty times afterward said, that the Lord made a covenant with them, or they with Him reciprocally. And yet, I suppose, none who ever really knew what this duty was, ever presumed either to enter into or perform the duties promised or engaged to, in their own strength, but only in and through the strength of Christ, "who strengtheneth us unto all things." But men may put what gloss on Scripture they please.

3. Our worthy Reformers and late sufferers made no scruple to call them covenants: nay, our English translation of the Bible above thirty times calls them so. But if it will please him better, we may as properly call them national vows or promissory oaths; and then the Gordian knot is loosed, and this great Achillean objection comes down topsy-turvy to the ground. Upon the whole, I would observe,

(I.) That covenanting is neither in form nor matter properly either the covenant of works or the covenant of grace; but an engagement to the duties we owe to God and one another. "And made a covenant before the Lord, to walk after the Lord, and keep his commandment and testimony." But more particularly,

1. That these covenants are in their nature morally binding, although there had never been the formality of a covenant: "Thou hast avouched the Lord this day to be thy God, and to walk in his ways."

2. They are sacred national vows: "Vow to the Lord thy God, and pay."

3. They are a solemn dedication of ourselves and all that we have to the Lord: "One shall say I am the Lord's, and another shall subscribe with his hand."

4. They are consonant to the law of nature, which says, If a man swear, it must be by the name of his God: "For men always swear by the greater."

5. They are a part of religious worship: "Thou shalt fear the Lord, and swear by his name."

6. Their ends are perpetually good, viz.: The propagation and defence of the true reformed religion.

7. They are of an hereditary nature, containing clauses expressing their binding obligation: "That the present and succeeding generations;" "We and our posterity," &c.

8. They are partly political, and twisted with our former national constitution, the *sine qua non* of government, as founded upon several laudable Acts of Parliament (Act v., Parl. 1647; Act v., 1644; and Act xv., 1640).

9. They are in their form *(formalis ratio)* formal and right reason: "Thou shalt swear in truth and in judgment." And

10. They are solemn oaths upon both sides, and if we shall grant a breach of these, then there could be no security of anything under the sun whereupon God's name is interponed. So that no mortal power can dispense with these under the penalty of running the dreadful risk of breach of covenant. All which I could prove more largely from these our covenants themselves, would time and place here permit.

(II.) Public as well as private covenanting has both been practised and

lieve an inspired apostle, when he says: "All Scripture is given ... inspiration, and is profitable for doctrine, for reproof, for cor- ... tion, for instruction in righteousness."

5. In the following discourses, a doctrinal banner is lifted up ... the divine right of Presbytery—that is, the doctrine, worship, ... cipline, and government of the Reformed Church of Scotland, ... contained in her excellent Standards, Confession of Faith, ... techisms, &c. But how stands the case in this with us at ... esent? For, not to mention these Machiavellians, court para- ... es, Platonic saints, or baptized heathens, whose wit is either ... me lascivious hint, or some broken jest upon Scripture, and who ... profess one religion to-day and another to-morrow, or turn ... ery way wherever the ministerial magnet leads them; or these ... ntlemen of the *beau-monde*, who ofttimes distinguish them- ... ves by the name of free-thinkers, under which may be com- ... ehended all Atheists, all Deists, Unitarians, Pelagians, Socinians, ... minians, &c. How many different sects are there amongst us ... ose principles (if they have any) say that the government and ... cipline of the Church of Christ is a thing purely ambulatory, ... t may be moulded or metamorphosed into any form or fashion ... t best suits their local circumstances and the political consti- ... ion of the kingdoms of this world will admit of. For, not to ... ntion Episcopalians, Independents, Anabaptists, Glassites, ... reans, Methodists, and Moravians, such a loose and vague ... eme of sentiment now obtains amongst many of the Presbyterian ... rsuasion that, under the notion of what they call charity, moder- ... on, and liberty of conscience, they can admit of almost all the fore- ... ntioned tribes unto their communion upon a bare supposition of ... ir visible saintship, or what they term sincerity in the main, ... thout any other text of orthodoxy than what they define the funda-

... roved of by the Lord in all ages of the Church under the Old Testament. ... tness that under Moses, Joshua, Asa, Joash, Hezekiah, Josiah, Ezra, ... l Nehemiah; and under the New, in the churches of Macedonia, France, ... rmany, and in none more remarkably than in our own land. Both in ... Reformation from Popery and Prelacy, these covenants were the means ... ereby they were excluded. And should you only acknowledge them as ... occasional duty, sure there was never more occasion for their revival ... n when both these now appear on the carpet. Scotland's Covenanting ... es were her best times. She was remarkably blest with heaven's ... ntenance in this by a further accomplishment of these promises (Psa. ... 3; Isa. xl. 1, 5, 6). And,

... inally, They were vindicated by, witnessed to, contended for, and ... led by the blood of our late sufferers (whose authority this anti-Cove- ... ter has rejected), and the Lord will yet vindicate them in His own due ... e, when perhaps neither he nor any of his fraternity are above ground ... ppose them.

row, contracted judgments, and illiberal sentiments; "The Word of God (say they) is our testimony." But what is all this? Almost every heretic that appears in the Church will tell us the same. Indeed a better testimony than this cannot be. But then the Word of God properly can be no man's testimony, it is God's own testimony. It is above eighteen times, in one portion of Scripture so called (Psa. cxix.). "We declare unto you the testimony of God," says the apostle. It is also called the testimony of Jesus, "The testimony of Jesus is the spirit of prophecy." And unto every truth, particularly that called the present truth, every one of His professing people is to give an explicit adherence, and this is called their testimony. "And when they shall have finished their testimony," and they "overcame by the word of their testimony." But to tantalize or soothe up the minds of the credulous they must needs own the thirty-three chapters of the Confession too. And who thanks them to own that which their own hand-writing binds them unto? But as this seems now a point of mere form, it will likely in a little go out of fashion; for, while some are using means to be disentangled from that obligation, others subscribe with a mental reservation (like Arius's paper) in their bosom; a third, to anticipate all this, must needs engage with his own explanation upon it. But hear the divine mandate, "Son of man, shew them the house, and all the forms, and all the ordinances thereof." "Hold fast the form of sound words."

6. In the following sheets a doctrinal testimony is displayed against Popery, Prelacy, &c. (whether by establishment or toleration), and all that is contrary to sound doctrine and the power of true godliness. But, oh! a different principle seems to be the distinguishing characteristic of this age; for Prelacy, the mother, is become so fashionable and necessary that its ritual forms have of a long time been made the test or essential qualification of membership in the highest courts of Britain.* And for Popery, the daughter, the most nefarious of all factions, it is not only palliated and connived at, but even tolerated now by those in supreme authority. Did I say tolerated? Might I not have said established by law in some parts in these dominions? And this is more than what the great-grandfather, the father, or his sons the two tyrants could ever get effectuated, for they never got Popery established in any part of their dominions, however deep their

* This is called the Test Act, "which requires all officers civil and military to receive the Sacrament according to the Church of England," and received the royal assent, March 29th, 1673.—*Vide* Salmon's Revol., and Memorable Events of England.

covenants) against an inundation of Popery must be repealed, and without one dissenting voice notwithstanding so much altercation about things of a petty nature. No faithful Murray, no honest Argyle, no courageous Loudon, or long-sighted Belhaven, here to interpose in behalf of liberty and religion. No, the infamous B—v—le approaches the walls with his Trojan horse, and there is not so much as a plain, free-spoken Chatham to oppose him. The necks of the civil and religious liberties of these nations must be cut off at one blow, and the very spirit, principles, and religion (might I call it a religion) of Antichrist, that man of sin *and son of perdition*, must be brought under the patronage and legal security of these nations again, and all to serve a political turn in views of worldly gain or secular advantage, upon a supposition of its professors taking the political test in form to the present government. Strange! to require oaths from men the very soul of whose principle is to keep no faith with Protestants. The Pope may as soon cease to be Christ's infallible Vicar as Papists can be bound by any obligation sacred or human. Oh! the infatuation. Must these lands become the asylum of that cursed brood of bloody Jesuits, trafficking priests, monks, and mass-mongers again; and all after that deadly wound was given unto the beast by the instrumentality of our Reformers and renowned ancestors. "And I saw one of his heads as it were wounded unto death, and his deadly wound was healed." We must be cemented unto that Scarlet Whore Mystery Babylon, "The mother of harlots and the abominations of the earth" again, for it seems these nations must go to Rome before the Church be delivered. "They have made void thy law." "But shall the throne of iniquity have fellowship with thee, which frameth mischief by a law?"

And for almost all other errors and heresies, they now magnify, multiply, and increase. The red dragon of persecution, who killed his thousands in the last century, now kills his thousands by that deluge of errors out of the mouth of the beast. The poet, when describing the ruins of ancient Troy, could say *(nunc seges est, Troja fuit)* "now corn grows where Troy stood." But to our sad experience, we may say that where the corn of truth and pure gospel ordinances once grew, or was produced, little more grows now than the noxious weeds of error. Nugatory fables, demented divisions and delusions, whereby men's minds are become stagnant, either with empty volumes of mere speculative amusements, or the doctrine or some old condemned heresy varnished over. And how can it be otherways, when almost every heresy or erroneous system of religion is tolerated by law, and hatched under the warm wings of that Government, upon whose streams flying appears this glaring excerpt of this doctrine itself. "That though every religion were enumerated that now exists from the rising to the setting sun, the Christian religion will tolerate them all, providing they teach no opinions that are destructive to the State, or dangerous to the particular members of it. Every man hath a right to judge for himself in matters of religion. He received this privilege from God. It is confirmed to him by the religion of Jesus."† Doctrine strange enough indeed, wherein allegiance or loyalty to the State of every nation is made the essential qualification of religion; a doctrine (1.) expressly contrary to the divine law (Deut. xiii., Ez. xliii. 8, Rev. ii. 2), where all idolaters, or setters up, or enticers to a false religion, are to be put to death and thrust out of the Church. But here Judaism, Mahometism, Popery, nay Paganism itself, must be tolerated and patronised by the Head and great Author of the Christian religion.

(2.) It is most inconsistent with a Christian constitution; for every Christian magistrate ought not only to profess the true Reformed religion, but also to exert all his power in defence of it in a subserviency to the advancement of that kingdom of Christ. But by this principle, the Church must only be an appendage to the State, and no limits set upon it. Be good loyal subjects, and profess what principle you will, here is the *primum mobile* of religion, and unto the secular nadir the sacred needle must be always pointed.

(3.) It not only inverts the very order of religion, but in some sense makes God the author of evil. For we are sure His word ought to be the alone rule for all Christians in principles, practices, faith, or manners: but here conscience is not only exalted above God's Word; but God Himself is said to have given men liberty to walk directly contrary to His own law. But "if they speak not according to this word, it is because there is no light in them."

(4.) It is repugnant unto our covenants, wherein we are bound to extirpate Popery, Prelacy, superstition, heresy, schism, profaneness, &c., and whatever shall be found contrary to sound doctrine, &c. But this can be of no weight with the abettors of toleration principles.

(5.) It is of bad consequence; for show me one church or nation in the world, where toleration in its full extent took place, that ever prospered in either religion or morality. Nay, the quite reverse of this immediately ensues, and the Lord evidences His divine disapprobation of it. Witness our own land, wherein as long as these covenants, the palladium of our Presbyterian constitution, were made the test of admission in both Church and State, the Church had both purity in doctrine and unity amongst her members, and the Lord's remarkable presence attended her ordinances; but as soon as Cromwell's toleration commenced (which was none of the worst), then the Lord's presence, comparatively as with a blush, withdrew, and both peace and unity among her members bade her a final adieu.

And lastly, It not only binds men down from using all lawful means for propagating the true religion, unless directed by the State, but also, in some cases, cuts down defending our religious liberties by arms; and however much defensive arms be now condemned by the generality, yet it is a truth confirmed in Scripture, founded in nature, consonant to the law of nations, sworn to in our covenants, and conformed to all the practices of all Reformed churches. And

1. It is confirmed by multifarious texts of Scripture, such as Jud. v. 26; Prov. xxiv. 11, 12; Neh. iv. 14; Luke xxii. 36. Says the Lord expressly

† Doctrine of Toleration, page 13.

E

heathen monarch, who, after he had commanded the Jews to set up the true worship of God at Jerusalem, under penalty of being hanged and having their houses made a dunghill, said, "And

by the Prophet, Zech. ii. 7,—"Deliver thyself, O Zion, that dwellest with the daughter of Babylon."

2. It is founded in nature. It is congenial with, and irradicated in man as a creature, to repel force by force; and to deny that power and privilege to man, which the brutish creation do enjoy, were irrational; neither can religion or policy irradicate sinless nature, nay, they are rather cumulative to it.

3. It is founded on and conformed unto the laws of nations. What kingdom or commonwealth but their laws allow them to defend their rights and liberties; and what privilege more momentous than religion? The poet in prospect of this could say,—

"*Armaque in armatos sumere jura sinunt.*"
"To meet armed men with arms, all laws allow."—OVID.

4. It is engaged to in our covenants, "To assist and defend all who enter into the same bond in maintaining thereof." And

Finally, We find it practised by all the Lord's people, wherever religion was embraced in an embodied corporation under the Old Testament. Witness Israel in the time of the Judges; the Jews in the time of Ezra and Nehemiah, and after the famous Maccabees and others. Under the New Testament witness the Waldenses about 1174; the Bohemians under the brave Zizica about the year 1420; the Germans under the D.S. and Landgrave of Hesse, 1546; the French Protestants, 1557; that little handful in Piedmont, 1560; the churches of the Netherlands, 1570; with many others, yea, and our own land both in the first and second Reformation (not to mention the persecuting period), wherein it is more than probable that if religion had not been defended by arms we had not had the face of a church this day. Nay, such is the malice of Satan and Antichrist against the true religion, that there is scarcely a kingdom or commonwealth in Europe where the Reformed religion is professed, but it had to be defended by arms before it was established. It is true that *(preces et lachrimæ sunt arma ecclesiæ)* "prayers and tears are the arms of the Church"—and the best arms of a church, as a church, too—for without these all others will prove ineffectual. But then church members are men, and as such they may use the same weapons that others do. If prayer resistance be lawful, why not forcible resistance against unjust violence also? Defensive arms are not only vindicated in some of the following discourses, but even one of these authors died in the practice of it, for which he received this testimony from his enemies, "That he lived praying and preaching, and died praying and fighting." So we must both pray, praise, and fight, if need require. "Let the high praise of the Lord be in their mouth, and a sharp two-edged sword in their right hand," &c. For defensive arms see the authors of the "*De jure Regni,*" "*Lex Rex,*" Prin's Appendix, "*Jus Populi,*" "Hind let Loose," "Apol. Rel.," &c. But after all I hear a general cry, "Liberty of conscience; let no man be troubled for religion, but give no liberty to Papists. Let not the Penal Statutes be repealed"—sentiments, I should think, as opposite to, and remote from one another as the arctic and antarctic poles; for if all religions may be tolerated, why not Popery amongst others; and if Papists must have no

decree; let it be done with speed," which must include different ways of worship, as well as the worship itself. But here every man may live as he lists, similar to the case of Israel in the time of the Judges, when it is said, "Every man did that which was right in his own eyes."

7. Unto these I might add, that there is a vein or tincture of true zeal and faithfulness (equally applied unto the sins of both Church and State) running through the whole of these discourses; and this is not only what the Lord ofttimes blesses with success (witness both Reforming and suffering periods), but what He also commands, acknowledges, and hath a particular inspection of. "Lift up thy voice like a trumpet, and show my people their transgressions, and the house of Israel their sins." "Ye are my witnesses," saith the Lord, "and mine eye shall be upon the faithful of the land," says the Spirit of God by the Psalmist. And what can be the proper cause why the gospel has so little success in these dregs of time wherein we live? You may say "The Lord withholds the Divine influence of His Spirit." True, but what can be the reason of this? Is it not our misbelief, neutrality, carnality, indifference, worldly-mindedness, barrenness, and supine security? But from whence flows all this? Is it not from our apostacy from God, breach of covenant, want of true zeal and faithfulness in the matters of the Lord, and the concerns of His glory, novelty striking the fancy more than truth in this

---

benefit of toleration, why may they not be prosecuted? "No, Popery is inimical to the Protestant interest, subversive of the Claim of Right, and happy Revolution, and contrary to the Union; and Papists are men of bloody principles, and dangerous to civil society." Wide steps indeed. All this is true, and it is good to see any opposition made unto Popery and Papists. But what is become of the word of God, our Church standards, Confession of Faith, &c.; our covenants, Christ's headship, and the many laudable acts in Church and State asserting the Divine right of Presbytery and Presbyterian Church Government? Are these become stale, or is Popery a friend unto any of these? No, these would affect Prelacy also; we cannot look without ministerial optics: we must not twit the Supremacy, and English Constitution, the source of all these evils; but if Popery becomes fashionable in England, it will soon become more general in Scotland, when time and cool persuasion have removed all prejudice, as Papists call it.

It is true, to soothe up men's minds and mend the matter a little in this alarming crisis, a motion is made now in part to give more freedom to English Protestant Dissenters, and here the awful catastrophe must terminate: bring Dissenters on an equal level with Papists, and then Papists, Prelates, and professed Presbyterians must be all good friends together. A striking evidence, indeed, of the fascinating influence of self-interest, while God's glory, Christ's cause, and the good of immortal souls are overlooked.

we are to have no man's person as the object of our _____ ;, we must not sacrifice or make a compliment of truth to gain applause, or gratify the ambition of any. Indeed, it is a long time since PEACE, PEACE, has been the war-word of this generation ; and yet they have but badly succeeded therein, for never was a time of more division than now. But if truth and faithfulness had been as much in men's mouths as peace and unity (however commendable these are), perhaps things might have been otherways than what they now are. For although every gift and grace has its own proper reward; yet this of faithfulness has the crown appended unto it, "Be thou faithful unto the death, and I will give thee a crown of life." *

There is yet one thing more which perhaps may crave the reader's attention a little; and that is, those prophetical expressions that are interspersed through the following discourses, concerning the awful strokes and judgments that are to be poured forth upon these lands for their dreadful apostacy from God, breach of covenant, contempt of the Gospel, and shedding of the blood of His servants : which expressions are not only treated with scorn and buffoonery by the profane now ; but even many professors tell us, "That it is long now since the spirit of prophecy ceased. We shall never see French or Spaniards here with our eyes." It is true, that with regard to the coming of the Messiah, the end of all prophecy is fulfilled ; but with respect to threatened judgments and promised mercies, they must be always the same in all ages or periods of time : and whether these expressions may be defined prophecy or not, it is not my province at present to determine. But I dare say, they had the mind of the Lord : and we are assured from His word, "That the secret of the Lord is with them that fear him." And as many of these men's words are already come to pass, there is but little ground to doubt but the rest shall yet be accomplished. These lands had a reforming time ;

---

* It is observable that many times ministers of the greatest talents are not the most faithful. For instance, the indulged were as great Gospel preachers (if not greater) than usually the more faithful were. And yet it is evident from the following discourses, that they had no such success upon the hearts of the hearers. What could be ascribed as the reason of this, but the want of faithfulness. For example, none were more faithful than the two Messrs. Guthries, Messrs. Cargill, Cameron, and Renwick ; none in that time were more remarkably blest in their labours than they. Yea, they all finished their ministerial labours upon a public theme. Witness all their last Sermons now in print. And even the Revolution church had some success, while she retained what faithfulness she had. But still as she resiled or departed from this, the Lord withdrew the tokens of His comfortable presence ; and it were to be wished, that the same were not applicable to the different denominations of Dissenters, who have appeared since that time.

strokes and calamities also? And if we shall compare times and events of the Lord's procedure with other sinning lands, churches or people; then we may conclude, "That the Judge standeth at the door." For if apostacy from God, breach of vows, contempt of His word, unfruitfulness under the gospel, scoffing at religion, atheism and ignorance of the true God, idolatry and idolatrous worship, unnecessary oaths and profane swearing, profanation of the holy Sabbath, disobedience to parents, even to the more exalted acts of revenge, innocent blood unpurged, unnecessary wars, homicide and suicide of all kinds, notorious thefts and robberies, open and avowed uncleanliness, perfidious perjury, covetousness and oppression, wherein extortion goes under the notion of improvement, and the most fraudulent practices under the pretence of good management, refuse to retire. Add to all these, insensibility and incorrigibleness under the most compulsive allurements to amendment of life; if these, I say, be either God-provoking or heaven-daring sins, or fatal symptoms of approaching ruin; then we have the Word of God and all the reason in the world to make us believe that these judgments, now impending over our heads, will not be long delayed. Indeed things have already a very gloomy aspect; our horizon darkens apace; and there is " a sound of abundance of rain." *

And what mean all these combustive commotions both in Church and State, division and sub-division, some running upon one extreme, some upon another, but mostly pointing at the trinity of the age, secular advantage, increase of proselytes, or popular applause; while the measures of the leading men appear more like the actions of men under an infatuation, or delirium, than of those endued with rational sagacity. Is it not, because we have forsaken the Lord, and He hath given us erring leaders? "The leaders of this people cause them to err;" who have brought us into the utmost imminent danger, out of which there is little probability at present of extricating ourselves. Similar to the case of Tyrus of old, "Thy rulers have brought thee into great waters." And yet who knows but these reeling confusions, armaments, wars and rumours of wars, both on the isles and continent, may bring about both good to the Church of Christ, and destruction to her enemies, by a further accomplishment of that ancient prophecy, "For my determination is, to gather the nations, that I may assemble the kingdoms to pour upon them mine indignation, even my fierce

---

* "Then issues forth the storm with sudden burst,
    And hurls the whole precipitate air
    Down in a torrent."—Thomson's Seasons, "*Winter.*"

Now, from these few strictures, the more intelligent reader may have a short but just view of these two particulars :—

1. That there is almost no principle, truth, or point of doctrine handled in the following sheets, but what is more or less controverted in this deluded time, whereby they again become the present truth, or " word of Christ's patience,'' and therefore merit the closest attention.

2. It is demonstratively evident, that these isles of the sea, Britain and Ireland, once famous for reformation, have now of a long time, not only been making unto themselves captains to return back to their Egyptian bondage of anti-Christian delusion ; but also by a rapid movement are taking a straight course with crowded sails back unto the gloomy shades of heathen darkness, from both of which we were once, by the good hand of our God, happily delivered. It might once have been said unto us, as to Israel of old, " O Israel (O Britain), who is like unto thee ? a people saved by the Lord." Our " Shittim was then well watered : our desert blossomed like the rose ! Our beauty was like the olive tree, and our smell as Lebanon." Here was a " river that made glad the city of our God !" even the pure preached gospel which replenished the hungry, and refreshed the souls of many. Our renowned ancestors braved all hazards, in handing down a system of pure gospel truths unto us. They separated and set apart themselves to the Lord. They set the crown upon the head of Immanuel. Our " Jerusalem was like a city, and carved like a palace." And who then could behold Scotland and not cry out, " How goodly are thy tents, O Jacob? and thy curtains, O Israel?"

But *Ah, quanto mutati sumus ab illis !* " Alas, how far are we degenerated from them !" How is that glorious work of Reformation tarnished, which in its very first dawn displayed more than a meridian brightness ! Has any nation of the world so far changed their glory for that which is their shame as we have done ? We have well nigh now quitted mount Zion, and shifted ground towards the valley of Hinnom. Nay, such is our temerity that it will not suffice us to desert the walls, unless we also storm the citadel, by a stated emulation, who can go farthest and run fastest from that depositum of truths left us by our forefathers. Christ is exauctorated from His kingly office, and His crown and dignity complimented to another. The Lord has not been ashamed to avow His covenant relation to us ; but we have not only been ashamed to own, but have even denied our covenant relation to Him. " The fear of the Lord is taught by the precepts of men."

---

\* "But now the clouds in airy tumult fly,
The Sun emerging opes the azure sky."—Parnell's Hermit.

lamentation, and shall be for a lamentation.

Secondly, as to this publication itself, I am now to acquaint the reader, that these discourses (excepting a few formerly in print), were collected from ten or twelve volumes mostly in an old small cramp hand. Some of them, I suppose, were wrote by famous Sir Robert Hamilton, and worthy Mr. Robert Smith. * For their order, I have arranged each author's sermons according to the different periods of time in which they were delivered. And as these manuscripts came mostly from different hands and distant quarters, where there were more copies than one sermon, which was often the case, I judged it best in transcribing to compare them, and take that which was most proper for the purpose. But as many of them had no certain date of the time and place when and where they were delivered (which might proceed either from the inadvertency of the writer, or designedly for fear of these places being put to further trouble, had they fallen into the hands of the enemy), I thought it most proper to put these which had any in a foot-note; and for the other notes I have added, they are intended either for explanation or illustration of the subject.† As for the

---

* If any person wants to know what these men were, for the first of these see his life, Biography (page 595). And for Mr. Smith take the following hint :—He was born in the Parish of Closeburn, in Nithsdale, about 1666 ; was brought up in the Episcopal persuasion. Near the end of the persecution, he went to the University of Glasgow, where falling acquaint with a Highland student, from whom in the night he got information of some things concerning the testimony of our sufferers, and the loan of some of Mr. Cargill's sermons, and some Martyrs' testimonies ; which, through a divine blessing, proved a means to convince him, and confirm him in the truth. Afterwards, he went to hear Mr. Renwick upon Heb. xiii. 13—which proved farther means of his conversion. After which he joined the United Societies, and was very useful and helpful to them, both before and after the Revolution, when he was instrumental in gathering the scattered remnant again, after they had been carried away by crafty compliers. After the year 1692, he was by them sent to Holland to the University there, in order for the ministry : but his ordination being frustrated by means of Mr. Linnings, he returned, and laid out himself to propagate true practical religion and stedfastness, in which he continued under many difficulties, until he died with much joy and assurance in believing, December 13th, 1724. He was a man of a tender disposition and acquainted with grief ; and yet, when in company, often most facetious and cheerful. What his principles were is to be seen in his own dying testimony in MS., unto which, for brevity's sake, I must now refer the reader.

† There is one Note, page 181, concerning church deliverances, where the Princes of Orange and Hanover are mentioned, which perhaps some may scruple at. But by the first could only be meant a deliverance from Popery, slavery, and arbitrary power ; and by the last a delivery from Popery (as these nations were then threatened with the accession to the throne of a

delivered, every one's expectation may not be fully met;
it this may be somehow accounted for, under a few considera-
ns. And

1st, With respect unto the fulness of the matter, it will be easily
unted that in several places they were neither so full, nor so
rect as could have been wished; but this need be no wonder if
consider—

1. The circumstances of the preachers. They were deprived of
external conveniences and worldly enjoyments. They laboured
ongst a poor despised remnant, who, for their faithful adherence
the cause and interest of Christ, were persecuted, robbed, and
iled of all that was near and dear unto them. So that there
uld be no pleasing views of lucrative gain; no cringing before a
dly patron in prospect of a large stipend, fertile glebe, and
tely manse; no attendance at the levees of gentlemen in hopes
a sumptuous dinner; no well-furnished room, and large assort-
nts of authors here. No, they were persecuted and hurried
m place to place, hunted like partridges upon the mountains;
y were in continual fear of their life; they had little time to
dy anything, and ofttimes less to deliver what they had pre-
ditated or prepared for that purpose, being many times alarmed
the approach of a fierce, cruel, and bloody enemy.

2. If we consider that, as is both usual and reasonable, when
hors have the opportunity of publishing their own sermons,
y are rather enlarged than impaired or curtailed. But it is not
iere; these discourses being mostly taken from their mouths in
rthand by the common auditory, and mostly by men of a rural
cation, so that they behoved rather to lose, both at first and at
ind hand in transcribing, than to gain; hence they may be more
perly called notes than sermons, for, if we may credit one who
rd several of them preached, they are far inferior (particularly
Cargill's) unto what they were when delivered. *

ndly, For the method, it may be easily accounted for. Every
of the Church has its own method. Nay, I had almost said
t every man has a method or way of delivery peculiar to himself;
.e in the haranguing way, some by doctrinal propositions and
eral heads, and some by general heads and particulars only.
ie may think these discourses somewhat scrimp in the applica-
.; but, upon mature deliberation, they will find little necessity
a long application where the doctrinal part is wholly practical
applicable. However far a good method in preaching may be

sh pretender); otherways the Church of Christ in these lands have met
no real deliverance at or since the Revolution. Nay, each reign has
a us recent and repeated instances to the contrary.

* Viz., Patrick Walker in his relation of Mr. Cargill.

it be otherwise in the matter sound, solid, and agreeable to the text and to parallel texts of Scripture, and faithfully applied unto the sins and duties of the time and particular cases of the auditory unto whom it is delivered.

3rdly, As to the style of language, any person who knows anything of the literature of these times may easily conclude that they were never designed for the reflections of critics, nor calculated to please the taste of those who affect nothing more than a bombast style of sentiment, embellished with scholastic phrases and grammatical oratory, with flights of fancy and terms of art, pronounced in a south British accent. No, they were delivered in such a sense and dialect as was best understood among common hearers, even those amongst whom they were most conversant. It is true that things would have passed then which cannot well pass now, when a plain and handsome style of English language seems more necessary as being now what is universally taught in this island. For which cause any little freedom I have taken in transcribing of these discourses by deleting tautological redundancies, supplying words or parts of sentences deficient, adding elyrtical bars, and placing or replacing figurative distinctions in their proper position, comparing the Scripture texts, and putting them in their own proper words, and translating some of these old-fashioned words or expressions—some of which are yet used in our common country dialect—into more proper English, will be the more easily pardoned by the more intelligent reader, as they are no way intended to detract from the spirit, sense, or meaning of the worthy authors. As to what escapes and typographical mistakes may have crept in at the press, I cannot, from the distance of the place, be otherwise answerable.

There is, indeed, one formidable objection that some of these sermons, viz., Mr. Guthrie's, have to encounter, which arises from the memoirs of his life prefixed to his treatise (now called his work), where it is said, "There were indeed, after the Restoration, some sermons of Mr. Guthrie upon Hos. xiii. 9, and a few other texts published from very imperfect notes, taken by a hearer, by some obscure person." But as these in no just sense could be accounted Mr. Guthrie's, being corrupted and defective, they were injurious to his memory, Mrs. Guthrie, his wife, published an advertisement, and spread it as far as she could, to prevent the public from being imposed on by these spurious sermons. To obviate any scruples arising from these, I would observe—

1. In the negative, this militates nothing against the authenticity of these sermons now published, for it does not say that there

ut that they were corrupt and deficient, as ...... coarse and unguarded expressions, which were made a handle of by prelatic writers against the Presbyterian interest. I shall not say but Mr. Guthrie's memoirs and sermons both might be injured by those incendiaries. But Mr. Guthrie was a very free and faithful man, and had done much for the covenanted interest; and when he beheld that glorious work of reformation wholly effaced and overturned after the Restoration, and Prelacy substituted in its place, no wonder that his zeal began to warm, and that he let fall some harsh expressions, especially when he saw all his faithful brethren thrust out, and poor people persecuted, teased, and tossed for adhering unto that noble cause he so much loved. And this he had no incitement to, neither from the time nor subject, when his treatise was published; but,

2. And more positively, I could produce several instances to prove that he had sermons circulating amongst the hands of our sufferers. But I shall satisfy myself with one, because just at hand in the following collection, preached by Mr. Richard Cameron, and published some time ago, under the title of "Good News to Scotland," of which I have three manuscript copies before me, in which he says:—"Now I would advise you to look much over the prophetical sermons of Mr. William Guthrie, for he speaks clearly of what is now our lot, and many things he pointed out as marks of the Lord's return." Now, if there had been no sermons of Mr. Guthrie, or if these bearing his name were not genuine, what reason in the world could have moved him to recommend that which had no existence, or at best was altogether spurious.

As for that canting objection to publications of this nature, viz., "We have more books than we can make good use of, and greater gospel sermons than what you can pretend these to be," I shall make no other reply than this: That it is granted, we have more books than we rightly improve. But here the fault is our own, and not in the multiplication of them more than in any other means of instruction and edification. And why should we deny these a place amongst others? And there is no question but there are many sermons more full and elegant daily delivered from both press and pulpit; and although what is just and necessary needs no commendation or apology, yet unto what I have said I may farther add—

1. That in them the merit of the creature is disclaimed; free grace exalted through the merit, death, and righteousness of Christ; cases of conscience resolved; the marks of the true believer given; contrary objections answered, and the sins and duties of the time faithfully pointed out unto us; which salutary

martyrs who heard many of them delivered, we must believe that they were in general as remarkably blessed with the powerful energy and down-pouring of the Spirit from on high, upon the hearts of the hearers, as in any age since the Reformation commenced in Scotland; I had almost said, since the primitive times. And, moreover, there is no positive truth handled in these sermons, but what is contended for and sealed by the blood of these martyrs,* nay, some of the worthy authors sealed them with their own blood. And it is a question, if these ministers and professors in this generation, who have either tacitly smothered, or practically, doctrinally, or judicially denied, or impugned these truths which they taught and suffered for, have not their blood yet to account for; seeing by this Italian stab†, they have served themselves heirs unto them that killed them. "*Malus filius, malus pater.*" "Wherefore be ye witnesses unto yourselves that ye are the children of them that killed the prophets."

But, after all, I might tell thee, reader, that, had these prefaces, lectures, and sermons been transcribed by a more dexterous hand or able pen, they had, beyond all doubt, appeared unto the world with more symmetry in parts and accuracy of style, than rationally can be expected. But it sometimes falls out that those who are best furnished for a work of this kind oft-times cannot find leisure for such employment. However, I have aimed for the best, and so far as I have failed therein I have fallen short of my

---

* That this is no empty compliment, hear a few of their own words. Says John Malcolm (who suffered Aug. 13th, 1680), "I am sure the gospel preached by Mr. Richard Cameron especially, was backed with the power and presence of Christ. As much of Christ and heaven was found as finite creatures on earth were able to hold; yea, and more than they could hold. The streams of living water ran down amongst His people at these meetings like a flood, upon the souls of many, who can witness, if they were called to it, that they would not have been afraid of ten thousand." To the same purport are the words of John Potter (who suffered, Dec. 1st, same year), "And now, when I am stepping out of time into eternity, I declare that I adhere to all the doctrines that ever I heard Mr. Richard Cameron or Mr. Donald Cargill preach. And my soul blesses God that ever I heard any of them; for my soul has been refreshed to hear the voice and shoutings of a king in these field meetings, wherein the fountains of living water have been made to run down amongst the people of God in such a manner that armies could not have terrified us." I could produce a number of the like instances; but I shall only notice a few of the words of our own countryman, James Nisbet, who, when speaking of faithful ministers, says, "Only these two, viz., Mr. Donald Cargill and Richard Cameron, which I desire to set to my seal to the faithfulness of these two men's doctrine; for my soul has been refreshed by them; and I set my seal to all their proceedings and actings in the work they were called to; and my soul blesses the Lord that ever I heard them preach."

† An Italian stab is to stab one after he is killed.

is accepted according to that a man hath, and not according to it he hath not."

Before I conclude, I cannot but acknowledge myself and the ᵇlic indebted unto the encouragers of this undertaking, and ᵉse worthy persons from whom I received the manuscripts (from ᵢich they are transcribed), who, I flatter myself, wish well to ᵉ character and works of these worthies. At the same time, I ght signify to the reader, that although I had the pleasure to ᵃ pretty large quarto volume of Mr. Guthrie's sermons, or ᵗes of sermons (said to be wrote with his own hand), yet, at the ᵉne time, I had the mortification to find that I could not obtain from the worthy and reverend person in whose custody it was, my intended purpose. I needed not have mentioned this, had not been surmised that I had received the said manuscript. ᵢd as I have said nothing hitherto out of prejudice, or at ᵢdom, but upon relevant grounds and with regret*, I would not shᵗ to be too censorious in this. Yet I cannot help thinking ᵢt this and like instances are too glaring an evidence that ᵇatever be the pretence) little encouragement is to be expected the publication of the labours and contendings of these worthy ᵗhors, from many of their successors, whether in place or ᵢce. Nay, it would appear rather a burden and grief unto ᵉm. "It grieved them exceedingly, that there was come a ᵈn to seek the welfare of the children of Israel."

But let me conclude with this: May the "Sun of righteousness ᵒ walks in the midst of the seven candlesticks, and holds the ᵉen stars in his right hand; whose voice is as the voice of many ᵗers, and his countenance as the sun shining in his strength," ᵉse, and scatter His enemies and anti-Christian foes, and diffuse radiant, pacific, and sanative beams in the glorious orb of ᵉ gospel, not only in the hearts of the people of these backᵢling lands, but even unto the distant parts of the earth, "whose ᵇitations are yet full of horrid cruelty." And while He shakes ᵗribly the earth, may He shake these kingdoms out of their ᵒstacy and defection from Him; that the cry may not only

---

* No question but some will condemn what I have here said; and others ᵢ think many things here unnecessary for a preface. I grant that large ᵈfatory discourses are not always expedient; but these are truths, and ᵗtroverted truths. It is true, there are some of them largely handled in ᵉeral detached pieces already published; whereas they are little more ᵑ named here, and passed. But truth can never be the worse for being ᵈce told over. We commonly say, "Abundance of law breaks not law." ᵈ what influenced me the more, is, that it is more than probable that ᵇ publication will come into the hands of many who will not allow themᵛes either to purchase or peruse what they call the controverted ᵖphlets of the time.

the Gentile Church, that her converts may be like the pure and numerous dew from the womb of the morning; that it may be said with the spouse, " For lo ! The winter is past, the rain is over and gone : the flowers appear on the earth ; the time of the singing of birds is come, and the voice of the turtle is heard in our land." And while Sharon's rose, who is white and ruddy, is in the small still voice of the gospel, saying, "Arise, my fair one, and come away," let us obtemperate the divine call with this reply, "Behold, we come unto thee, for thou art the Lord our God."

And if the following discourses shall, through a divine blessing, prove useful to any soul for information, instruction, direction, conviction and conversion, and in fine to their edification, spiritual comfort, growth in grace, and the saving knowledge of our Lord and Saviour Jesus Christ, then I shall account all my pains (which have been somewhat considerable), more than fully compensated. For that " the earth may be filled with the knowledge of the glory of the Lord, as the waters cover the sea," is and ought to be the prayer and earnest desire of one, judicious reader, who remains thy soul's Ever-Well-Wisher,

JOHN HOWIE.

Lochgoin, *March 19th,* 1779.

THE CANONGATE TOLBOOTH,

EDINBURGH.

# WILLIAM GUTHRIE.

## BIOGRAPHICAL NOTICE.

## SERMONS.

# WILLIAM GUTHRIE.

## BIOGRAPHICAL NOTICE.

WILLIAM GUTHRIE, the author of seventeen of the sermons that follow, was a native of Angusshire, and was born in the year 1620. He was the eldest of five brothers, four of whom devoted themselves to the ministry of the Gospel. The youngest, John Guthrie, was the author of the sermon that appears last in this Collection.

After a careful secular and religious training, preparatory to his higher studies for the great work of his life, William Guthrie became a student at St. Andrews. Under the direction there of James Guthrie, his cousin, who suffered martyrdom in 1661, and Alexander Rutherford, he completed those higher studies in moral philosophy and theology, and received license to preach the Gospel. It was while studying at St. Andrews, "by the ministry of that excellent person," Rutherford, that William Guthrie had that gospel "revealed in" him which he was to proclaim to others. "His conversion was begun with the great terror of God in his soul, and completed with that joy and peace in believing which accompanied him through life." His consecration to the service of His Redeemer was marked from that time forward. He freed himself of all worldly entanglements, and gave himself up to labour in love for the salvation of souls, and in zeal for the Divine glory.

On November 7th, 1644, he was ordained minister of the newly erected Parish of Fenwick, in Ayrshire. The moral and religious condition of the people of his charge was such as to require all the consecration that the young minister brought to the discharge of his duties. An utter indifference to religion and many sinful customs prevailed throughout the district. But every proper expedient that could be thought of to reclaim them and make them servants of Christ Jesus, Guthrie employed. In a disguised manner he visited those who wholly neglected ordinances and had never seen him, and conversed and worshipped with them; he promised

F

gled with the people generally in their harmless games, and
braced opportunities in this way of speaking words for the
ster—shooting arrows at a venture which reached many con-
nces. The main motive that seems to have actuated him in
his pastoral relations was that of the Apostle—"I seek not
rs but you."

[is excellence and eminence as a preacher of the Gospel, his
1fulness to covenanted attainments, and specially his opposition
1e Resolutioners, drew upon him the envy and wrath of the Pre-
s. The Archbishop of Glasgow resolved upon his deposition
1 the office of the ministry, and his extrusion from the manse
rights of Fenwick. Even among the fawning curates it was
cult to obtain a man to carry out the iniquitous resolution.
1ere was an awe upon their spirits which scared them
1 meddling with this great man." For the sum of five
nds the curate of Cadder undertook the work, and pro-
led with a party of soldiers to carry out the sentence.
hrie and his attached flock observed suitable services
riew of the trying ordeal through which they were to pass.
text of the last sermon preached by Guthrie in the Church
from Hosea—"In Me is thine help." Having presented
self in the manse, the curate read his commission from the
bishop, and enumerated several offences which he laid to
hrie's charge. The answer of the accused was fearless and
le. Guthrie assured his accuser and those for whom he acted
the crimes alleged against him were utterly false, that he laid
veight upon their sentence, that those who assailed him were
ty of defection from the cause of Christ, that upon them, in the
t of God, were chargeable all the consequences of the interrup-
of his ministry, and he continued in these words :—"And here
further declare, before these gentlemen, that I am superseded
1 my ministry for adhering to the covenants and Word of God,
1 which you and others have apostatised." To the curate, who
rrupted him by remarking that the Lord's work was carried
before the covenants were entered into, Guthrie replied:
is true the Lord had a work before that covenant had being;
it is true that it hath been more glorious since that covenant :

open resistance, and the curate, after going through the form of deposition in a deserted Church, returned to Glasgow, but died in a few days thereafter "of great torment, of an iliac passion," according to Wodrow, who adds, "Such a dangerous thing it is to meddle with Christ's servants."

Like many eminent ministers and other devoted servants of Christ, William Guthrie suffered long under a sore affliction. He was subject to severe attacks of the gravel, which caused him extreme pain, and brought him down frequently to the very verge of the grave with prostration. Being once in a meditative mood in the company of his cousin at St. Andrews, and being asked what he was thinking of, he replied—"I'll tell you, cousin, what I am not only thinking upon, but I am sure of, if I be not under delusion. The malignants will be *your* death, and this gravel will be *mine;* but you will have the advantage of me, for you will die honourably before many witnesses, with a rope about your neck ; and I will die whining upon a pickle straw, and will endure more pain before I rise from your table than all the pain you will have in your death." Yet amid all his racking pains, his Christian fortitude did not forsake him. He was still strong in the Lord. "Though I should die mad," he said on one occasion after a violent attack, "yet I know I shall die in the Lord. Blessed are the dead which die in the Lord at all times, but more especially when a flood of errors, snares, and judgments, is beginning or coming on a nation, church, or people." The deliverance he long sought for was at length granted him. On the 10th of October, 1665, in the forty-fifth year of his age, William Guthrie entered into the joy of his Lord.

His character is described by Livingstone, partly in the following terms:—"In his doctrine he was as full and free as any man in Scotland had ever been ; which, together with the excellency of his preaching gift, did so recommend him to the affection of his people, that they turned the cornfield of his glebe into a little town, every one building a house for his family on it, that they might live under the drop of his ministry." He was "a man of most ready wit, fruitful invention, and apposite comparisons, qualified both to

n tempted to leave Fenwick for larger parishes and a more
aential position, he preferred abiding with the people among
im he first began his ministry, and where he had many clear
lences of success. Many souls from that parish, saved by his
rumentality, preceded and followed after him to the Church
mphant. "For what is our hope, or joy, or crown of rejoicing?
not even ye in the presence of our Lord Jesus Christ at His
ing? For ye are our glory and joy."

# SERMONS.

## SERMON I.

*"But it is good for me to draw near to God."*—Psalm lxxiii. 28.

THESE words are a part of the result of a very strange exercise, which a godly man had, being much stumbled and troubled in heart at the prosperity of the wicked, because they got so much of their will in the world. But now having surmounted the temptation, and got a second view of all things, relating both to the prosperity of the wicked, and to the afflicted condition of the godly, in contemplation of which he resolves to draw near to God. "It is good," says he, "to draw near to God." As if he had said, "I trow I am neither wise nor happy to intermeddle so much with these things, and I wot well it is my best to 'draw near to God.' It is good for me to flee in unto Him, and, as it were, to look out at my windows, until I see how all things here will roll." Now there is no great difficulty here, in the words now read, but what we may reach in the doctrine. We may consider them either—

1st, Simply or absolutely; or,

2nd, As they have a reference unto what goes before in the same place or portion of Scripture. And,

First, Consider these words simply or absolutely, from whence for doctrine we observe.

DOCT.—*That* IT IS GOOD TO DRAW NEAR TO GOD; *or good by way of eminency; it is truly and really good. It is an advantageous good. And it is enough for confirmation of the doctrine, that it is not only positively asserted here in the text, but it is also commanded as our duty by the Apostle James. "Draw nigh unto God, and he will draw nigh unto you."*

Now, in speaking of this we shall,

I. Show you what it is to draw near unto God.

II. Show you what are the advantages of drawing near to God, or how it is good to do so.

I. To show you what it is to draw near unto God. And,

1. A man should make his peace with God in and through the Mediator Jesus Christ; for until once that be done, a man may be said to be far from God, and there is a partition-wall standing

e with him, and so good ___

God and all shall be well with you. Ye must come up unto
e measure of conformity to the blessed will of God, and quit
life of estrangement from Him, as is evident from that fore-
l text: "Draw nigh unto God and he shall draw nigh unto
" And this is explained in the words following: "Cleanse
: hands, ye sinners; and purify your hearts, ye double-minded:"
is, Quit that filthy life of estrangement from God, in being
e conformed unto Him and His will, as He hath revealed unto
in His word.

It is to seek more after communion and fellowship with
, and to pursue after intimacy and familiarity with Him, and
ave more of His blessed company with us in our walk and
ersation; according to that word: "Blessed are the people
know the joyful sound: they shall walk, O Lord, in the
t of thy countenance." This is to walk through the day,
ng a good understanding between God and us; and so to be
ys near unto Him in keeping still up communication with
t. And,

As it stands here in the text, it is the expression of one who
made up his peace already, and is on good terms with God,
doth differ a little from what the words absolutely imply; and
e may take it thus:—

.) It implies the confirming, or making sure our interest in
, and so it supposeth the man's peace to be made with God;
whoever be the author of this psalm, it supposeth he hath
e his peace, and therefore in the following words it is sub-
ed, "I have put my trust in the Lord," &c., that is, I have
ted my soul unto God, and made my peace with Him through
ediator. It is good whatever comes; it is always good to be
unto God that way, and to be made sure in Him.

.) It implies to be more and more conformed unto the image
lod, and therefore his nearness to Him is opposed to that of
g far from God. "It is good," says he, "to draw near to God
ly duty, when so many are far from Him."

.) It implies that which I was hinting at before, to lay by all
gs in the world, and to seek fellowship and communion with
; and to be more set apart for His blessed company, and to
: with Him in a dependence upon Him, as the great Burden-
rer, as Him who is to be all in all unto us. In a word, to
v near unto God is to make our peace with Him, and to secure
confirm that peace with Him, and to study a conformity unto
l, and to be near unto Him in our walk and conversation; in
fellowship, and whole carriage and deportment to be always
unto Him.

happy consequences that follow upon it.

1. It is a pleasant good. "Wisdom's ways are pleasantness, and all her paths are peace." And although many of you think that the people of God have a sorrowful and sad life of it, yet this flows not from their nearness unto God; but it is because they depart out of His way, or step aside from following Him.

2. As it is good in itself, and a pleasant good, so it is a creditable and honourable good. Is it not good to be at peace, and in good terms with God, to be conformed unto His will, which is the supreme rule of all righteousness, and to have intimate fellowship with Him? We would think it a very honourable thing to be in favour and on good terms with a man that ruleth over all nations, supposing him to be a good man, and that our intimacy with him were not scandalous and offensive. But it is quite another thing to be in favour and on good terms with Him who ruleth over all laws and all men as so many insects; under whom the inhabitants of the earth appear as so many grasshoppers in His sight.

Oh, but it is good in respect of the circumstances and consequences of it, and so it is also a profitable good! Yea, it secures a man's soul and eternal well-being. It keeps him in perfect peace. It has many testificates and outlettings of God's countenance, which is better unto him than barns full of corn, or cellars full of wine and oil. Yea, He is all good. "The Lord will give grace and glory, and will withhold no good thing from them that walk uprightly." And who are these? Even such as are near unto God; so that it is a good thing to draw near unto Him.

USE.—Would you be for ever happy in the enjoying of that which is supremely good? Well then, draw near unto God. Everyone readily follows after something that he thinks to be good. There are many that say, "Who will show us any good?" The most part would be at some visible or seeming good. Yes, but this is a more sure and permanent good, that will fill your hand. Then go and acquaint yourselves. Seek to have communion with Him, and to be confirmed and conformed unto Him. In prosecuting of this use we shall speak a word unto these two sorts of people :—

1. To some who are wholly estranged from God, although I know there are many of you that will not take this charge, go and acquaint yourselves with Him, if you would be for ever happy. And what is this but to know Him, and make an offer of yourselves unto Him? How is it that ye make your acquaintance with one come from France, or so, having some knowledge of him, and expecting great favour at his hand? You offer your

d? You will do it the better when you know how far heaven
l you are from one another. For your better understanding of
s, I will give you a few marks of those who are far from Him.

1.) Have you known anything of His voice? Ye will say, "If
ere near such a one, I would know his voice." If you do not,
ι are yet far from Him. "My sheep hear my voice, and I know
m, and they follow me." What God speaks in this gospel is
lishness unto many; but those who are His sheep know His
ce, and unto them this gospel is the wisdom and power of God.
ιld ye never lay claim unto that word, "It is the voice of my
ʒved that knocketh"? I know whose voice it is. Were ye
er persuaded that this gospel was the most wise of all devices
t ever was contrived, or thought upon to save sinners? This is
ɪnow His voice. You that count the preaching of the gospel
babbling, ye are far from God in hearing of His voice, and
not but expect to stumble upon what ye hear concerning Him.
2.) Know ye His face? Who is he that says, "Stay till I be
r unto Him, and then perhaps I shall know Him"? But if ye
ɪot know His face, ye are far from Him. And yet I am per-
ded that there are many hearing me, that know not what I
ιn. But pose yourselves. Know ye anything of the difference
wixt the smiles and frowns of God; or what it is to have your
rts and souls warmed with the heat and light of His countenance?
th ever your soul been made to weep within you with His love?
ιot, it is a bad token; for the people of God know His face;
whenever they hear Him named, their affections go out after
n.
3.) What dealings have ye in your ordinary way and walk with
1? Do ye acknowledge Him in all your ways? He knows the
ked afar off, and hath no dealings with them. Do ye venture
n nothing without God's counsel? Do you keep your eye upon
n in your ordinary business? And do ye give an account
reof unto Him? If it is so, it is well. But if ye have no mind
ɟod; only when ye put on your clothes, and wash your hands,
nay be ye retire a little in secret, and then lose any thought
have had of Him all the day long; that is a bad token that ye
yet far from God: and if death shall meet with you in this
ιation, your hearts shall be roughly handled by it.
ʔ. The second sort that I would speak unto are those who are
ly godly. Would you be happy and good in the land of the
ng? then draw near to God in all these respects formerly
iced. And that ye may do it, it were good for you, that,
1:) Ye were convinced of your being in a great measure far
n God; and in that respect unlike what I formerly spoke of.

And what is that? It is even to remove whatever stands betwixt Him and you. When ye go unto prayer, or when you would lay claim unto any promise; then "do not regard sin in your heart." Put away all idols of jealousy. Let none of them come in with you before the Lord; for if ye do, He will never regard your desires in prayer: and this is a time wherein there are many loose hands in this respect. Therefore it were good for you to step home, and be sure where ye are to take up your lodging at night.

(2.) Study to be convinced, that ye are by nature far from God, and in your walk and conversation, from that communion with Him that ye might attain unto, even while here. And if once ye were at that, you would think it your unquestionable duty to "draw near unto God," in all these respects before mentioned. But where is that labour of love, that unweariedness in duty, and that disposition to suffer everything for Christ? Are not all these, in a great measure, gone? What fainting, failing, and scaring at the cross? So that but scratch the clothes of many Christians, and they will be like to go beside themselves. Where is that appetite and desire after Christ, and His righteousness, which folk sometimes so vigorously pursued? Where is that estimation of, and enquiry after, marks of grace in the soul, that hath sometimes been? How perilous hath a mark of grace sometimes been, and how did it alarm you when it was observed? And where are that sympathy and longing for the discovery of duty, submission unto reproof, that were wont to be amongst you? Are ye not rather afraid to hear your duty laid out before you? And where is that simplicity of the gospel, or that happiness people had in hearing the gospel, when they had not such skill to shift, or evade the word, and to put all by, except those sentences that pleased their own fancy; and when they durst not entertain a challenge of conscience all night but it behoved them to mourn for it before the Lord, until it was removed? Hath not many of you got the devil's wisdom to lodge a challenge all night, and not be troubled with it? And where is that tenderness of conscience, that would have made people abstain from every appearance of evil, and would have made them walk circumspectly in regard of offences, and mourn for them before God? And where is that true zeal for the interest of Christ that was once in our corporations in these dominions? Is not that gone, and are there any rightly exercised when they see the matters of God going wrong? Now ye should draw near unto God in all these things. Now,

(3.) Is there any pursuing after this nearness unto God that was wont sometimes to have been a case of conscience? But now to mend our evil faults, of all cases this is the most remote from us.

undle of myrrh, between your breasts." But, oh! is not this ost gone? Oh! therefore draw near to Him. Again, it is good we commonly say, to come to old use and wont again, if ye come farther. But,

Secondly, I come to speak of the words as they have a reference o what goes before the text. And,

st, They turn upon this:—he had seen the wicked prosper and much of their will in the world. When he beheld this, he s made to stumble at it; but after recollecting, and considering a little, he recovers himself, and begins to speak of what he had merly said concerning it. And here, says he, "It is good for to draw near unto God." Whence I observe,

l. That a godly man's heart should satisfy itself, over all the sperity the wicked hath, or can have in the world; and there-e the word in the original imports a gaining of God unto me. is good for me; it is an only good for me, to draw near to God, I that is enough to satisfy me, over all and beyond all the sperity of the wicked in the world. And so much is insinuated the wicked that prosper in his way. What should we then do? hy, trust in God! Be satisfied in Him as your blessed choice I portion. And the grounds on which a godly man's heart uld satisfy itself over all that he sees in the lot of the wicked, these:—

(1.) The fountain itself is better than any drops that come to wicked. God Himself is better than the creature. He is ter than ten sons, yea, He is better far than any good thing t proceeds from Him. Therefore, he says, in the words pre-ing the text, "Whom have I in the heavens but thee, and re is none on the earth that I desire besides thee." When he counted all, this is the sum of the whole reckoning.

(2.) He goes further on the same ground, as if he would say, see that all this folk, viz., the wicked, stand in slippery places. vould not be in their place for all that they enjoy, and as much it. But as for me, 'Thou wilt guide me with thy counsel, and erwards receive me unto glory.'" No other good thing is so d as God. God is good in Himself, and He commands all that eally good unto that man that draws near unto Him, even from shoe latchet unto the salvation of his soul, and makes every-ng turn to him, as it were, in the hollow of His hand. "The rd will give grace and glory; no good thing will he withhold m them that walk uprightly." And may not that satisfy us ly?

For Use 1.—This reproves the godly, who grudge and fret at prosperity of the wicked. "Fret not thyself because of evil-than many portions. Oh! learn to compare your lot with the lot of the men of this world. Count, and count on, and see whose number exceeds. Tell, and tell over, and see who tells longest, for there is much counting in your lot compared to what is in theirs. That is a strange word, "Was not Esau Jacob's brother, saith the Lord ; yet I loved Jacob, and hated Esau, and laid his mountain and heritage waste." Esau had the dominion for a time, yet the headship or superiority belonged unto Jacob. And that might satisfy him, though he had not so much worldly substance as Esau. Believers may sing that song with David, when near his end : "Although my house be not so ordered with God, yet he hath made with me an everlasting covenant, ordered in all things and sure."

USE 2.—Although there be a party of wicked men, men of Belial, that we have to do with in the world—a party that are like briers and thorns, so that the people of God had need of gauntlet gloves when dealing with them, yet the covenant is enough for that also, for "this is all my salvation, and all my desire," although He make it not to grow.

2. Observe, That the more the wicked get their will, the people of God should still draw the more near unto God. And this is imported in Psalm xxxvii. 3, "Trust in the Lord, and do good ; delight thyself also in the Lord." This is opposed unto fretting at the prosperity of the wicked. This is the duty of all the godly when the wicked get most of their desires in the world, and that for these reasons :—

(1.) Because they may be satisfied in so doing. Do the wicked get much of their mind in their lot and portion ? Well, the people of God should fill themselves full of their portion, for there is a reality in it, but there is none in the portion of the wicked. What are houses, lands, gold, silver, or ease, to eternal life ? Oh, take a good draught thereof by drawing near unto God. And

(2.) Because your trials and temptations are coming. And if the wicked get up and have the dominion, as it is likely they may, then the godly may make for their sheet and their shoes, if they can come at them.

(3.) Because this is the way to preserve you, and to guard your hearts from mistakes, when you meet with the temptation this man met with. A sad temptation, when godly folk get not their will in what they would be at, for God and His interest, and godless folk get their will and design. Then they are ready to misrepresent and mistake the voice of Providence. You see this godly man accounted himself as a beast under this. But a drawing near unto God will prevent every mistake in this case. And

stroyed for ever." Then may the Lord save the innocent, for
re will be stirs. Therefore flee into your windows. Draw near
to God.

USE 1.—Ye hear what is your duty when wicked folk get most
their designs and commands over all. Here it is; draw near
to God, and thus hold you out of harm's way in an evil time.

USE 2.—See how ye may be put into a capacity for a day of
al and be creditably carried through. And if ye would be even
th wicked men, and guard against mistakes, and be enabled to
faithful, and forthcoming for or to God, then draw near unto
m in all He has commanded you.

USE 3.—This reproves those who are resolving to take another
y, and cast about to the leeward, and row to the shore, to see
at friends they may have at court, to curry the favour of great
n, to get their own business well managed, and to tell ill tales
the godly. Be sure ye shall meet with a mischief. It is good
all times, but especially at such a time, to draw near unto God.
d if ye do not this ye shall never have safety in any other way.
t,

2ndly, Take the words as they are, an inference from these
rds before the text, in the 25th verse; "Whom have I in
ven but thee; and there is none upon earth that I desire
ides thee: my heart and my flesh faileth me," &c. Here we
the Psalmist very near unto God, and yet in the text he says,
t is good for me to draw near unto God." Whence
[ observe, Let a man be as near unto God as he can imagine,
; it is good to draw near unto Him, and to seek to have nearer
owship and more intimate acquaintance with Him. This man
s near, yet he seeks to be nearer unto Him; even to have his
ns full of God, so to speak. And the reason is

1. Because the life of true religion in the world is but a strong
petite, and a heart hungering after God. And therefore folk
uld still be hungering and seeking after more from Him. And

2. Because even that which ye have got ye cannot keep, unless
a be still in the pursuit of more. You lose what ye have got,
d scatter as fast as ye have gathered, if ye be not still making
gress and increase. Therefore, "Hold up my going in thy
h, that my footsteps slip not." That is, hold a grip of me,
erwise I will suddenly go wrong. Ye will come unto a small
koning, if ye draw not near and more near unto God.

USE 1.—This serves for trial of your reception of God. Try if
be still pursuing after more. Ye that think ye have got
nething from God, and are sitting down upon that, I am in
ubt whether that reception of God be at all real. For where it

in the pot of ointment.

USE 2.—And ye that have really got anything of God, work fast for more. Study to go forward; otherwise I defy you to keep what ye have already gotten. The devil will get his hand upon it, and then ye will be in hazard of losing what ye have once gotten.

USE 3.—"Open your mouths wide, and the Lord will fill them abundantly." There are treasures of good things with Him, that ye never yet beheld, or lighted upon; sweet fills of love, peace, joy; perfect victory over sin; self-denial, and dying to the world, being alive to nothing but Christ, being filled with all the fulness of God. All these, and much more are to be had for the seeking after.

3rdly, Consider the words, as they are connected with these immediately preceding the text. "Thou hast destroyed all that go a-whoring from thee." Hence observe,

That it is good to draw near unto God; the only way in all the world, to secure a man from the dreadful judgments that are coming upon men, is to draw near unto God.

USE 1.—It were good that folk considered, and were oftener thinking upon those judgments that are to be poured out upon wicked men. There was a generation of ungodly men in Scotland that were enemies to the people of God; and many of them are yet alive. God has dropped dreadful judgments on some of them, and yet continues to drop them upon the rest; and it is likely the dregs of the cup will be the bitterest. Ye may believe it, you that are the people of God have no other way to escape the judgments of God but by drawing near unto Him. Fancy not an immunity from judgment another way. There is a sword of the Lord that will cut off the wicked; and the righteous have no way of escape, but by drawing near unto God. And if ye would set yourselves seriously to it, God would meet you mid-way, and more; as it is evident from the forecited text.

USE 2.—It were good for all God's people in times of temptation and trials, to follow this godly man's example here. He hath been in a temptation, and he wrestles with it and carries off the spoil of the temptation, as it were, upon the edge of his hat, and comes off the field honourably.

Finally, Study to carry in this way whenever a temptation comes upon you, and ye are engaged in it. Thus bring some of the honourable spoil of the temptation with you. "It is good for me to draw near unto God."

# SERMON II.

*?or what is a man profited, if he should gain the whole world,*
*and lose his own soul? or, what shall a man give in exchange*
*for his soul?"*—Matthew xvi. 26.

CRIST had been pressing the company that were hearing Him,
d His own disciples also, to lay out themselves for the truth, at
hazards. In these words that I have read in your hearing, He
es a double argument. The one is, What is a man profited, if
should gain the whole world, and lose his own soul for that
rldly gain? The truth is, he is a perfect and an absolute loser.
cannot be told what loss he hath, and how bad a bargain he
th made. The other is, if a man lay his soul as a pawn, or
dge for this, he will not set it free again at his own pleasure.
e text says, "Or what shall a man give in exchange for his
il?"

Now, from these words, I shall hold out to you the following
ctrines.

Doct. I.—*The souls of men are highly valued and esteemed by*
*Jesus Christ.*

Christ Jesus hath valued the souls of men at a very high rate;
: He hath so computed that He sets the whole world at nought
comparison to one soul. He says, "Though a man should gain
e whole world, and lose his own soul, he is a perfect and an
solute loser." "Thou fool, this night shall thy soul be required
thee." Christ said this to the man that had enlarged his barns,
d had provided nothing for his soul. Christ values the souls of
en very much. And,

Here I offer you the following evidences of the doctrine, Christ
ghly values and esteems the souls of men. And,

1. That glorious contrivance of the gospel speaks forth what
high esteem God puts upon the souls of men. Great has been
e work and business of its contrivance, in order that His will
ay be revealed and made known to men: all is done with a
sign to save the soul. And if there were no more to speak of
im than the Bible, it sufficiently shows how He values and
teems the souls of men. He can make thousands of worlds at
e word; and yet He has taken much pains in contriving a way
w to deal with men's souls, and about that great and glorious
siness of man's redemption.

2. This also says that Christ values the soul much, that He took
Him our nature, and subjected Himself very low, for such
worthy worms of the earth. None knew how to value the

soul. There is not an up or down, a dethroning of kings, or pro-tectors,* or princes, but it is done with an eye to the good of the soul. He carrieth on some things in order to the good of the souls of men. If there were no more but the keeping up a standing ministry, and the vindication of that ordinance which He keeps up at a great expense, it shows that He values the souls of men at a very high rate.

3. Let us come and take notice of another evidence just at hand. Consider the particular care that He takes of particular persons; even a poor boy or girl. He will be speaking unto them, rebuking, exhorting, comforting, instructing them particu-larly, and singularly; waiting upon their ups and downs; to ratify the thoughts of their hearts, as if He had no other thing to do; though He has great kingdoms and sceptres besides to rule. All this shows how highly He values the souls of men.

Now what are the reasons of this doctrine? It is not because of any good works we can do unto Him. But,

1st, It is because He values the souls of men, at least compara-tively with other things, as more glorious pieces of His handy-work than any other thing in this lower world. These glorious lumin-aries, the sun, moon, &c, are nothing to the soul. All the pleasant things that you ever saw, even heaps of gold, and silver, and streets garnished with pearls or precious stones, are nothing in comparison to a rational soul. There was never anything made upon earth that bore the image of God so eminently and singularly as the soul. And this is one reason why the Lord values the soul so much; because it doth represent Himself more than any other creature upon earth.

2ndly, The Lord values the soul of man very much, because He carrieth on His work by the soul more than by any other thing. He gives the most glorious displays of His power and mercy, by the souls of men. He proves Himself Lord over heaven, earth, and hell, by the souls of men. And,

3rdly, I may say, the Lord values the soul much, because it is of the highest concernment. And this is one of the reasons God lays so much weight upon it; "For the redemption of the soul is precious, and it ceaseth for ever."

What use then can we make of this doctrine? God loves the soul so much, and we value it so little. It holds forth this unto us :—

That we differ exceedingly in our thoughts from the Lord. He hath put an high esteem on the soul, and we do not esteem it

---

* This sermon seems to have been preached about the time of Oliver Cromwell.

appear. And,

1st, Try whether ye have any serious thought concerning your souls. Do ye value your souls much, who have never a thought of them to see in what case and condition they are, and what will become of them in the end? Dare ye say, in the sight of an all-seeing God, that ye had serious thoughts of your soul, and what would become of it in the end? If ye dare not say that, your value for your soul is a fancy indeed. And I pose you all, this day, that hear me, if ever you had deep thoughts concerning your soul's case and condition, answer me to that. You that cannot answer in the affirmative, ye are not far from the wrath and vengeance of God. Ye that cast your souls at your heels, and undervalue them, and spend more time and pains on the poor perishing things of the world, would ye be called Christians? Nay, rather limbs of the devil, worldly worms, and moles of the earth.

2ndly, Do ye value your souls much, who make no endeavours for your souls. Ye can tell every year how far your labour is advanced at such a time; that you have now got your oat-seed, or your barley-seed into the ground. But what have ye done for your soul? Surely everyone must give an account unto the God of heaven for their souls. I dare boldly say, that some of you lay more weight on six or seven steps of a rig's end to sow a little flax seed on, than ever you did upon your precious and immortal souls.

3rdly, Do ye value your souls much, when for a thing of nought, for a very little, or frivolous thing, ye will venture upon the wrath of God; when ye will swear and profane the name of the Lord for a thing of nought; when ye will lay down your soul against twopence; as if I were to throw down my gold ring, and play it against a few pennies Scots. And so you venture upon the wrath of the Almighty for a trifle.

4thly, Another evidence of it is given, when other things come in competition with the soul. Here is something that concerns the soul; there is something that concerns the world; I will refer it to your own conscience, which gets the first place. Here is a thing that concerns the soul; but ye are called to yoke the plough. Now lay your hand to your heart, and judge ye whether ye value your soul or the world most, and look which of these gets the priority.

5thly, Do ye value your souls much? Ye can hear threatenings concerning the destruction and ruin of your souls, and yet never be affrighted or alarmed. There is no need of greater

no reason to think that thou valuest thy soul much, and thou hast need to be laying thy soul's case and condition to heart.

DOCT. II.—*Though the soul of man be a precious thing, and much valued by the Lord, yet He hath committed it unto man's keeping for a certain time ; and it is the business God has put you upon, to look to your souls.*

But ye will say, "We have no leisure for this." But tell me, when get you time to go about any other business? What is your work? Is it about your soul; or is it about other things? When got ye leisure to eat, drink, and sleep, and to go about your other worldly affairs? Remember that the Lord hath committed the soul to your keeping, as your principal work and business. And,

1st, In some respects, God hath allowed you more time to go about your other business. Yet in other respects, God has allowed you to take more time about your soul's case; much more, at least, than probably you do.

2ndly, Know, there are few in all the world that can give a faithful discharge of their souls as well kept. Look if ye be of the number of those few. But if ye can find no good reasons that ye are of these few, there is little hope of you. Are ye not afraid of these words, "Many are called, but few are chosen." There are but few that enter in at that strait gate, and walk in that narrow way that leads unto life. There are but few to whom God discovers the worth and preciousness of their souls. Ye would do well to remember that a very little thing will wrong or injure the soul. We commonly say, and I wish it were more noticed by us, "That a little thing will harm the eye." But a far less thing will harm the soul. A thought will put the soul out of case for many days. And a wrong word spoken will put the soul out of order, so that perhaps it may never afterwards get the comfort of its peace with God in this life.

USE.—Now, ye should be making your peace with God; for ye know not if ever ye shall get another day after this. Yea, there is a day appointed when the Lord will take back again the souls of men; "O fool, this night shall thy soul be required of thee." There shall be no delay. It shall be taken from thee this same night. As thou doest, so shalt thou receive according to thy works. If thou hast dealt well with thy soul, the Lord shall deal well with it also. And if thou slightest it, He will slight it also. And do not think that because the soul is a precious thing, and the Lord values it much, that He will not assign such a precious

G

eality, " What account can ye give to God,.." He should require an account of you before ye sleep this night?" Can ye not answer? Are ye speechless? And how much more shall ye be speechless when God shall put that question unto you, and shall command you to be taken and bound hand and foot, and cast into hell-fire, "Where the worm dieth not, and the fire is not quenched."

Doct. III.—*The Lord cares little for the world.*

He values the souls of men much; and we value them little. He values the world little; and we value it much. Although a man should gain the whole world, and lose his own soul, he is but a fool, and he hath made a very bad bargain. Christ values the world very little. I offer you these evidences of the truth of this doctrine.

1st, When Christ was in the world, He made a very mean purchase of it for Himself. He had not where to lay His head; and sometimes He could not command a drink of water therein. He made a very poor purchase of it to Himself. "The foxes have holes, and the birds of the air have nests, but the Son of man hath not where to lay his head."

2ndly, He usually gives least of it to His dear friends and followers. I do not say but some who have much of the world may be gracious folk; but ordinarily God gives least of the world to His own people. Where ye will get one rich man that is godly, ye will get ten that are atheists. "He hath not chosen many mighty men of the world, not many wise men, after the flesh, not many mighty, not many noble, are called."

3rdly, The Lord has given a considerable portion of the world unto His avowed enemies, who fight against Him, and improve it against Him. He gives much of the earth to profane atheists, profane beasts, and renegades, who are His avowed enemies; for the earth is given unto the wicked."

4thly, And ere long He will set it in a flame. He will burn it up with fire. The earth is, as it were, withered already, and ready for burning. And what makes the Lord care so little for the world? "The earth also and works thereof shall be burnt up."

But what are the reasons for this doctrine?

It is because by man's transgressions it is made subject unto vanity. "For the creature was made subject to vanity, not willingly, but by reason of him who hath subjected the same in hope." All things are properly diversions from God, from the living God, and there is not a dumb beast, but it is for man's sake plagued of him, and so made subject unto vanity.

it very much, and care for perishing things, even trifles of the world. But ye will perhaps say, that ye do not value it much. But this will appear in these few things following.

1. A man values that much on which he spends his strength voluntarily, and with complacency and delight. Ye say the world pulls the life out of you. But yet ye suffer it to do so willingly, and with delight.

2. A man does that most willingly on which the affection of his heart is most bent. And do not your hearts run out most after the things of the present world? Hence your fear, love, hope and delight run out after a present world. What makes you glad and cheerful, but something in the world that prospers, and is going well with you? And what makes you afraid, or sorry? Is it not because the world seems to frown upon you?

3. This proves that you value the world much, that ye will not take a rebuke, but will eagerly follow on in the pursuit of it, although it has failed you often, and given you many a disappointment; and although the Lord has blasted that which ye have been following after.

4. A fourth evidence is, That ye will venture to lose the friendship of God for a very frivolous thing. Ye will venture to wrong the God of heaven for a little worldly enjoyment. But I go no further at present, only I shall notice these two things following:—

(1.) Although the soul be very precious, yet we value or esteem it very little: and although the world be a poor ambulatory thing, we put a very high price or esteem upon it. And,

(2.) Although your souls be threatened with utter ruin on that account, yet ye are not afraid, which shows that ye care not much for them. You cannot be put off the cutting and carking cares of this world, even though God has corrected you, and given you as it were, over the finger ends for them. And yet do your best ye cannot take delight in serving God half an hour. Look then to your souls in time; slight them not; otherwise God will slight them, if you mind them not in time. "For what is a man profited, if he should gain the whole world and lose his own soul? or, what shall a man give in exchange for his soul?"

*"For I will pour water upon him that is thirsty, and floods upon the dry ground: I will pour my Spirit upon thy seed, and my blessing upon thine offspring.—Isaiah xliv. 3.*

WE have heard of the two commands that make way for the promise, and ye have heard of the grounds on which they are pressed. When His professing people hear of their danger, and try not to seek after a remedy, but turn their back upon God, He cries, as it were, after them, and says, "Hear another word, and take not away an ill report of God and His ways." But may we say, "What is that word?" Why, it is just to hold by the covenant. The covenant is given, not only to satisfy all your desires, but even to hold by until ye hear a better word come forth from the Lord.

But, say ye, "If ye knew my condition, ye could not bid me but fear." It is true I know not your condition, but He that formed you from the womb says, "Fear not, O Jacob, my servant, and Jeshurun whom I have chosen." "Our iniquities are like to take hold upon us," say ye, "but sink them into the covenant," says He. "Lean down your burdens there," says He; "and speak a word to Me, and if I answer not your condition, then take it up again, if ye be able, and go your way." "Well," say ye, "we are content to lean down our burden upon the covenant. Now what hast Thou to say unto us, Lord?" "Then," says He, "I know ye want much, and I know the chief of all your wants. I know ye want My blessing. Then stay and take it, and ye shall prosper the better. I know that ye would have drink, although ye will not grant ye are thirsty. Can ye not say dry ground? Then come and set to your mouths here, and I will let out waters unto you. But know ye what I say?" says He. "Not very well," say ye. "Then," says He, "I will tell you in plain terms. 'I will pour out my Spirit upon you; for I will pour water upon him that is thirsty, and floods upon the dry ground.'" "But there are many," ye may say, "that get that, who do not bear much fruit." "But," says He, "I will bless it and make it grow, and ye shall avow your profession before the world; you shall not hang down your heads when ye meet with a professor, but ye shall avouch your interest in God, while He allows His Spirit and good-will to do you good."

I. The first point of doctrine. The Lord allows the pouring

---

* An afternoon sermon.

high places, and fountains in the midst of the valleys; I will make the wilderness a pool of water, and the dry land springs of water." And so (Joel ii. 28) when He has forbidden them to fear He says, "I will pour out my Spirit upon all flesh; and your sons and your daughters shall prophesy, your old men shall dream dreams, your young men shall see visions." The Lord holds out the covenant to a trembling soul, or people. And He says, "Lean down your burden there, and hear what I have to say to you." The man is content to stand and hear, but is not content to lean down his burden, lest he be not able to raise or lift it up again, till once he hear the covenant branched out to him. "Fear not, for I have redeemed thee, I have called thee by thy name, and thou art mine."

Now, the reasons why the Lord allows His Spirit for the satisfying of His people who are thus afraid, are

1. Because the Spirit can answer all ye can object. There is nothing ye can want, but His Spirit makes way for it, and follows all your doubts and fears. And

2. The Spirit differences the godly from the wicked. For there are many who would rather have an outward delivery, than a delivery for their soul. And therefore the Lord takes this way to satisfy His own people.

USE.—Then try what ye take up with, when ye are afraid and in trouble. And if ye be spiritual, ye will desire the Spirit; but if otherwise, ye will desire an outward delivery. I say, "Take hold of this promise to satisfy all your doubts and fears." But ye may say, "Ye know not what ye want." Ye must have this much, and that much. I answer, "If it be offered unto you to satisfy, and solve all your doubts and fears, take not another way of it, for God will not be mocked. If ye will take it, it will satisfy all your desires; for there is in Scripture to satisfy them all, be what they will." But ye may say, "I want faith." "Then welcome," say I. "He is the Spirit of faith." "But I want a promise." "Well, He is the Spirit of promise." "I want holiness." "Then He is the Spirit of holiness." "But I trow, I want all grace." "Well, then, He is called the Spirit of all grace and supplication, yea, and glory too." "But I have an ill-natured, passionate spirit." "Then He is called the Spirit of meekness." "But I have no understanding." "Then He is called the Spirit of understanding that searches all things, even the hidden things of God." "I am a fool, and destitute of counsel; and I know not what to choose." "He is the Spirit of counsel and direction." "But I cannot pray."

mourn over my sins and wants. ~~~~~ ~~~~ ~~~~ ~~~~
makes one mourn as for an only son, or first-born."

Then what do ye want? He is the Spirit that worketh all things in all cases in all His people. Therefore has He not good reason to offer His Spirit to answer all their doubts and fears? It is like Fortunatus's purse, to use the similitude; ye shall always find something in it. Sit down, then, and devise wants, and He has something to answer them all; therefore seek the Spirit above all things. Those who esteem not the Spirit above all things, know nothing of the Spirit of God. This Spirit teaches humility, and teaches to call God Father. But ye may say, that ye find it is elsewhere said, "Grieve not the Spirit;" "and that," say ye, "we do continually." Well, to satisfy you in that, He not only promises His Spirit, but He promises His blessing also with His Spirit. "Thy blessing is upon thy people." So John vi., when He blessed the five loaves, then they were enough to satisfy all the multitude. And at the word, "Take up the fragments," who could bear that which was blest? The Spirit and the blessing answer all doubts and fears.

II. The Spirit is called water. Then observe that God's Spirit is compared unto water. Now would ye know the reasons why God's Spirit is called or compared unto water. They are these,

1. Because water is of a cleansing nature. It cleanseth; and so doth the Spirit. "Then washed I thee with water; yea, I thoroughly washed away thy blood from thee." He makes them clean and holy, that is, by the Spirit of truth.

2. The second reason wherefore the Spirit is compared unto water, is, that as it cleanses, so it cools. It is of a cooling nature; and so is the Spirit of God. Know ye what it is to be scorched with a spark of hell, so to speak, and to have the hot displeasure of God burning in your bosom. Then this Spirit cools and quenches this. "The water that I shall give him, shall be in him a well springing up into everlasting life." It quenches terrible threatenings. Then whenever ye have terrible challenges for sin, take the Spirit and quench them.

3. The third reason wherefore it is called water, is, because as it cleanseth and cooleth, so it also makes fruitful, as water makes dry barren ground fruitful. So where the Spirit comes, and the blessing with it, then the soul grows in grace. Now the fruits of the Spirit are peace, love, &c. And if ye would know wherefore, He says, "I will pour floods upon the dry ground," it is just because God's Spirit is all in all; and I defy you to step this or

the mountains of Bether."

USE.—Are ye unclean, and would be cleansed from sin; or would ye be cooled from the heat of God's wrath? Are ye fruitless, and would ye grow? Then come and lay hold of this promise. "I will pour my Spirit upon thy seed, and my blessing upon thine offspring." By faith we hear that word, that He bids all come that would be cleansed. "But to whom is that promise made?" say you. Even unto those that are thirsty. "Then that cuts us off at the web's end," say ye; but I say, "Ye shall be knit or cemented to again."

III. The next point of the doctrine answers your objection. The Spirit here is promised to be poured forth upon the thirsty, and on the dry ground. "I will pour water upon him that is thirsty, and floods upon the dry ground." Then we see the party that He pours out His Spirit upon. They are those that are thirsty, and the reasons why they are called thirsty, are:—

1. Because a thirsty man is pained; he is pained at the heart with drought. Say ye, "That cuts me clean off." Now this is the pained man, that is pained with fear of challenges, and the threatening of God's holy law. "That is not me," ye may say. Well then; the thing that one will not, another will, as we commonly say. Some will take hold of this word of promise, because they are pained at the heart for sin indeed.

2. It is a reason wherefore he is called thirsty, that he is not able to delay drinking. So in like manner those who are pained with the threatenings and challenges of a broken law, are not able to delay the taking hold of some promise answerable to their condition. "But," say ye, "that belongs not to me."

3. Bring water unto a thirsty man, and yet give him none of it to drink, and he is just like to faint, or die away for thirst. In like manner, a man pained at the heart with challenges, when a day of the promises comes, and he gets none ready to answer his case, then he becomes almost faint.

But some of you may say, "That is not my case; for I can hear all that, and be in no danger of fainting at all." But here we shall descend a little lower yet. And,

1st, A thirsty man cannot eat his meat well. Now if ye take this with regard to your natural food, ye will think it as hard and difficult as the rest; but I mean spiritually. So it is with the man that is pained at the heart with thirst for God. He cannot eat well; because he must have a drink of water. Now, if thou

not applicable to me," say some of you; "for I can speak enough about anything in the world." But, let me ask you, "Were ye ever in such a case that ye could pray none?" then be what thou wilt, thou art a thirsty man.

3rdly, A man is not able to work well, but hangs down his head at his business. Well, art thou in this case that thou canst go about no duty, but thou still thinkest thou wantest something. That is the man that the promises of the water of His Spirit have respect unto; a man that is not able to speak well, eat well, nor work well. But after all, ye may say, "I cannot think that is the man He offers His Spirit unto." But when the people of God see a promise that requires a brave qualification, they think that none should take that, but those that have this qualification, as that promise, "Come unto me all ye that labour, and are heavy laden, and I will give you rest." And, "Ho, every one that thirsteth, come ye to the waters: and he that hath no money, come ye, buy, and eat: yea, come, buy wine and milk without money, and without price." Ye think these are only to those that are pressed down with the sense of their sins, and those who are pained with such a great thirst. But indeed ye are mistaken. The Lord speaks unto them only; and why! Because it is only these who are most loath to meddle with it. He gives it out under their name, but everyone may take it under that name.

But ye will say, "That is a strange doctrine that ye preach, for who may lay claim to, or take the promise, but those who have these qualifications therein required?" But will ye tell me in a word, 'What is the least qualification that ye may take a promise upon?" Indeed I dare not name one, that we may take a promise upon, under the pain of God's displeasure. I may not judge upon that; for, "Cursed is he that addeth any thing to God's word." For He will seek a less qualification than we would require. But I will tell you somewhat of it. If ye have any need of a promise, that is a qualification good enough. For if ye see that the promise can do you any good, and that ye have need of it, that is a qualification to take the promise. "But how can these things be?" ye will say. Ye would think it strange for me to prove it from the word "thirsty." Yes, for the Lord neither says, those that have a great thirst, or a burning thirst; but He sets it down so universally, that all are bound or commanded that are thirsty under heaven, to take it; because we must not make the promise more narrow than He hath made it. "And let him that is athirst come

"But what," say ye, "if we be thirsting for nothing." Then ye are a piece of dry ground. And you have it in the text; "I will pour floods upon the dry ground." This is what I was saying, that it is to the thirsty that could not eat, speak, or work well; but if they will not be satisfied with that word, "I will pour water upon him that is thirsty;" then He gives you another word to suit your condition; and will that satisfy you? "I will pour floods upon the dry ground." Which brings me unto

IV. A fourth point of doctrine is, The Lord will pour floods upon the dry ground. "Sing, O barren, thou that didst not bear; break forth into singing." What makes Him speak to the barren and dry ground? It is because all the world is dry ground. And are they not as dry ground that bear nothing? Are they not all dry, withered, and dead in trespasses and sins? And the reasons are :—

1. Because there is no such ground in the world but it is dry and barren until God gives it something. What is any in the world, but as dry barren ground? And therefore the wickedest in the world may come and take it freely.

2. The second reason wherefore it is offered unto dry ground, is, because God never put away any that came unto Him. "Him that cometh unto me, I will in no wise cast out." Wherever He comes in the word of His gospel, He excludes none but those who exclude themselves. And so the promises are holden out unto all. "For the promise is to you, and to your children, and to all that are afar off, even as many as the Lord our God shall call." That is, an outward calling them that are afar off. God offers the promises freely to all that will take them. "Whosoever will, let him come, and take of the water of life freely." God loves freely, and He does not regard whether they be wicked, or not wicked, if once they will come unto Him. Nothing in this case will hinder them from receiving the promises.

3. The third reason for which He calls it dry ground, is, that He may meet with the cases that His people are most often in. Therefore, anyone that is useless, fruitless, hopeless, and helpless; come; this is the word that He has bid you abide by, and take with you. But ye will say, "We are very barren." So is the world until God cultivate it. "Sing, O barren, thou that didst not bear; break forth into singing, and cry aloud, thou that didst not travail with child; for more are the children of the desolate than

of the land, and they shall no more be remembered." "Instead of the thorn shall come up the fir-tree; and instead of the brier shall come up the myrtle-tree; and it shall be unto the Lord for a name, for an everlasting sign that shall not be cut off." And whereas ye say ye are useless and fruitless; you see here that it shall be to the Lord "for a name, and for an everlasting covenant that shall not be cut off."

Objection 1. If this be the case, then any man or woman in the world, in a natural state, may take a promise.

Answer. And what dare you say to the contrary? What were any that ever took a promise but runaways from God? All that are spending their money for that which is vanity, may come and take it if they will.

Objection 2. But we find many in a natural state taking, or laying claim to, the promises, that have no right to them.

Answer. I am very sure that these folk take none; for,

(1.) No person takes a promise, but those that have a right to it.* And prove it by this: they have no particular needs to be answered by the promise, or to meet the promise with; and therefore they have no right to it.

(2.) They were never caused to take it. "Remember thy word, on which thou hast caused me to hope." They were never *caused* to take a promise, and therefore they never took one.

(3.) Tell me when thou wast served heir to the promise; for one must know when he was served heir to the promise. And that the natural man does not; but the child of God knows when and where this took place.

(4.) The natural man never took it, because it was never sealed over unto him as to those which believe. "In whom also after ye believed, ye were sealed with the Holy Spirit of promise." They think they have a right to it, because they can speak well of it, or about it; like a beggar, who can tell over the several parts of a charter very distinctly, but yet he has no right unto any article therein at all.

(5.) I prove that thou art a natural man, for thou never knewest the different parts or dimensions of the promise; thou never drewest

* By RIGHT here must be meant an actual interest in the promise by faith; for with respect to a right of access, all gospel-hearers are on a level, that is, they are equally warranted to receive and apply the promises to themselves; since the promise of the gospel is directed (as it is suitable) to sinners of mankind without exception. (Acts ii. 39. Prov. viii. 4.)

the flesh and spirit, which it does indeed unto the spiritual man. "Having these promises, dearly beloved, let us cleanse ourselves from all filthiness of the flesh and spirit." It makes the spiritual man never rest till he attain unto a cleansing of the soul in some measure.

Now, finally, I say the natural man has not these things now noticed, and therefore he has never yet taken hold of the promise; and if you get it you shall, sooner or later, know when and where you got it. "For I will pour water upon him that is thirsty, and floods upon the dry ground: I will pour my Spirit on thy seed, and my blessing upon thine offspring."

*Come now, and let us reason together, saith the Lord; though your sins be as scarlet, they shall be white as snow; though they be red like crimson, they shall be as wool."—Isaiah i. 18.*

THE Lord is here speaking unto a stubborn and rebellious people, who thought themselves far on in religion because of external things; and now the Lord, who loves the welfare of His people, resolves either to bring them home unto Himself or leave them inexcusable. In the former verses, the Lord, finding them to have made some kind of reformation in their lives by outward ceremonies, tells them it was nothing but lies; when they trusted unto their outward service, it could not pass in heaven, because it was not found on both sides, and therefore He calls both their practices and their worship a lie. Having convinced them of this, He comes now to lay down the true and living way, that if they would take Christ for their Prophet, Priest, and King, and His righteousness and holiness, then although He and they were strangers to one another before, now He would admit them into near fellowship with Him. "Come now, and let us reason together, saith the Lord; though your sins be as scarlet, they shall be white as snow; though they be red like crimson, they shall be as wool. And whatsoever ye can object against your well-being, I shall answer it if once ye will come and make use of the suit. Come, and I will take away your sins;" and He says in the sixteenth verse, "Wash ye, make you clean; put away the evil of your doings from before mine eyes, cease to do evil."

We have in the text so many reasons to press the point upon them.

Reason 1. "Come," says He, "let us reason together. And if ye will do so, I will admit you into near fellowship with Me."

Reason 2. The second reason is, "If ye will come and make use of the fountain, or remedy, that I have laid out unto you, then come; I am content to debate, or reason the matter with you in a gospel way."

Reason 3. The third reason is, If ye will come and make use of the fountain, be your condition what it will, it shall not be remembered: "If your sins were as scarlet, they shall be white as snow; though they be like crimson, they shall be as wool."

I. The first is the word "Come."

II. The second is, "Let us reason together."

---

* It is supposed that this sermon was preached at Irvine on a sacramental occasion.

Now we come to the explication of the words. And,

I. The first reason, as we have said, is "Come." And to come is several ways taken in Scripture. And,

1. To "come," sometimes signifies to appear. "God came from Teman, and the Holy One from mount Paran." There, coming is taken for appearing.

2. Sometimes "coming" is taken for believing. "He that cometh unto me shall never hunger." There it is meant of believing.

3. Sometimes, in Scripture, it is taken for going from one place to another; and in this sense it means a piece of reformation in life; and so it may be taken in these words.

4. "Coming" may be also taken for a heavenly joining together. "And many nations shall come, and say, Let us go up unto the mountain of the Lord." That is, Come let us join ourselves in a heavenly way together, in the Lord's service.

Now we say all these significations may be contained here, in the word "Come." Now,

1st, The first signification was, to appear. In the former words He has laid out a fountain unto them, and has bid them come, and make use of it; and it is well. "Come," says He, "and let me see thy countenance; let me hear thy voice, for sweet is thy voice, and thy countenance is comely."

2ndly, This word "Come" may be taken for believing. "Ye are guilty of all these things," says He. "Now if ye will come and take My advice, and submit unto Me, then I allow you faith to believe upon My Son, and you shall have life."

3rdly, As it signifies to come from one place to another; and this expresses some piece of reformation, as I said before, says He, "If ye come and make application to this fountain, then I will command holiness for you." "Now ye are clean, through the word that I have spoken unto you." By what word? Even by that word that He had spoken unto them and that they had believed. So says He, "Come, ye shall be cleansed; I will command holiness for you." But,

4thly, The word here is principally to be taken for a heavenly or close joining together. "You are guilty," says He, "and ye cannot be cleansed, but by the fountain; and if ye will come, whereas ye were but strangers and outlaws before, and I took no gracious notice of you; now I will admit you to be near unto Me, and I will notice and look into your case and condition." But there is a coming two ways.

ure thinks the command of God very unreasonable, as in this instance that the like of it should come and believe, and yet necessity and the command press unto it. And,

2. There is another sort of coming, and that is not so much out of obedience to the command, and of necessity, as it is out of love to God. This kind of coming is rather a reward for the creature, than a duty; for it may be the creature has stayed itself upon God, and yet comes to God but as a law-giver; and because of the command, it goes about duty. But when one comes out of love to a loving invitation, then it becomes rather a reward than a duty.

II. I come now to the second reason that is given to press this point on these people—"Let us reason together. Let us humbly and mildly debate the matter as to whatever concerns your well-being. I am now upon speaking terms with you, which I was not before." Now there are sundry sorts of reasoning between God and the soul. And,

1. There is a law-reasoning between them. Sometimes when the Lord, as a just and holy God, sets all the sinner's iniquities before him, and then He appears as a lawgiver unto him. Now, in this law-reasoning, all the acts of parliament are from the covenant of works; and this is one act, "Cursed is every one that continueth not in all the words of this law to do them." And when He comes to this creature, this clause is in its bosom, "Depart from me ye workers of iniquity." Now, in these acts there is nothing given unto the creatures to work upon but their own strength. Neither do they admit of repentance, but persons are cursed for the least sin as a breach of that law.

2. A second kind of reasoning is a gospel-reasoning. The form of it is this: God enters into debate with the creature, only for the removal of its doubts. And He reasons with the soul only according to the acts or terms of the New Covenant, and this points out a pleasant way wherein the creature may be fully satisfied.

3. There is a reasoning which, in some sense, may be called a law-gospel reasoning, beginning in the spirit of bondage and fear, but terminating in the gospel. In this the Lord calls a rebel to an account, and at length he finds all he has forfeited, he is made sensible that there is not so much as a dish or a spoon that he possesses but he, as it were, steals it from God, as having no proper right in law to it. Now, after all this, the criminal hears an ancient act, which was made in the reign of King Jesus, and it is found there that if any man, either in the person of himself

have wronged God greatly, but it shall be done away." And then out of God's own treasure He takes as much as satisfies God fully, upon which this promise comes out, "All that the Father giveth me shall come to me; and him that cometh to me I will in no wise cast out." "And let him that is athirst come, and whosoever will let him take of the water of life freely." Now this we may call a law-gospel reasoning.

4. There is a fourth way of reasoning, wherein the Lord reasons or speaks to His people by strokes. In this kind of reasoning He is said to contend, as ye will find it frequently expressed in Scripture. And this reasoning has its rise from the former. This arises from the gospel, in this sense, that it is a clause of the covenant to correct His people. "If his children forsake my law, and walk not in my judgments, then will I visit their transgressions with the rod, and their iniquity with stripes. Nevertheless, my loving kindness will I not utterly take from him, nor suffer my faithfulness to fail." If they stand in need, they must not want strokes. This is a clause of the New Covenant. But shut out faith and consolation from the creature, and debate only for sin in the creature, then it becomes a law-reasoning. Therefore He has said, if He sees it needful, He will strike them. But judicially, or aiming at satisfaction, He could debate with Christ only, so that He does not strike His people to get satisfaction from them; no, but for their good. "All things work together for good to them who love God, to them who are the called, according to his purpose." Though it may not seem good for the present, yet it shall be for their good at the long-run, as the Scripture says, "No affliction for the present seemeth joyous, but grievous." Besides, the apostle says that He "afflicts us that we may be partakers of his holiness."

Now, there are also other sorts of reasoning between God and the creature, as when the creature reasons from arguments taken from the Lord Himself, such as Moses or Jeremiah used. The latter says, "Why shouldst thou be as a mighty man who cannot save."

Again, sometimes the creature reasons from his own holiness or uprightness. "Preserve my soul, for I am holy; save thy servant that trusteth in thee." "O that I knew where I might find him, that I might come even to his seat! I would order my cause before him, and fill my mouth with arguments. I would know the words which he would answer me, and understand what he would say unto me." There the righteous might dispute with you in a gospel way; I will answer all your doubts, and let the Mediator be Judge of all."

III. The third thing was, "Though your sins be as scarlet, they shall be white as snow; though they be like crimson, they shall be as wool." Their objection was, "Why should we reason; we can look for nothing but death." "No," says He, "though your sins be as scarlet, though they be of a double dye, yet they shall be blotted out." But how is it that He says "they shall be made white?" Why, He makes them as if they had never committed them. "For if once ye will yield," says He, "and come to the fountain, ye shall be freed from the pollution of sin." Moreover, if ye will yield to Jesus Christ He shall make you holy, and ye shall be reformed more and more, and made thoroughly holy.

And the authority for this is, "Thus saith the Lord." "Submit, I will reason calmly with you, and answer all your doubts." And for your warrant, ye shall have the word of Jehovah, who is absolutely in and of Himself; for "by my name, Jehovah, shall I be known." Before He was saying that He could not away with their offerings, and then in the sixteenth verse He says, "Wash you and make you clean." But here He gives them His word and His own great name as the security of their cleansing.

Now, if ye look on the command, and the necessity, you will see that the doctrinal point here is,

DOCT. I.—*That provided any abominable sinner will submit his way and himself to God, he may come boldly, and have access unto Him.* "Let us draw near with a true heart in full assurance of faith, having our heart sprinkled from an evil conscience, and our bodies washed with pure water." "In whom we have boldness and access with confidence by the faith of Him." "In whom you are also builded together for an habitation of God, through the Spirit."

So that if any sinner, however so great, yield once to Him, he may come with boldness and have access unto God. And the

Reason is : If once the soul come and yield itself to God, it has got a full right and title to the heavenly inheritance. "But ye are come to Mount Sion, and to the city of the living God, the heavenly Jerusalem, and to an innumerable company of angels, to the general assembly and church of the first-born, which are written in heaven, and to God, the Judge of all, and to the spirits of just men made perfect." And they get the new name and white stone. Moreover, the partition-wall that was betwixt God and them is now broken down. When the creature confesses his

His daughter-in-law should come familiarly unto Him : The real enjoyment of this access to God manifests itself by gospel-holiness. "If we say that we have fellowship with Him, and walk in darkness, we lie, and do not the truth : but if we walk in the light, as He is in the light, we have fellowship one with another, and the blood of Jesus Christ his Son, cleanseth us from all sin." Again, we have access unto Him because we are entered by the door. "I am the door; by me, if any man enter in, he shall be saved, and shall go in and out, and find pasture."

Use.—This doctrine is of use to comfort all those that are content to take Christ as their Prophet, Priest, and King; and yet dare not be bold with Him. But if you be content to submit to Him, ye may come boldly unto Him. But whosoever they be that will not yield to God, and lay down their arms of rebellion, they are proud rebels, and God knoweth the proud afar off. And they get all that God gives them as one would cast a bone unto a dog. If ye ask me, "What points of familiarity those who have submitted unto Christ may use?"

1st, You may go and tell God what is wrong with you, either with respect to sin or judgment. Ye may come and tell Him the greatest sin that ever ye committed; think it before Him when ye dare not speak it. Many a time the sin is so heinous that the creature dares not speak it. And yet ye may tell the thing to Him that ye dare not tell to a living creature, for He is the best secretary that ever one had.

2ndly, Whatever you have need of, you may get, and take, in and through Christ, even whatsoever can do your souls any good.

3rdly, Ye may use familiarity with God to know His will, or purposes, in so far as such knowledge may make you forthcoming to His praise. You may say, "Wilt thou let me know, Lord, what Thou wouldst have me to do in this case, and what is Thy mind in it." God allows you to be familiar with Him, so far as it may make you forthcoming in your duty to His praise.

"Come let us reason together." Thus God allows them in a peaceable way to come and reason the matter with Him ; and, says He, "You shall be satisfied concerning all your doubts."

Doct. II.—*If once poor sinners be content to yield to Christ, then He is willing to come into terms of speaking with them in a peaceable way; as ye will find in sundry places of Scripture.*

Now, for the reason of this point, we find in Scripture that the Lord uses to reason with His people.

H

Now,

1. For the first reasoning about the Lord's procedure. "Righteous art thou, O Lord, when I plead with thee; yet let me talk with thee of thy judgments. Wherefore doth the way of the wicked prosper? wherefore are they all happy that deal very treacherously?" "I will give Thee credit before I begin, that Thou art righteous," says he; "yet there is somewhat in my heart concerning thy dealings, and I would be glad to be satisfied as to that: Wherefore doth the way of the wicked prosper?" Here the servant of the Lord reasons with Him as to His proceedings; and yet at the same time acknowledges that all He did was righteous. When the Lord was about to destroy Sodom, He tells it to Abraham, who had some reluctance in his heart; "Wilt thou also destroy the righteous with the wicked?" "Shall not the Judge of the earth do right?" But, says the Lord, "I will satisfy you;" and then He falls a reasoning with him about His way of proceeding with Sodom.

Sometimes they reason about the work of God in themselves. Now, the creature's mind is not clear, but in doubts; and therefore he must reason thus: "Lord, if it be not so, that I have the work of God within me, whence is all this striving? If Thou hadst designed to have killed me, wouldst Thou have taken a meat-offering at my hand?"

Again, There is a reasoning concerning the creature's duty. The creature is at a stand in duty, and cannot go any further, till it knows the Lord's mind. "Lord, let me know what Thou wouldst have me to do in this, and in that cross, that is fallen in my way." Somewhat of this is expressed, "O Lord, why hast thou made us to err from thy ways, and hardened our heart from thy fear?" Lord, we would know why Thou hast let this and that come upon us. But the natural man doth not say so; for it were blasphemy for him to speak to God after this way and manner. And,

2. We say, "It is granted to the creature to debate with God;" and why?

(1.) Because it is one of the privileges of the creature to be of one mind with God; for God will seek the creature's approbation as to what He is about to do. And,

(2.) Because it concerns His glory, and their duty. For where they know not His mind, it is lawful for them to reason and plead with Him, in order to know it, that they may know their own duty concerning such and such a thing.

USE.—You that have fled to Christ, plead for satisfaction in the Lord's way. It is well known that the natural man many times is ready to curse God in his heart, because he cannot be content with His way. But iniquity shall stop the mouth of the wicked. But unto you that flee to that fountain He shall make known His covenant; that is, He shall make you read His covenant in that which does not resemble it.

The next thing in the text is the justification of the sinner, by taking away his iniquity. "Though your sins be as scarlet, they shall be white as snow; though they be as crimson, they shall be as wool." Hence,

DOCT. III.—*The most vile sinner that ever comes to Christ is welcome, and shall be set free from the debt of sin.*" "Him that cometh unto me," says Christ, "I will in no wise cast out."

The reason for this doctrine is, because the soul having once fully yielded itself to Christ, owes God nothing, so to speak; it is not a debtor any more, it is completely justified. God has nothing to say unto it when once the righteousness of Christ is imputed to it as, to everyone who savingly knows Him, he is fully justified "through His blood, which cleanseth from all sin."

USE.—This reproves all those who have God's testimony in them, that they are content to submit unto Him, and yet they have thoughts arising in their hearts as to what shall become of them for such and such sins; for the text says, "Though they be of a double dye, they shall be done away, and be made white as snow." Sins that are done against light, sins that are done against challenges of conscience, are sins of a double dye, and yet they shall be done away. Sins done against love, even against much of the good-will of God, are sins of a scarlet dye. Sins done against vows, making former vows lie like so many broken chains about your necks, are sins of a scarlet colour—such sins committed after sacramental occasions; sins relapsed into after you have been oft-times convinced of them; sins after fasting, when you have been duly warned by those who would not be found guilty of your blood. Sins against covenant engagements, sins against a profession, all these are sins of a scarlet colour and crimson dye. But I say, "Suppose your sins have been after communions, after-fasts, after swearing or covenanting, if once ye stoop and be content that Christ reign in you, the Lord will cleanse you, and make you white as snow or as wool.

"But what is the matter," say ye, "although I be clean to-day, I shall be as unclean to-morrow." But the text says that He will put holiness in you. Hence,

drunkards, and such were some of you; but ye are washed, but ye are sanctified, but ye are justified in the name of the Lord Jesus, and by the Spirit of our God."

Come then to Him, and He will sanctify you, and make you holy. The reasons are,

(1.) If you yield to Christ He is engaged to make you holy. "And the very God of peace sanctify you wholly." "Faithful is he that calleth you, who also will do it."

(2.) The soul now coming home unto God is under correction for misbelieving Him so long, and therefore is afraid to fall into sin again, and provoke God to be again angry.

(3.) A third reason is, that he has been far from God, and in the devil's service. He knows the subtle devices of that enemy, and therefore does all he can to evite them. But we do not wish tha any would take occasion from this to go far from God, that they may better know the subtle wiles of the devil. And therefore yield yourselves to God, and ye shall be purified, sanctified, and made holy.

But, say ye, "I would gladly yield if I knew my warrant, or ground whereon I would be better." I say, there is a command, and there is a word that says, "This is the command, that ye believe on the name of his Son, Jesus Christ, whom he hath sent." Here is a command and ye shall receive damnation if ye obey it not. "He that believeth on the Son hath everlasting life, and he that believeth not the Son shall not see life, but the wrath of God abideth on him." There is nothing within you that should be allowed to jostle out a commanded duty. "But," say ye, "I would yield unto Him if I knew that He would but accept of me, or the like of me." Oh, high blasphemy! To say that thou wouldst, He would not; to say that thy insignificant love would go beyond His infinite love; for He chose us before we chose Him; He loved us before we loved Him. His love has helped many, and drowned their iniquity—many who were loath to come to heaven. Hell, devils, and men have tried His love, but they have never yet found a crack or flaw in it.

Now, to put you out of all doubt, He doubles the expression, "For the mouth of the Lord hath spoken it." To satisfy them He uses two different expressions of one meaning, whereby we see that the Lord is pleased to answer the daughters of Zion with sundry expressions for one doubt. And He does so for this reason, that the creature is simple, and the devil is subtle; the devil who takes so many different methods to make the creature believe that these are new doubts again, which, indeed, are nothing but the

And then in a little he will come back again and say, "How know ye that ye are called?" "Because," say ye, "I have got mine ear opened to hear the word, and I love it better than I did before and it does me more good many times." "And how know ye,"-says he, "that God is your Father!" "Because," say ye, "I get my meat, drink, and all I have from Him." And then he will say, "How know ye that ye have true grace within you?" and so on, still one doubt after another, as long as he can make the poor jealous of God; and yet all these doubts are one and the same in substance; and therefore the Lord uses sundry expressions, though one and the same in substance, to answer all His people's doubts and fears.

USE.—Think much on the devil's subtlety, and God's goodness towards you, who takes such pains in answering your condition. Ruminate upon your own folly. Though God has forgiven you; never forgive yourselves. And for your security you have, "Thus saith the Lord," the greatest security Zion's daughters can have in the world; and the only security that can satisfy the soul. For if ye would speak never so much to the soul, if ye do not prove it by "Thus saith the Lord," the soul will not believe it. And moreover this security, or way of security, keeps God in much respect among His people; because all their salvation and the grounds of it depend on Him! and it makes much for our duty also.

Finally, If we had only a man's word for our security in any matter, would we not be more loath to offend that man? How much more careful should we be not to offend the Lord, whose word we have for our security? This security makes believers continually seek to have God honoured. "Come, then, saith the Lord, and let us reason together, though your sins be as scarlet, they shall be as white as snow; though they be red like crimson, they shall be as wool."

*"O Lord, why hast thou made us to err from thy ways, and hardened our heart from thy fear?"*—Isaiah lxviii. 17.

r is likely, if we all knew how it were with us, and if it were
ven to every man and woman in this assembly, to know our own
res, and the plagues of our wicked hearts, it is, I say, more
an probable, that there would be a very harmonious joining in
esenting this unto God, as the matter of our sad complaint, that
r hearts are hardened from His fear. But it may be, that it is
ith the most part of us, as it was with those that Elihu speaks
when he says, "The hypocrites in heart heap up wrath; they
y not, when the Lord bindeth them." Many are bound with
e bond of a very hard and obdurate heart. It is an evidence
at it hath gone a great length, and is come to a very great height
ith us, that we are not sensible of our bonds, and are out of
pacity to cry unto God, because of this strong binding where-
ith we are bound.

Now, these words are very sad words; the very mention of
em, especially when they are so descriptive of our own condition,
ight make our hearts to tremble. It is one of the heaviest and
ddest troubles from the hands of God upon men and women, to
ve their hearts hardened from His fear. And yet the business
not desperate, or past remedy, so long as there is so much
ftness of heart as to perceive or take up the hardness of our
arts, and to be capable of regretting it before God. Hard soft-
ss, as we may call it, is not the worst kind of hardness, or at
ast it is not the greatest degree of it. But alas! to be so
rdened that all sense of discerning or feeling of it is worn away
very sad. Although the people who spoke these words were very
r under this stroke; yet the Lord had so graciously set bounds
ito it, that it had not gone the full length that it would have done.
ence they take notice of it, and say, "Why hast thou suffered
r hearts to be hardened from thy fear, and to be so hard that
e should not fear thy name?"

But before we come to any observations from the words, lest the
pression should be mistaken, and lest any of our apprehensions
ould be intermingled with wrong thoughts of the majesty of
od, ye should know and consider,

1. That whenever it is said that the Lord hardens, it is not
eant that He does so by infusing any sinful qualities into the
art of man: as it is expressed by the apostle, "Let no man say
hen he is tempted, I am tempted of God; for God cannot be

the man to the hardness of his own heart, which is natural unto the sons of fallen Adam, but also when He withholds or withdraws somewhat of that grace given to the creature, on which hardness of heart follows; and the majesty of God being under no obligation to give grace unto the creature, either by a natural necessity of Himself, or yet by merit in the creature, that hardness of heart cannot be charged upon Him, nor yet can He be blamed for the withholding of abused grace from them. Besides this, He may present objects occasionally, which may be good, nay, are good in themselves, and yet by the person's own corruption abusing them, they may harden the heart. For instance, professors may make use of the ordinances of Christ, and their own gifts, unto their own hardening. Also, He may give up a person to his own lusts, and to the power or hand of Satan, to be hardened, as a punishment of his former sins and iniquities. As the Psalmist says, "My people would not hearken to my voice; and Israel would none of me. So I gave them up unto their own hearts' lusts; and they walked in their own counsels." And as this may come to a great height in the case of natural men, even so it may be in some degrees incident unto the people and children of God.

Having thus premised these few things for guarding against mistakes, ye must look upon the complaint as not being spoken in a way of proud or ill-natured expostulation laying all the blame upon God, and evading or shifting it off themselves; no, the words intimate the Lord's carriage towards the church-members who are speaking here. Nor are we to think that these words are spoken irreverently in the way of complaining of God; but only in the way of expostulation with themselves; as if they had said, "Lord, what have we done that hath provoked Thee to deal thus with us?" There is an insinuation of a desire to know what sin in them it was that had brought on this plague or stroke of hardness of heart, which was grievous to them beyond anything in their external condition and captivity.

Now having taken the words in this sense, we come shortly to draw some doctrinal observations from them. And,

I. In general, we observe, that a child of God, when in his own proper latitude, will be very diligent in taking notice of God's dispensations about and towards his own heart, and is in some case to make a representation to God how it is with his soul. Oh how sad is it when God is dealing with our hearts, and yet we are not so much as taking notice what either God or the devil is doing about them! If the Lord reach not the carcase with some

ır approaches to God, in any case to make a serious representa-
ɔn of the posture of our spiritual affairs, but just as if we were in
ıe country, and our hearts in another, we are become so great
rangers unto them. But,

II. And more particularly, I observe, that hardness of heart, or
ıart-hardening, is an evil incident unto the people of God. It is
ɤ such that this complaint is made, "Why hast thou made us to
r, and hardened our heart from thy fear?" And we think that
uch hardness of heart, or blindness of mind, could not have seen
ıd felt such a weight; and we think it is with much bashfulness
:tered; being spoken by those who before were ashamed, that
ıey could not plead an interest in God as their Father, being so
uch degenerated from their ancestors. Yet they are necessitated
ı lay claim to God. They are such as give much credit; as if the
ok of His eye could redress their condition, and they are in case
ı observe the former dispensations of God, and to compare them
ith their present case. They likewise take up a great alteration
: His kindness towards them. The case of David is a proof of
ıis, who for near the space of a year was bound up under hard-
ɛss of heart. Solomon is a proof of this, who for some time was
ıclined unto idolatry. Asa is a proof of this, who imprisoned
ıe prophet, and oppressed some of the people, and under his dis-
ıse sought unto the physicians, and not unto the Lord. It is
robable the time wherein we live affords us likewise many a sad
roof of the truth of it. Oh! hardness in part, and in many de-
rees is incident even unto the people of God. But that ye may
ıe better understand this, we shall hint at a few symptoms and
vidences of it. And,

1. Take this for one. When challenges for sin do not easily
ıake impression upon us, that is, when we are more hard to be
rrought upon by challenges than formerly we were wont to be,
nd become like green wood that, you know, is long a-kindling.
'or instance, when David was in a good case, and his heart tender,
e was instantaneously alarmed with any evil, such as the cutting
ff the lap of Saul's skirt; but when he was under hardness of
eart, there was much ado to get him convinced in general. Though
he case was particularly pointed out in the parable used by
Jathan, yet that would not do; he takes little notice of it in the
ʀay of applying it to himself, until the prophet said, "Thou art
he man." And is it not the case of not a few that a challenge
oth not so easily grip, or draw blood upon them, as formerly it
ısed to do? And,

2. When challenges are taken with, and sins acknowledged;

easily put off than sometimes it was wont to be—that is, when the impression of a sin or challenge for sin is easier worn off than formerly it used to be. I think if there were a spiritual dexterity learned of sinking challenges for sin in the blood of Christ, there were no great skaith. But when the challenge is thrown off through deadness, passes away we know not how, or else is forgot before any satisfying views of pardon, our case is not right. It is likely this is very common. We have frequent challenges that things are not right with us; that corruption is strong, and grace is under a decay; but we let them go. Such a course evinces hardness of heart, and hath a great influence in hardening the heart still more.

4. When the conscience hath lost a great deal more of the power of reflecting upon ourselves, or our case, as to what is sin or duty, this is another symptom of hardness of heart. But,

5. There is another great symptom of hardness of heart, and that is, when we are under cross dispensations, and yet prayer is restrained before God. This the people of God, or the prophet in their name, regrets. "There is none that calleth upon thy name, or that stirreth up himself to take hold of thee." The same is signified by Daniel. "All this evil is come upon us, yet made we not our prayer before the Lord our God, that we might turn from our iniquities, and understand thy truth." And,

6. It is another great symptom when fear is in a great measure cast off; yea, this is the first degree wherein hardness of heart doth appear. The soul can scarcely be under any degree of hardness of heart, but it will soon appear in the want or decrease of true fear. Say they, "Why hast thou hardened our heart from thy fear?"

7. A seventh evidence of hardness of heart is when persons become rash, heedless, precipitate, and fearless in worship and in walking, rushing forward without ever considering their own condition, without fearing lest God's name be taken in vain by them, in their worshipping of Him—or, at least, without fearing lest they should be deserted of God,—strengthening their own hands in their way, as if there were no hazard in people's walk and conversation ; taking every little discourse or common tale by the end, without fear of being indisposed for worship, or any kind of duty. When folk are become thus fearless, it is a great length they are come in hardness of heart. And,

8. In the eighth place, It is an evidence that there is much hardness of heart in this generation, that there is much fearlessness in

ady to comply with every snare and temptation. We are not
aid of catching skaith by our excess of mirth and jollity. So
at walking in the fear of the Lord all the day long is become a
re thing among Christians now-a-days. Standing in awe to look
th the eye, speak with the mouth, and to do or forbear doing
ything that may be displeasing to a holy God, without leave
ked of Him and obtained. There is little fear of abusing God's
odness, which says that there is little fulfilling of that promise,
And they shall fear the Lord, and his goodness in the latter days."
III. The third observation is, That felt hardness of heart is, in
e account of God's children, one of the heaviest and greatest of
rokes that come upon them from the hand of God. It is pitched
on here as the worst of judgments. I think their hearts were
their mouths, and the tear in their eyes, when speaking out
ese words, "Why hast thou made us to err from thy ways, and
rdened our heart from thy fear?" Here they do not complain
the majesty of God of their outward calamity, though it was
ore than ordinary; but this was the stroke that affected them,
en hardness of heart. "And there is none that calleth upon
y name, that stirreth up himself to take hold of thee; for thou
st hid thy face from us, and hast consumed us because of our
iquities." And "All this is come upon us; yet made we not
r prayer before the Lord our God, that we might turn from our
iquities, and understand thy truth."
Now, the reasons why the people of God look upon this as a sad
roke are these :—
1st, The first reason is, because it is a sad and angry-like stroke,
d hath somewhat judicial in it. As there is displeasure or anger
a stroke, so it is sad and grievous to a gracious heart. But of
l strokes, hardness of heart hath most of God's displeasure in it.
2ndly, Because it borders very near upon the condition of the
probate. I say it comes near to that which is their lot or con-
tion. God gives up His children unto some degree of a reprobate
ind, as He delivers them up to walk in the lusts and counsels
their own heart. Hence it comes to pass, that it is in a singular
anner puzzling in that case for a child of God to get himself kept
om concluding that he is none of His, and he is ready to say,
My spot or provocation is not like the spot of His children, and
nsequently my stroke is not like the stroke of His children, but
ly like that of reprobate or wicked men." And,
3rdly, Because this keeps back from a kindly resenting of all the
ils done by them that are labouring under it. Yet though they
e and know that they are in the wrong, yet they cannot mourn

there is no profiting under any of God's dispensations. But le¹
Him smite as He will, their hearts grieve not. So that they, i₁
this case, may say, "That all this is come upon us, yet have w₍
not made our prayers unto thee."

Use.—For use, I would in short pose you, and desire you t₍
put it unto yourselves:—What think ye of such a stroke as this
and how doth it affect you? Do ye feel it, and think it one of th
heaviest and saddest strokes? Do you seriously think that if i
were meet for you to enter into a paction with God, ye would b
content to take any other stroke from His hand, upon conditio₁
that this were removed? If ye were kept tender, and your hea₁
melting before the Lord, it were a good token. Ye will conceiv
that there is a merciful difference to be discovered betwixt a perso₁
that is plagued with hardness of heart, and one who is smitte
with it in a kind of fatherly displeasure; that is, there is in th
one a looking upon it as a grievous stroke, whereas in the oth₍
there is not. And therefore, I would say unto you that are und₍
these bonds, and yet not affected with them, wrestle with Hi₁
that hath the keys of hell and death in His hand, that He woul
loose your bonds. If ye be grieving for it, and yet your grievin
is not adequate, or according to your stroke, yet if it be looke
on as a stroke, and lamented by you as such, so that ye are sensib₁
of it, and that sense puts you upon making your complaint unt
God—such exercise says that there is so much softening as th₍
you have the knowledge of it. A quick feeling of hardness sa₎
ye are not given up altogether of the Lord, and "that there is y₍
hope in Israel concerning this thing," and ye are in the way ₍
getting your captivity turned back, as the streams in the sout₁
and ye should not look upon your case as desperate.

IV. The fourth observation is, that there will be in a child ₍
God, while under this stroke of hardness of heart, some serio₁
search or enquiry accomplished concerning what hath been t₁
procuring causes of it, and what hath provoked God to smite wi₍
this stroke. Therefore they say here in the text, "Why hast th₍
hardened our heart from thy fear?" Now there will and shou
be some search made into the cause where there is anything
God. And I would commend this unto you that have hardness
heart as your burden, that you would take it as a favour from G₍
that it was or is your burden. Perhaps that it is so little yo
burden makes you question if there be anything promising like
your case and condition. Search then into the causes; and ₁
your help in this, I shall only touch at a few things, which I c₍

1. Not taking notice of challenges of conscience and convictions, d trying to quench the motions of the Spirit, gradually harden e heart, and provoke God to let such a person alone. Smiting this kind may sometimes befall a child of God. But where con- ence tables a challenge, oh, then, let it speak out, and smite it t upon the mouth; when God hath given His deputy in the soul charge to arraign, then it well becomes you to listen to what it th to say. It is likely that David had his own stirrings of con- ence at the beginning of his fall, but because he listened not to them, he is smitten almost year and day with a benumbed d silent conscience.

2. Another cause may be this: When the Lord's calls are very gent and pressing upon us to entertain grace, communion, and llowship with God, when these are borne in upon a person or ople, and the soul listens not but lets them pass by, and takes notice of God's entreaties at all. This is observed by the salmist, "Open thy mouth wide, and I will fill it." There is e offer. "But my people would not hearken to my voice, and rael would none of me; so I gave them up unto their own hearts' sts, and they walked in their own counsels." There is nothing th more influence in hardening than this. Hence people that ve under an entreating gospel, if they get not God's grace, or if ey shift the offer of it, are the most hardened of all people. And hen this deadness in the people of God prevails, and they are dding after their idols, it brings on many degrees of hardness of eart upon them.

3. A third cause is: When any sin that we know to be a sin is ot seriously opposed, but gets leave to sit down upon the con- ience unrepented of. As every act of sin strengthens the habit sin, and disposes unto more acts of sin, so it hardens exceed- gly, thrusts out from God, and keeps the soul still under its ominion; and therefore says the apostle to the Hebrews, "But xhort one another daily, lest any of you be hardened through the eceitfulness of sin."

4. A fourth cause is: A continual custom of formal worshipping f God, either in public, in the family, or in secret; and when ye se no ejaculations in the time of your worship, and when ye eflect not upon it when it is over. Alas! we are killed in these ays with much formality. There are symptoms of it in this place, regard that there is so much sleeping even among good folk. here is much of it even where that evidence is wanting. And h, what lightness is in the duty of family worship, even to such degree that strangers may observe it! And,

mind or ask what becomes of these evils that they expostulated with themselves for; and so lie down, and as it were leave the door open unto wrath, &c. No marvel that, many a night, floodgates should break in upon them before the morrow. This is a very subtle cause. Many good folk have a custom of complaining of evils, who wrestle not with God for their pardon and victory over them; and hardness of heart is one of these evils. It is true there is a number under this evil that never complain of it, and it is a doleful prelude that it will be their death at last; but it is a good token, and some ground of hope, when a person is puzzled about it and burdened with it. The Lord convince us more thoroughly of it, and teach us to make use of the right remedy through Christ Jesus. Amen.

*Therefore I say unto you, What things soever ye desire, when ye pray, believe that ye receive them, and ye shall have them."—* Mark xi. 24.

Having formerly spoken unto divers things upon this subject of prayer, both as to its kinds and nature, and to the persons for whom we ought to make conscience of prayer to God, and likewise the persons against whom we may warrantably pray, I come, in the next place, to speak of those qualifications requisite in acceptable prayer—there being a vast difference between prayer and acceptable prayer—between our uttering words to God and praying by a gift, and praying by the promised Spirit of grace and supplication, in such a way and manner as to be accepted of God in what we pray for. This is the thing that doth so much take up the thoughts of the tender and serious Christian: Am I accepted of God in what I do? The words of the mouth many times run this way; and if ye heard the language of their heart, ye would hear much unto this purpose.

Now, the first requisite qualification of acceptable prayer to God is true and saving faith. And it is so requisite in prayer, that no man or woman can put up a suitable desire without it. And the having of this grace makes anything that they do in this exercise of a sweet smelling savour unto God. Hence,

I shall observe, That in order to acceptance with God in all our addresses unto Him sound, saving, and justifying faith is very requisite and necessary. And the method is the following:—

I. I shall show you from Scripture that this is the thing that God requires in prayer to make it acceptable.

II. Show you what it is to pray in faith.

III. Show you what is faith's work in prayer.

IV. Show you what is the nature and properties of this grace, which is so necessary in prayer, that without it God will not accept of prayer.

V. Show you how it is that this faith, which I shall describe as to its nature and properties, is so necessary in prayer.

VI. Show you in what respects this grace is requisite and necessary in prayer.

VII. Show you what are the helps to attain unto this grace of faith.

VIII. Show you some of the noble effects that faith in prayer hath. And,

IX. Lastly, make application of the whole.

therefore that men pray everywhere, lifting up holy hands, without wrath and doubting." That is, let faith be acted and exercised in our prayers. "Let us, therefore, come boldly unto the throne of grace, that we may obtain mercy, and find grace to help in time of need. Let us draw near with a true heart in full assurance of faith, having our hearts sprinkled from an evil conscience, and our bodies washed with pure water." So that the way to draw near to God acceptably is by faith. The apostle James allows any that lack wisdom, to ask it by faith. "If any of you lack wisdom, let him ask of God. But let him ask in faith, nothing wavering." So if you would obtain anything from me, says God, seek it in faith. And says the same apostle, " And the prayer of faith shall save the sick, and the Lord shall raise him up; and if he hath committed sins, they shall be forgiven him." Now, that which gives being and life to prayer is faith. Thus, for the first head, these Scriptures hold out that, in acceptable prayer, faith is requisite and altogether necessary.

II. The second thing is : To show what it is to pray in faith.

I shall take it up in these five or six things, which ye may endeavour to keep in remembrance. And

1. To pray in faith is to be endued with saving grace from the Lord. This grace of faith must be infused into the person that approaches unto God. For it is impossible that the person that wants faith can be acceptable to God—I mean not faith of miracles, or an historical faith, but true and justifying faith. This shows that all that are destitute of this grace are in a bad case. "For without faith it is impossible to please God." And this is the woful case they are in that want faith, that never anything they do is acceptable to God; and this, again, is the noble privilege of those that have it, that all they do in duty is accepted of Him.

2. To pray in faith is not only to have this grace infused into you, but it is to have that grace in exercise in and about the particular petition ye would put up to God. Whatsoever thing ye ask, ye must have faith exercised about that particular, whether it be for soul or body; for yourself or for the Church; for spiritual or for temporal things.

3. To pray in faith is to make use of the grounds of faith in our praying, viz., the word of promise; for the promises are the ground of our suit. So that in acceptable prayer faith makes use of this and that promise and turns the promise into a petition. This is faith's work. It is neither humility, nor self-denial that

Mediator. So that the soul will never go to God but in the Mediator; and it looks for a return to its suits or petitions, only in and through the Mediator, Jesus Christ, and Him crucified. Says He Himself, "Whatsoever ye shall ask in my name, that will I do." That is, "Expect access to the Father in and through my name; look for a return in and through my name." We pray in faith when in all our addresses we are actually endeavouring to improve the merit and mediation of Him who is at the right hand of God the Father.

5. To pray in faith is to pray over the belly of all opposition. When, in human appearance, there is nothing but anger and wrath from God, and when the soul is under the apprehensions of His wrath, yet faith will come over all these unto God. When He is inflicting some judgment upon the person, and seems to be angry with the person, then faith goes over all and presses in unto God; that is to pray in faith. For instance, "I cried by reason of my affliction; I said, I am cast out of thy presence." Yet what does faith when in sense he is cast out of God's presence? Faith puts him upon supplicating God again. "Yet will I look again to thy holy temple."

6. To pray in faith is this: When the soul promises to itself on the ground of God's word an answer to the particular petition it is putting up to God. To pray in faith is not only to know well that the thing ye are seeking is warrantable and according to His will, but in some measure to have assurance (or endeavour after it) of an answer in absolute things, that is, if it be absolutely necessary they believe it shall be granted. As to conditional petitions, they believe that if it be good for them, they shall have what they ask. If they present a petition for those things that are absolutely necessary, whether in respect of themselves or His Church, it shall be sure unto them; and if their petition is for things conditional, either to themselves or the Church, if it be for their good it shall not be wanting. Ye see an instance to this purpose in Mic. vii. 7. All was then going wrong, yet, says he, "I will look unto the Lord; I will wait for the God of my salvation; my God will hear me;" as if he had said, "What then? I answer myself that God will hear me." Remember these six things which show what it is to pray in faith.

III. The third thing is: What is faith's work in prayer, or what is the work of this grace in a believer in his suits and supplications?

1. It instructs the person of his own need of the unsearchable riches that are in Christ. It makes him cry out, "O sinful man

there is a perfect and complete fulness in Christ, as ye may see in the case of the publican. What was the thing he prayed for? Says he, "God be merciful to me a sinner." Faith instructs as to his sin, and then as to the way of his relief and help from sin, viz., in Christ; so that faith's first work in prayer is to instruct a sinner of its own condition, and then of its supply, and help. And poor, poor are they that want this grace of faith; and rich, rich are they that have it.

2. Faith's work in prayer is to be the hand by which the soul takes hold of the remedy and relief that is in Christ, and offered by Him to us in the gospel. It is the soul's hand to lay hold of Christ and His fulness, as He is offered and held forth to us. As a poor man puts forth his hand to take that which is offered unto him, so it is with faith in prayer. It is called a receiving, and it is the very hand whereby Christ, and all that is to be had in Him, is to be received or laid hold of. This is an excellent mark in prayer.

3. The work of faith in prayer is, to enable the soul to wait patiently on God for a return of the petition it hath put up. Faith says, "Ye have prayed, and that is your duty; but see, Sirs, that ye stay still at His door until ye get an answer. Be not like those who shoot blunt-shot, and never look where it goes. 'I will hear what God the Lord will speak.'" "I will stand on my watch, and set me on the tower to see what He will say to me," says faith to the soul. This is a good work of faith in prayer, to make our souls wait patiently on Him, while He is trying them with delays. It is faith that puts strength into our souls to make them patiently wait on, till God send an answer unto them.

4. It is true faith's work in prayer to make them judge aright of all the Lord's dispensations towards them, especially in or about the exercise of prayer. Faith says, "Look that ye construct aright of Him, and entertain not wrong thoughts of Him: although He gives you not His presence now, yet He will come." "He that will come, shall come, and shall not tarry." If He give you not in that measure that ye propose, see that ye fret not. If He seem to frown, you are then to abase yourselves as miserable wretches. What says David, "O my God, I cry in the day time, and thou hearest not. But thou art holy, O thou that inhabitest the praises of Israel." There is faith's work; he cried to God, and is not heard; but says he, "Thou art holy." As if he had said, "I aver that He is holy, if He should shut out my prayers, as it were, with hewn stone, and refuse to answer me till my dying day, yet Thou art holy." That is faith's work in prayer.

I

of Canaan in her prayer, when Christ upbraided her, saying, "What have I to do with thee? Should I give the children's bread to dogs?" "Truth, Lord," says she, "Thou hast given me some ground to expect help from Thee. Truth, Lord, I acknowledge that I am a dog; but it is as true that dogs eat of the crumbs which fall from their master's table." Whereupon Christ says unto her, "O woman, great is thy faith. Thy faith hath taken hold of the least intimation, or may-be, as a ground of hope. Be it unto thee even as thou wilt." And this reproves those who fret if they get not what dish of meat they please; or if it pleases them not, they cast it from them. But if thou knewest what thou art, and how little thou deservest, thou wouldst bless God, that thou art not in hell already.

6. Faith's work in prayer is to enjoin every praying faculty, or all that is within the soul, before God. For faith sets its desires in order. Faith makes it desire nothing but what God hath allowed in His word, and it will be nothing short of this. Again, it orders our zeal, so that it is not blind and preposterous: where faith rules it orders humility, so that the soul does not say in a sullen fit, "Lord, depart from me for I am a sinful man." It orders sorrow for sin neither to be too little nor too great. It is faith's work to make the soul sorrow heartily before God: on the other hand it makes us guard against anxious sorrow. Then it orders hope that the soul may wait patiently for the answer or accomplishment of prayer. Thus it is faith's work to order all things within the soul, and put all things in a composed temper. So commanding is the grace of faith in a soul where it is, that it will let nothing be out of order.

7. Faith's work in a soul in prayer is to make it importunate in pressing for that which it prays for. Having the word of God for its ground, and the name of Christ for its encouragement, it importunately presses for the thing desired, and when He seems to say, "Ye shall not have it;" it says, "I will not let Thee go." It was faith that made Jacob wrestle that night with God; says the angel, "Let me go, for the day breaketh. And he said, I will not let thee go, except thou bless me." And, "Moses," says the Lord, "will ye let me alone, that I may destroy this people." But says Moses, "If thou wilt forgive their sins; and if not, blot me out of thy book, which thou hast written." And the woman of Samaria, say what He would, harped still upon this string, "Lord, have mercy upon me."

8. Faith's work in prayer is to undertake for the soul to God, and for God to the soul. This is the very kernel of prayer. Faith

performed." So that this is the work of faith in prayer, to engage for the Lord that all the promises that He hath given shall be made out and fulfilled unto them. On the other hand, faith engages the soul to wait patiently on for the accomplishment of all that the Lord hath promised. So that this is one of the mysteries of God; and it is lamentable that so many souls live strangers to God and to this work of faith, and do not consider the worth and excellency of this grace of faith. I dare say that we, His Church and people, would be as far above trouble this day as we are under it if we had faith and the lively exercise thereof. Those that have this are of all men the most happy, and those that want it are of all men the most miserable.

9. Faith's work is to make the soul to plead with God upon Scripture argument. Faith looks to what God hath promised, and makes use of all these promises in its approaches unto God in prayer. This ye may see in Moses' pleading for the people. He pleads upon all the promises the Lord had made unto them, when they had provoked His anger to burn against them. And so Jeremiah pleads upon scriptural arguments, not for himself only, but for the people of his time, that the Lord would do some great thing for them. So that this is faith's work, to gather all the arguments contained in Scripture, and to pray that the Lord would do this and that according to His promise.

10. The work of faith in prayer is, to turn over all the suits that the supplicant puts up into the hand of Christ the Mediator, that for His sake, intercession, and mediation they may be accepted of God, and answered in things according to His will; which implies a disclaiming of any works or merit in the person's self that is praying. Says Daniel: "Cause thy face to shine upon thy sanctuary that is desolate, for the Lord's sake." Not for my sake, nor the people's sake, nor for anything that we can do, but for the Lord Jesus Christ's sake. He puts all the suits upon Christ's account, that in His name they may come before the Father and be accepted.

11. This is faith's work in prayer, to make the person praying keep at a due distance from God. Faith makes the person keep its own due room as unworthy—as dust and ashes. It teaches persons to give God His due room, as He is the high and lofty one; to have low thoughts of themselves, and high thoughts of God. Faith says to the soul, "Carry in subordination unto God; let not your words be rash, nor your thoughts and conceptions of Him unsuitable." Faith made Abraham say, "I have taken upon me to speak unto the Lord, which am but dust and ashes." It is an

subject-matter of prayer, viz., to gather the promises that are here and there in the Bible. And then it not only furnishes matter, but it furnishes a mouth to speak unto God; it opens the mouth to speak unto God that which the soul hath gathered. Nay, it furnishes feet to go unto God with the matter gathered. Nor does faith only furnish matter, and a mouth to speak it, and feet to go to God with it, but it is as wings unto the soul, whereby it flies as it were with wings unto heaven with the petition that it hath to put up to Him for itself, or for His work, or for His Zion. Oh, but this is an excellent work of faith! It makes them that wait upon the Lord "mount up as on eagles' wings; and walk, and not be weary; and run, and not be faint."

13. It is faith's work in prayer to enable the soul to wait patiently till God give an answer to prayer. Faith is still petitioning and supplicating the Lord till He give a gracious return. To renew the self-same thing in prayer again and again, it being according to His will and warranted in His word, in the exercise of the self-same faith, is no tautology, though it were a hundred times to have the self-same suit. It was the way of the woman of Canaan. "I am not sent to thee," says Christ; yet she prays still, "Have mercy upon me, Lord." And it made Paul return his suit again and again. "For this thing I besought the Lord thrice." This is also an excellent work of faith. Nay, I may say, they never can do anything in the exercise of prayer that want this grace. Their prayers have no bones, strength, nor edge. They will never pierce heaven.

14. Faith's work in prayer is, to make the petitioner take up God aright as the object of prayer, and Christ Jesus as the only Mediator, and take up their own condition aright, that they may apply the promises accordingly. For faith's work is to apprehend aright our Lord Jesus Christ the Angel of the covenant, and to apprehend our own soul's case and condition aright; as in Isa. xli. it is called a looking; as it makes them take up Him whom they are seeking, and themselves aright. This is faith's work in prayer. And,

Lastly, I shall add this. It is faith's work in prayer to enable the soul to prevail over, and, as it were, to command the Lord. The prayer of faith has a prevailing and commanding over the great and dreadful Lord. Hence it is said by James, "The fervent prayer of the righteous availeth much." And it healeth the sick. It is said of Jacob, "He had power over the angel, and prevailed." Says the Lord, "Concerning my sons and my daughters, command ye me." Thus the Almighty Maker of heaven and earth is content

of Canaan—" ᴅᴏ ɪᴛ ᴜɴᴛᴏ ᴛʜᴇᴇ, ᴏᴠᴇɴ ᴀ̀s ᴏɴᴏᴜ ᴡᴀᴀ ᴀ ᴏᴜ ᴀ ᴄᴀᴜᴜᴏ· keep it from thee. Thy faith has prevailed over Me."

Now from all these, you may see the woful case they are in, who want this grace; and the good and desirable case they are in, whom God hath endued with it.

IV. The fourth thing is, What is the nature of this faith, which is a necessary and requisite qualification in prayer? That we may show you the worth and excellency of this grace, and the need folk have of it, I shall in these particulars hold it out, that ye may know it, and how to come by it. And,

1. This grace of saving faith is one of the main, choice and principal graces peculiar to the elect, and is the very root of all other graces. It is in a manner, the kernel and life of all the rest, it being the only grace that closeth with Christ. "Add to your faith virtue; and to your virtue, knowledge." It is the first ground stone, and then add to it all the rest. All that folk go about, all the moral duties that some professed Christians perform, are but mere shadows for want of this.

2. This grace is one in all the elect, but not in a like measure in all. It is the self-same grace in all the elect. But you will say, How is that? For then one's faith would serve all. No, there are as many faiths, as particular persons of the elect; for it is not one in the elect as to the measure of it; for some may have a less, and some a greater degree of faith. But in this respect, it is one as to its closing with Christ, and embracing of Him as offered unto them in the gospel. It is the very self-same faith in all the elect. It was the self-same faith that was in Abraham, Isaac, and Jacob, that is in all the believers after them. The poorest as well as the greatest hath the self-same faith in substance. If this were considered, it might be comfortable to us. You will say, "The apostle Paul, and the rest of these worthy men, might plead confidently with God in their own behalf, and in the behalf of others." But, I say, if ye have fled to Christ, and closed with Him, ye may with confidence draw near to the throne of grace, to plead with God on your own, and on the behalf of others also.

3. This grace of faith may, yea, ought to increase in the saints of God. See Mark ix. 2., 2 Cor. x. 15, where the increase of faith is mentioned. And, "Remembering without ceasing your work of faith, and labour of love." This grace is said to grow. "The righteousness of God revealed in the gospel from faith to faith." It is a sin and a shame for Christians to be and continue at the same degree that at the first they were at. Where it is sound and real, it grows. And oh, but the Lord's people should

4. Ye should know that as it ought to grow, so some... ay come under decay, as to the exercise of it; though there can-t be a decay of it as to its foundation. But I say, it may come der a decay as to its exercise; which proceeds either from urity, or from Christians being too much elated in duty. hen these give a stroke to faith, it may come under a decay. ristians, beware of security, for it is the bane of faith. Beware uplifting in duties, for it likewise is the bane of faith. And in ur afflictions pray to God for the increase of your faith, for als and rods of affliction are for trials to faith, therefore ye ght to pray for faith that are bearing the burden in the heat of day.

5. The grace of faith is that which renders all that ye do eptable unto God, "For without faith it is impossible to please d."

6. This grace of faith hath always with it obedience, and the nging forth of good fruit to the glory of God and the edification others, which fruit is called "the obedience of faith." Wherever is, it leads still to sincere endeavours to keep up all the com-ndments of God. By this, folk may know whether they have s grace or not."

7. This grace of faith apprehends things altogether beyond the ch of human reason, and brings these things home unto the n's own bosom. It makes things that are absent as if they re present; it brings that into the man's heart that he shall e to all eternity; it brings in God to the man; it brings in rist to his bosom; it brings in the joys of heaven to his soul— ice it is said to be "the substance of things not seen." It was s that made Moses see Him that is invisible, and the eternal ry and happiness of the saints in heaven, whereupon he refused be preferred in Pharaoh's court; and this is the nature of this ce which is so necessary and requisite a qualification in the y of prayer. And,

. This grace of faith is a most sincere cordial grace. It is ed "faith unfeigned." It knows not what it is to have the ding by-gates that carnal reason and hellish policy find out. s grace of faith is downright and without guile.

. The nature of this grace is, that it is firm, stable, and sted-, and renders the person stedfast in whom it is: "Rooted and lt up in him, and stablished in the faith." They are like wing trees that cannot be shaken; they are like mount Zion, t cannot be removed. When they are in a right frame, let the ld turn upside down, they will not be afraid. But folk

God, and hath nothing of our own power in it. "Faith is not of ourselves, it is the gift of God." It descends from the Father of lights, and by this ye may know where to find it; and if it be once infused into you, it can never be plucked out of your hearts again. They are fools that think to believe, without knowing God the Author of faith.

11. This grace hath the Word of God for its ground. It is not this or that minister said it; not this great man, nor that great man that said it; no, nothing will serve the believer until he gets this, "Thus saith the Lord."

12. This grace of faith is a knowing and intelligent grace, so that they in whom it is know somewhat of God, and of Jesus Christ, who is the immediate object of faith, and of the promises of the Gospel, and of their own case and condition. Says Christ, "And have known surely that I came out from thee, and have believed that thou didst send me,"—hence sometimes it is called knowledge.

13. This grace is a lively, operative, and working grace. It makes the soul in which it is lively, diligent, and active in working the work of God. It is called "the work of faith." It puts folk upon working. Ye shall never see one who hath true faith, though he discerns it not, but he is busy; even though believers were not bidden—yea, though they were forbidden—they would read the Scripture, pray unto God, speak and confer with the Lord's people when under trouble or disquiet of mind, if they knew them to be such as they might safely communicate their mind unto.

14. This grace is a most precious grace in respect of God, the author of it; in respect of Christ, the object of it; and in respect of the Gospel, the means of attaining to it; and in respect of salvation, the end of it. Oh, but it is precious, and makes those that have it precious unto God.

15. It is a most conquering and overcoming grace; "It overcometh the world and the devil;" it is the shield that quenches all his fiery darts.

16. I shall add that it is a purifying and cleansing grace, for it gives the person no rest until he has recourse unto the fountain of His blood. Says John, "He that hath this hope in him, purifieth himself, even as he is pure." Not only to be reformed outwardly, but inwardly. By these things ye may see what this grace of faith is; and by some of them ye may know if ye have it, and how ye may get it. Withal ye may see the need ye have of it.

it will be enough to hear them; for how will ye look death in the face who never studied this grace? How will ye wade the fords of Jordan to eternity? And how shall ye be able to answer God in the great day of accounts? If ye would get safe through all these, labour to obtain this grace of faith. The Lord help you·so to do.

*" Therefore I say unto you, What things soever ye aesire, when ye pray, believe that ye receive them, and ye shall have them."*—
Mark xi. 24.

I OBSERVED the last Sabbath from this verse that sound justifying faith is a necessary and requisite qualification of acceptable prayer to God. In prosecution of this point I went through these things in your hearing.

I. I proved from Scripture that faith is a necessary and requisite qualification of right and acceptable prayer unto God.

II. I observed in several particulars what it is to pray in faith.

III. I showed you what is faith's work in prayer.

IV. I cleared a little what is the nature and the properties of this grace of faith which is so necessary a qualification in acceptable prayer. Now I come,

V. To the fifth thing in the method. And this is to show you how it appears that the grace of faith, as I described it in its nature and its properties, is required in acceptable prayer. It will appear that sound and saving faith is requisite and necessary in prayer, if we consider

1. That the Lord commands absolutely that in our prayers to Him we pray in faith. He enjoins by His authority that every petition we put up to Him be put up in faith—"Let him that prayeth, pray in faith, nothing wavering." And here in the text it is said, "What things soever ye desire, when ye pray, believe that ye receive them, and ye shall have them." So that in respect of the Lord's command it is highly necessary.

2. Consider this, That there is no prayer acceptable to God, nor well-pleasing to Him, without faith. No performance nor duty that we can do, or go about, and consequently no prayer is acceptable unto God without this grace. "But without faith it is impossible to please God."

3. Consider that it is by the grace of faith that the saints repel all Satan's temptations, and quench his fiery darts, wherewith they are afflicted, especially in time of prayer. And hence it appears that faith is necessary in prayer. Persons cannot stand it out without this grace; they cannot endure his fiery darts, but must be burnt up by them. Says the apostle, "Above all things, taking the shield of faith, wherewith ye shall be able to quench all the fiery darts of the wicked." This is the grace that resists when he sets upon them to divert them in prayer.

---

* The second sermon on this text.

e studious of holiness. "I will wash my hands in innocence; ᴐ will I compass thine altar." And this will make it appear hat faith is necessary in prayer, if ye would be kept in a fit isposition for it at all times and seasons.

5. Consider that it is the grace of faith that makes the soul ᴐntinue in prayer till it obtains its answer or request. It is ᴜith that is the strength, or bone of the soul, enabling it to go on ᴧ prayer, and not to take a refusal from God till it obtains an nswer, as appears in the woman of Canaan. It was her faith hat would not take a refusal, but she continued praying and ʹrestling out her soul until she got an answer. It was faith that ᴧade Jacob refuse to let the angel go until he blessed him. Thus ; appears to be requisite, because it makes the people of God con-ᴧnue to wrestle with God in prayer. Folk that only pray by a ift will soon take a refusal; but it is not so with faith, it will ot be refused.

6. Consider that it is this grace that mainly and principally lorifies God, and therefore it is most requisite in prayer, in scribing majesty, power, honour, and dominion unto God. And ᴜust not that be necessary in prayer which glorifies, magnifies, nd honours Him to whom we pray? And,

7. Consider that the grace of faith is the means and way to see, ehold, inherit, and enjoy the glory of the Lord. And oh! but ᴧith is necessary in prayer, as ever ye would behold His glory and ower in that duty. "Said I not unto thee, that if thou wouldest elieve, thou shouldst see the glory of God." And is it not then ery necessary that souls have faith, seeing it is the way and means ʹ getting a view of His glory? From all these we may see how ecessary faith is in all our performances, and especially in prayer.

VI. For the farther prosecution of this subject, I shall show ou in what respects this grace of faith is necessary in prayer; nd in clearing of this, I shall sum it up in the following par-culars. And,

1. The grace of faith is necessary in respect of God the object ʹ prayer, as of every other act of worship.

2. It is necessary in respect of Christ Jesus the Redeemer.

3. It is necessary in respect of the promises of God.

4. It is necessary in respect of God's providences.

1st, I say, in our praying to God, faith is necessary in respect ʹ God Himself, the object of prayer. For faith looks unto Him. He that cometh to God must believe that he is, and that he is ᴧe rewarder of them that diligently seek him." And particularly observe,

have builded?" We should take heed to His omnipresence; that is, His being everywhere present. Thus faith takes Him up as present with the person wherever he prays.

(2.) In our prayers, faith is necessary in respect of His omniscience, by which He is intimately acquainted with our case and ways,—acquainted with the sighs and groans of the soul. Jeremiah, in praying to God, says, "For thine eyes are open unto all the ways of the sons of men, to give every one according to his ways, and according to the fruits of his doings." Faith looks unto Him as one to whose eyes all things are naked and bare. Christ says, "Pray to your Father in secret, and your Father who seeth in secret, shall reward you openly." So that there must be faith in His omniscience in one praying to Him in an acceptable way.

(3.) In our prayers, faith in His all-sufficiency is also necessary. There must be faith in Him, as one who hath to supply our needs and necessities to the utmost. His supply and help is broader than all our wants. He hath a sufficiency to help our need, without any mean or instrument. There He holds out His all-sufficiency, as one who needs neither bullock nor goat. "For," says He, "every beast of the forest and cattle on a thousand hills are mine. I need none of these. I have enough for thee; only call thou on me. But look by faith unto my all-sufficiency." So that there must be faith in God's all-sufficiency in prayer. And oh! but it is necessary to take Him up in prayer as one who hath to serve our turn; as one who hath mercy to pardon us; life to those that are dead; healing to those who are sick and diseased; righteousness unto those whose righteousness is as filthy rags; peace unto them that are confused; light to them who are in darkness; and strength to them that are weak, and not able to go about duty.

(4.) Faith, while we pray, must be exercised in His omnipotence and almighty power, in respect of which there is nothing we stand in need of but He is of power to give it, and able to perform it for us. He can do it without the concurrence of second causes; nay, His power can do it above natural causes. "Behold, I am the Lord, the God of all flesh. Is there any thing too hard for me?" What is it He cannot do? What is it thou standest in need of that He cannot do? What evil is there that a soul is under that He cannot take away? What evil is it that ye are troubled with that He cannot remove by His power?

(5.) It is also necessary and requisite in our prayers that we exercise faith in His gracious nature, as one that is gracious and

all your sins. Oh, but that is necessary in prayer.

(6.) In our prayers faith should be exercised in God's simplicity and spirituality, as He is a Spirit invisible and cannot be apprehended by our outward senses, and therefore one that requires to be worshipped in spirit and in truth. "God is a spirit; and they that worship him must worship him in spirit and in truth." Ye must be spiritual in your worship, that so ye may not have gross and unsuitable conceptions of the Lord whom ye worship.

(7.) In our prayers faith must be exercised in His eternity, as He is an eternal and everlasting majesty, without beginning or end; as one who was from all eternity contriving the salvation of sinners; as one who had time enough to do good to His creatures: as one who endures for ever to be their happiness. Says Habakkuk, "Art thou not from everlasting, O Lord my God?" We are to look on Him as one with whom a thousand years are but as one day. The faith of this might damp all the perplexed thoughts of our hearts, as if He were long in performing His promises.

(8.) In prayer we must exercise faith in His unchangeableness, as He is unchangeable in all that He is in His nature; in His goodness. "He is the same yesterday, and to-day, and for ever: without variableness or shadow of turning." The Psalmist looked upon God as one who changeth not. "But thou art the same, and thy years shall have no end." There is great need of faith in this respect, that the soul may be fixed on God as one that hath done such things and can yet do such things for them.

(9.) Faith should be exercised in Him in prayer, as He is holy and of purer eyes than to behold iniquity, that with all due reverence the soul may draw near unto Him. "Thou art of purer eyes than to behold evil, and canst not look upon iniquity. Wherefore lookest thou upon them that deal treacherously, and holdest thy tongue when the wicked devoureth the man that is more righteous than he?" Think ye that men and women durst wallow in sin if they exercised faith in God as a holy one, as one who cannot look upon iniquity.

(10.) In prayer faith must be exercised in His justice, as He is a just and jealous God, and will by no means acquit the wicked; that the sins persons are guilty of may be the more grievous unto them; considering that God will not let them go unpunished if they get not true repentance.

(11.) Faith in prayer must be exercised in the relative titles that God hath come under unto His people, as that He is their Former and Maker. "We are the clay, and thou art the potter;"

covenant with them. "O our God, wilt thou not judge them;
for we have no might against this great company that cometh
against us, neither know we what to do, but our eyes are upon
thee." How sweet the relation faith looks to in prayer! They
should look to Him in prayer as their Husband, considering themselves as His married people, called by His name, and having His
name put upon them. "I will be their God, and they shall return
unto me with their whole heart." This then is the first thing in
regard of which faith is necessary.

2ndly, I told you faith is necessary in respect of Christ the
Mediator; for in going to God in prayer we must have an eye to
the Mediator, for His sake, not for our own sake, looking to be
heard. There are particularly these things in Christ that faith
looks to in prayer :—

(1.) It looks unto Him as one in and by whom the person
praying gets access to the Father. It is in and through Him that
we ever had nearness to God; no coming unto this holy God but
in and through Christ the Mediator.

(2.) It looks upon Him as one in and by whom the supplicant
finds acceptance, and not only access. One may, in some cases,
get access and not get acceptation; but says the apostle, "He
hath made us accepted in the Beloved."

(3.) Faith looks upon Him as one who offereth up incense with
the person's prayers, that the value of Christ's sufferings may make
the prayers acceptable to God. Faith looks much unto the obedience and sufferings of Christ, through which it gets acceptation
before God and remission of sin.

(4.) Faith looks on Him as one who intercedes with the Father.
The praying person finds there is this and that he cannot say to
God, and in what he says there is this and that wrong. "But,"
says he, "I have all my dependence on Christ's intercession in my
prayer, therefore do I look to Him that is at the Father's right
hand interceding for sinners."

(5.) It looks to Him as one who is the agent or advocate with
God for the person praying, seeing he cannot plead his own cause
in the court of heaven. "And if any man sin, we have an advocate with the Father, Jesus Christ the righteous."

(6.) Faith looks upon Christ as one appearing before God for
sinners, and presenting the person unto God; as praying like the
high priest who had the twelve tribes upon his breast when he
went in unto the holy of holies, that he might present them unto
God. "Such is this person's case, and such is that person's case,"
says he to God. "For Christ is not entered into the holy places

for sinners to pay their debt, and to answer for them when the principal debtor hath nothing to pay. "By so much was Jesus made the surety of a better testament." God substituted Him as their Cautioner and Surety. What they could not do for themselves He did for them. Faith looks upon Him as satisfying justice and responsible for the believer.

(8.) Faith looks on Him as compassionate, merciful, and pitiful to poor sinners; He having our nature, and so a fellow-feeling with us. Hence He is held out and typified by the high-priest as one compassionate on the ignorant and those who are out of the way. Thus there must be a mystery of the exercise of faith in God, the object of prayer, and in Christ the Mediator and Redeemer, otherwise ye are not the wetting of your finger in water the better for your prayers. They will never ascend above your heads. He will regard them no more than the barking of dogs, or the offering of swine's flesh, or the cutting off a dog's neck. The Lord rejects all these; and so without this grace of faith folk "spend their labour for that which profiteth not, and their money for that which is not bread." How very necessary is it to exercise faith in Christ the Redeemer; and oh! if many would reflect how they have gone about this duty, they would look with black countenances, and they may say, "That in effect all our prayers are lost; we have not taken the right way in it."

3rdly, I told you that faith was necessary in prayer in respect of the promises of God. We have examples of the exercise of it in many places of Scripture, as in 2 Sam. vii. 28, David makes much use of God's promises by faith in his prayer to God; and 2 Chron. xx. 7, Jehoshaphat is praying, and in this exercise he makes much use of the promises by faith. Now in prayer faith is requisite in respect of the promises.

(1.) Because faith gathereth the promises that are interspersed here and there in the revealed will of God, as a hungry man his food, or a thirsty man his drink, or as a naked man his clothing to keep him from the chilling cold.

(2.) Faith not only gathers God's promises, but it makes application of them to the heart of the person in particular, as if the person had been set down particularly by name and surname. Faith makes the promise directed to sinners in general one's own in particular.

(3.) Faith chooses promises suitable to the case and condition that the soul is in; for such a case such a promise, and for another case another promise. If the soul be dead, it looks to the promise God hath made of life; if it be under the sense of guilt, it looks to the promise God hath made of the pardon and remission of sin;

the heart and giving a heart of flesh, taking away the stony heart.
Thus faith chooses suitable promises to the man's case and condition, as a hungry man chooses meat, and a thirsty man drink, and a sick man physic, &c.

(4.) Faith makes persons urge in prayer all the promises of God, that He would perform and accomplish them unto them. It looks through the Scriptures, and chooses such and such promises: and goes to God with them, and begs God that He would make them out unto them. "For thou, O Lord of hosts, God of Israel, hast revealed to thy servant, saying, I will build thee an house." What does David with the promise? Why, he goes unto God with it. "Now therefore, let it please thee to bless the house of thy servant, that it may continue before thee for ever; for thou, O Lord God, hast spoken it." Faith having found out the promise, goes to God with it, and puts Him to it; turning the promises into petitions to God. There is no grace in the soul besides faith, that can put it upon wrestling and pleading earnestly with the Lord, that He would make out His own word, even His gracious word of promise.

(5.) Faith having gathered the promises, chooses them, applies them, and urges them; and then it will make the soul patiently wait on, without fretting, or wearying, till God make out His promises to it. Thus in respect of the promises of the gospel. Oh! but faith is requisite in prayer, if ye consider these five things already noticed.

4thly, I told you that faith is requisite in prayer, in respect of God's providences. This ye may see in Psalm xxii. 4, where David prays earnestly, and his faith is exercised in reference to the dispensations of providence. There are three or four things that faith does under providences. And,

(1.) It makes the person wisely observe every passage of God's providences, to himself, or others. "Whoso is wise, and will observe these things, even they shall understand the loving kindness of the Lord." And "Hear ye the rod, and who hath appointed it." Faith makes a person careful to observe God's providences.

(2.) Not only doth faith make them carefully observe God's providences, but it makes them have errands to God as to all the occurrences of providence. If it were but something happening one's beast, or one's child, nay if it were but a forefinger, forehead or the toothache, it goes to God with every such passage of providence, whether it be of mercy, or of judgment; nothing else that faith can or will do this effectually.

(3.) Not only doth faith observe and make errands of occurrence

get the sacrifice." But says he, "God will provide himself a lamb for a burnt-offering."

(4.) It makes this of providence, that it refuseth to make it the ground of the person's walk, when it comes to contradict the promises. For the Lord's providences are not the ground of our walk. Oh! but faith is necessary in prayer. Without it, folk will never observe God's providences, nor make errands of providences, nor shall they wisely interpret providences; nor shall they refuse providences to be the rule of their walk. But those that have faith and look to the object of prayer; to Christ the Mediator, to the promises, to the occurrences of providence, know certainly that this grace of faith is highly necessary in prayer; even so necessary that persons cannot make a right use of God, of Christ, of the promises, and of providences without it.

VII. But say ye, "What shall they do that have not found saving faith, it being so absolutely necessary that without it they cannot pray one word acceptably to God? Now what shall we do, who think we have it not?" Now, that I may answer this, ye must consider that those who have this question, scruple, or doubt, are,

1st, Either such as have no sound saving faith at all; or,

2ndly, Such as have it, and cannot yet discern it. Or,

3rdly, Such as do but make a question, or scruple about it in words, to fill the field (as we sometimes say) but use not the right means to get it. Or,

4thly, Such as in sincerity are making the doubt, or scruple, whether they have faith or not, and are using the means for it, and would gladly have it.

First, For the first of these, I would have them that have no faith, consider these two things; 1. The danger of such a case. 2. Consider that they are yet in the place of hope, and therefore ought to use the means to attain it. I say, those who have not true faith, as there are many who have it not, should consider the case they are in. And what is that?

(1.) They are a prey unto the devil, to do with them what he pleases. "Who are taken captive by him at his will." They curse, they swear, they debauch, they profane the Sabbath-day, they lie and deceive; for it is impossible to resist the devil, that is "going about as a roaring lion, seeking whom he may devour", without this grace of faith.

(2.) And not only are they a prey to the devil, but they are a prey to their own lusts. "My people would not listen to my voice; and Israel would have none of me." But what comes of it? "So all ranks of men are given up to profanity, to their own hearts lusts; to all sorts of wickedness. Scotland, since any can remember, was never so full of abominations as it is at this day. And,

. (3.) It deprives them of fellowship with God, and with Jesus Christ. They that have no faith, can have no communion with God. For it is by faith that Christ dwells in, us. And is not this a doleful thing to be without God, and without Christ in the world? One is without God, while he lives without that precious grace.

. (4.) The want of this grace brings on more obduracy and hardness of heart. In Mark xvi. 14 ye will find that unbelief and hardness of heart go hand and hand together. Is it not a sad case to be bound up in stupidity and hardness of heart. But so is it with those who are destitute of faith.

(5.) They not only cannot pray acceptably; but unbelief also takes away the gift of prayer, and the mouth, so that they cannot speak to God. "Behold thou shalt be dumb, and not be able to speak until the day that these things shall be performed, because thou believest not my words, which shall be fulfilled in their season." It makes the person a slighter of prayer in secret, and if they have a family, in their families; so that there is never a day goes over their head that they pray a word to God. "Thou shalt be dumb, and not be able to speak," &c.

(6.) They that want faith cannot bring forth fruit unto the glory of God. No more than these branches broken down can bear fruit, no more can a man without faith bring forth good fruit unto God. What is that which makes folk like briers and thorns? Whence their profanity, ungodliness, and throwing out oaths for every trifling matter? Is it not owing to their unbelief? And,

(7.) This is the wofulness of their case that want faith, that whatsoever they do is sin. "Whatsoever is not of faith is sin." Everything that people do is sin, if they believe not. The very work and labour they are about is sin. Their ploughing, their eating, their drinking, their walking, their sitting, their sleeping, and all that they do is sin. Their hearing, their reading, their praying is sin. And is not that a deplorable case, to have all that a man doeth looked upon as sin? And so it is with such as are destitute of the grace of faith.

. (8.) This is also a branch of the wofulness of that case, that they are obnoxious, and liable unto the wrath and curse of God, here and hereafter. "He that believeth not, shall not see life; but the wrath of God abideth on him." God's wrath and curse are

K

eternally, that do not believe. "For if ye believe not that I am he, ye shall die in your sins."

They that have not found faith would do well to consider that they are yet in the land of the living. Your case, however deplorable it may be, is more hopeful than that of those who are already in hell. The means are therefore to be gone about, such as reading, hearing; and be busy in prayer to God for it, and say, "Lord, increase our faith." Be convinced of the want of this grace, and of the evil of the want of it, if ever ye would attain unto it. So that this is the answer to the first sort, viz.: Those who have not found faith (1.) They should sincerely consider their case and condition. (2.) They should consider with themselves, "I am yet in the land of the living, and in the place of hope." Those who find it to be so with them, should seriously say unto themselves, "I will set to now, as if I had but one night or one day to live in the world. I will not take rest, until, in some measure, I get it made out unto me, that I have faith."

Secondly, For the second sort, viz.: Those who have it, and yet do not discern it. To such I may say these few things:—

1. Consider that the having of faith is sufficient security for folks happiness and well-being, though they know it not; seeing the having of it interests them in God as their own, in heaven as their own, in the promises as their own, and in the righteousness of Christ as their own; in justification, adoption, and sanctification as their own. I say, the having of faith is sufficient to secure salvation, though ye know not that ye have it. Although their not having the knowledge of it tends much to the sorrow of such, yet the having of sound saving faith is a great matter. It is true they have most comfort that know that they do believe, and can say, "I know in whom I have believed."

2. Consider that the Lord in His revealed will hath laid down several signs or marks of true faith; and therefore the Lord's people should try and examine themselves by those signs, marks, and evidences of faith set down in Scripture, whether they have them or not, so that ye may not only have it, but know that ye have it, and take the comfort of it. There are these marks and evidences of sound faith in Scripture, which I shall briefly mention here. And,

(1.) Those excellent graces, gifts, and fruits of the Spirit are where this grace of faith is. See Gal. v. 22,

(2.) Where those Christian virtues and graces are linked together as in a chain. "Add to faith virtue; and to virtue knowledge; and to knowledge temperance; and to temperance

that begat. "Whom having not seen, ye love; in whom, though now ye see him not, yet believing, ye rejoice with joy unspeakable and full of glory."

(4.) Wherever faith is, there is sincere love to all the saints of God. "Since we heard of your faith in Christ Jesus, and of the love which ye have to all the saints." So that faith and love go hand in hand together.

(5.) Wherever faith is, there is a patient waiting for the promises. Faith makes no haste, but waits for the performing of the promises. It is by faith and patience that the glorified and redeemed have obtained possession of the promises. "Be ye also patient; stablish your hearts: for the coming of the Lord draweth nigh."

(6.) Where faith is, there is a patient enduring of affliction. What God carves out unto them, the apostle tells them they were to endure in faith. Faith keeps patience in the soul where it is.

(7.) Where it is, it weans the heart and affections from the earth and earthly things; they are not desirous of them. "I glory in the cross of our Lord Jesus Christ, by whom the world is crucified unto me and I unto the world." It is by faith in the cross of Christ that the heart is taken off the earth and earthly things, where it is real.

(8.) Faith, where it is in exercise, resists temptations to sin, whether from men or from the devil. The grace of faith cannot enter into any communication with the devil. It is not good communicating with him, lest ye give way. Therefore faith rejects all his temptations with this, "Get thee behind me, Satan."

(9.) It is serious and studious of holiness in the heart, life, and conversation. Believing will not tolerate sin in the heart or conversation. It makes the soul say, "Should such a man as I yield to sin, should such a man as I go on with the world in their corrupt courses, who am an adopted child of God." "Be ye holy, for I am holy." Faith purifieth the heart.

(10.) Again, where faith is, oh! but it puts folk upon being serious and fervent in prayer to God. "Lord, I believe; help thou mine unbelief." Now, are ye bowing your knees to God and confessing your ill-spent time, your ignorance, and the plagues of your corrupt hearts?

(11.) Where faith is, persons are very sensible of the unbelief of their hearts; and gladly would they have their unbelief cured. "Lord, I believe; help thou mine unbelief."

(12.) Faith leads the person in whom it is to make conscience of yielding obedience to God only in Christ's strength. It sets

are not studying to keep His commandments. And,

Lastly, Wherefore it is they are longing for Christ's second coming, that they may be in His company never to be out of it again, as ye may see in 2 Cor. v. 1. There is a great longing to have the house or tabernacle of clay dissolved, and to be possessed of that "house not made with hands, eternal in the heavens." Take a believer in his right frame, you would find he does not care if the day of judgment were ere he slept; he does not care if all the world were in a red flame, as it will be when that day comes; he does not care if the sound of the last trumpet were going through the four winds of heaven. Therefore, believers are described to be those who are hasting unto the coming of Jesus Christ. They are waiting for His appearing in the clouds. Where faith is not, they cannot endure to think of the judgment, because the Judge and they are not friends. The sight of the Judge shall be the saddest sight that ever they saw. Then they shall cry out, "Hills and mountains fall on us, and cover us from the face of the Lamb." But where faith is, there is a crying of the soul, "Haste, Lord." The Spirit says "Come," and the Bride says "Come." So much for the second sort, viz., those who are not clear, and cannot discern it. I daresay that it is folks lying in their sins that makes them uncertain of their faith.

Thirdly, For the third sort, viz., those who make some words or noise about the want of it. Say they, "What shall I do without faith? Why should I pray since I want faith? My praying will not be acceptable to God." Such are Gallio-like, indifferent whether they do it or not. To these I would say these two things :—

1. To make words of that kind, and not to have any hearty concern for the want of it, is altogether unprofitable.

2. While folk continue in that case, they cannot see the Lord, heaven, or eternal happiness. "But the fearful, and unbelieving, and the abominable, and murderers, and sorcerers, and idolaters, and all liars, shall have their part in the lake which burneth with fire and brimstone, which is the second death"—that is, all that are such shall be excluded the kingdom of heaven. But,

Fourthly, For the fourth sort, even such as seriously think that they want faith, and would be glad to use the means of getting it. To these I would only say :—

1. Consider that faith is the gift of God.

2. Consider that the way to draw this faith from God is by prayer; for whatsoever they need, let them seek it by prayer.

3. Consider that as it is God's gift, and that which we should seek from Him by prayer, the Lord hath promised to give what-

whatever we ask agreeably to His will. As this is so, I shall add no more. But remember the absolute necessity of faith, and the good and desirable case and condition they are in that have it; and the woful condition those are in who want it. Remember that He is both the Author and Finisher of faith. He hath promised to give it, if ye seek it. Continue in so doing, and ye shall receive it according to His own promise.

*N.B.*—It appears that the author preached another sermon upon this subject, as the last head and the application are not discussed.

*'We have been with child, we have been in pain, we have, as it were, brought forth wind, we have not wrought any deliverance in the earth, neither have the inhabitants of the world fallen. Thy dead men shall live, together with my dead body shall they arise. Awake, and sing, ye that dwell in dust: for thy dew is as the dew of herbs, and the earth shall cast out the dead."*—Isaiah xxvi. 18, 19.

As this people had before heard of many judgments, and likewise of many good days to come; so, in the first and second verses of this chapter, Zion begins this song, "In that day shall this song be sung in the land of Judah, Open ye the gates, that the righteous nation which keepeth the truth may enter in." And well she sings, and desires to have possession of that of which she sings. That shows what was in her heart, for she sings with the tear in her eye. She sings a song of that which is coming on; she invites all to come and take a trial of the Lord, for "Thou wilt keep him in perfect peace whose mind is stayed on thee." And then, "Trust ye in the Lord for ever." And then she begins to look what way he will do it: "For he bringeth down them that dwell on high; the lofty city, he layeth it low; he layeth it low, even to the ground; he layeth it low, even to the dust." And then she and her daughter come to say, "Yea, in the way of thy judgments, O Lord, have we waited upon thee: the desire of our soul is to thy name, and to the remembrance of thee." And at length she takes the promise boldly: "Lord, thou wilt ordain peace for us; for thou also hast wrought all our works in us."

In the words we have read, she shuts up her song, as if she had said, "I can sing no more, except it be in complaints; we have been with child." We may take this to have been spoken when she was in captivity. She says, "We have been in pain; we expected a deliverance; but when we thought to have brought forth a man child, then we only brought forth wind. We have not wrought any deliverance in the earth." But Christ answers her thus, "Although thou be dead, and lying in the dust, yet sing, 'Thy dead men shall live, together with my dead body shall they arise.'" Or the prophet says it, in Christ's name, "I am fully persuaded that ye shall be well, and I would engage to sink and swim with you. I shall," says he, "desire to be no better

---

* This sermon was preached immediately before the celebration of the Sacrament of the Lord's Supper at Fenwick.

unto themselves. The Lord begins to bear in the upper the point upon them; then they all consent to sing, and they encourage one another, saying, "Our dew shall be as the dew of herbs; and the earth shall cast out the dead."

Now ye have heard of the close of the song. And now in this, and the preceding verses ye have—(1) A complaint, (2) a promise, and (3) an application of the promise.

As to the complaint, it consists in three things:—(1.) "We have been with child." This is their condition. (2.) They are pained. (3.) The continuance of the pain. "We thought to have been delivered, but our thoughts and expectations are frustrated, and we bring forth wind, instead of a child."

Doct. I.—*When ye find such a woful condition, and yet a song appended to it, observe that sometimes Zion and her daughters sing with tears in their eyes.*

Now, for proof of this, there are many mournful psalms of David that bear this title or inscription, "A Song or Psalm of David." The Church of God is represented in a sad and woful condition in this place, and yet the prophet calls this representation a "song." The reasons are threefold:—

1. The first reason why she must sing with the tear in her eye, is because it is a commanded duty. Though she can give no reason of a song, either internal or external, yet she must sing. If it should be to run over some precipice, and dash herself to pieces, if she hath a command, she must obey the charge. Whatsoever stands in her way, she must go through it; and then He allows Zion to sing. She must sing a song.

Use.—This reaches a reproof unto the natural man, for he knows not what it is to obey a command out of regard to God's authority. He cannot do it in remembrance of Him; but the spiritual man must essay it, and he dares not say anything to the contrary. Says Job, "Yet in my flesh shall I see God;" that is "My dust shall yet praise God." Thus the children of Zion must go on in obedience to a command. And,

2. She must sing. And why? That she may engage others in this work; "For although I never thrive," says the child of God "yet I wish all Zion's daughters to thrive and prosper." So that Christians, you should not suffer any of your jealousies to frighten others from coming to God in Christ. Zion's daughters will smil when they hear the word preached, although it should sting then to the heart.

3. The third reason why she sings is, she knows that if ther be any means under heaven to engage God to work for her and t

Him. The soul knows that it never got God's approbation for disbelieving. "Many times," says the soul, "hath He frowned upon me for it; and therefore I would strive against unbelief." Now when the soul can plead this way from experience, then it is encouraged to sing. But again, as Zion sings, she sings with the tear in her eye. The reasons for this are :—

(1.) Because, although she sees she is bound to sing, yet she sees a debt in her bosom that she will never be able to pay. This makes her weep because she hath wronged Christ; and when she sees how far she is fallen from God, and from that sweet and desirable condition she was in, as the Psalmist expresses it, "When I remember these things, I pour out my soul within me: for I had gone with the multitude, I went with them to the house of God, with the voice of joy and praise, with a multitude that kept holy-day." Thus he begins to sing, and then the tears start into his eyes, and he thinks, "Oh, that it had been with me as formerly, then I might have sung cheerfully."

(2.) The second reason why they sing with the tear in their eye is, because their enemies thrust sore at them. When they begin to sing, the devil perhaps starts up and says, "O thou blasphemer of God, how canst thou sing? for thou but dishonourest Him with thy song." Then the tears start in their eyes. "Thou hast thrust sore at me, that I might fall; but the Lord helped me." And then she sees that she hath reason both of singing and complaining. At last she finds out a way to unite them, and sings with the tear in her eye.

(3.) The third reason is, because ye know singing is a token of hope. When she begins to think how many vain hopes she has had, she is troubled, and that makes the tear to start into her eye.

Now, we think there are some people this day that would sing, and they must sing, and yet the tear appears in their eye when they think how many vain thoughts and vain expectations they have had, to be loosed from their bonds. Now, we would wish the Lord's people would not plead their duty of praise out of doors. For be your condition what it will, sing; for the worst condition ye can be in gives you no liberty to thrust out a command. If ye will give this place, we defy unbelief to prevail with you. But you may say, "Ye know not what condition we are in, and yet you bid us sing." Indeed, I know not your different conditions; but they can be no worse than the condition the Scripture here speaks of. "We have been in pain; we have brought forth wind; we have not wrought any deliverance in the earth."

2ndly, This conception comes to the ———

3rdly, They were disappointed in this.

DOCT. II.—*Great troubles and afflictions are in the lot of the people and children of God.*

But you will wonder that we took such a text or subject on this day; but as we essayed to pass it by, but could not get liberty, so we think that many of the people of God are come to this pass.

I say, outward afflictions are the lot of the godly; for "we must through much tribulation enter into the kingdom of God." "Many are the afflictions of the righteous: but the Lord delivereth him out of them all." Some have troubles on their bodies, some upon their names, some upon their goods, &c. But why is it so with Zion?

1. The first reason for this is, because it is to scour off the rust, so to speak, of their armour, that it may be put to use or practice. Sometimes when a man doth not his duty to God, then He lays trouble one way or another upon him to stir him up to his duty. He will suffer this man's character to be tossed as a foot-ball up and down the country, and by that means will set the man upon working. "Knowing that tribulation worketh patience; and patience, experience; and experience, hope: and hope maketh not ashamed." Acquainted with troubles, people grow more patient; they will bear with a wrong now, that they could not have endured or borne with before.

2. A second reason is, that they may know that the full enjoyment of their peace is not on this side the grave. For when they begin, as it were, to lay in a stock for themselves to live peaceably upon, then he cuts the sinews of their expectations. That which they leaned unto fails, so that they can find no comfort in it. But says the apostle, "Let us go forth therefore unto him without the camp, bearing his reproach. For here we have no continuing city."

3. The third reason why God lays troubles upon His people is, that the rent of these troubles may be paid unto Him. There are a great number of outward strokes that He lays upon the men of the world, and they never acknowledge God in or for them; and therefore He lays them upon Zion, that He may get the tribute of them from her. He will have His people declare what they can pay to Him out of any year, accident, or the like. He will have them give a proof before the world what may be made of that which the world can make nothing of. And, we dare say, that if people knew this, they would walk more sure, more safely, in and under troubles. Pay thy dues then, O man, or woman, before the world. "I will pay my vows now, in presence of all his people."

therefore you of Zion shall get them laid upon you. "We have been in pain; we have been with child."

The trouble is as that of a woman with child; that is, great trouble in itself; but the thoughts of being a mother to a child mitigates the pain unto her. Hence,

Doct. III.—*That outward trouble is grievous in itself.*

Therefore it reproves these who may be saying, "Oh that I had some cross, I would wait better upon my duty." But fools, I say, that trouble is altogether grievous in itself; it is as a woman with child in pain to be delivered. It is true, the man is blessed that gets the right and satisfied use of it. "Blessed is the man whom thou chastenest, O Lord, and teachest out of thy law." But without teaching of His law, trouble is an impediment, and hindrance unto many. I say, a cross laid on you, if ye get not the sanctified use of it, will bring one trouble after another daily, as so many strangers that will hold you so busy, that ye shall not have time or leisure for prayer to God. Therefore let none of the people of the Lord, now approach unto His table, with these thoughts in their hearts. For crosses of themselves are an enemy to godliness. For instance, some men will have a bad wife, and some women a bad husband; some bad children, and these troubles occasion new ones, so that they are in pain to be delivered, and yet oftimes bring forth nothing but wind. And troubles are grievous,

1. Because the Lord hath hidden, as is were, His face; and that makes it troublesome. For it is impossible for one to be much subdued with any affliction, if he have the Lord's countenances. But when He hides His face, then trouble becomes more grievous. "Thou hidest thy face, and I was troubled." Now we would wish, that those who have trouble, and from whom the Lord hath hid His face, would pray unto God, that He would, as it were, draw the curtain, and that would make every trouble sweet and comfortable unto them.

2. A second reason why trouble becomes grievous is, because ye have not a clear conscience, but have challenges along with the cross; and then the least cross hath the sting in it. For if I am not consumed with guilt lying upon my conscience, then I can plead with God more cheerfully.

3. The third reason why your troubles become grievous to you is, that when ye see these things come to pass that ye proposed unto yourselves, yet have not got that in them which ye expected. This brings forth wind, and makes your trouble grievous unto you. For example, a man that, perhaps, hath a bad wife takes comfort in this: he thinks, "I shall have good children, and I shall have

He deliver you, although it should be till your last breath.

4. The fourth reason that makes your cross grievous unto you, is because ye will not bear one day's cross alone ; as if the cross ye have were not enough, ye cut and carve out crosses unto yourselves. Ye think, "What if this and that shall be, then I must be still worse and worse." Thus the man is vexed with his own vain thoughts. "This and that will come," says he, "and then I shall be ashamed ; then I and my house will be ruined." "But is not every day sufficient for the evil thereof," says Christ. And can He not send as much strength with the cross, as shall make you bear it. These sad thoughts of the cross make it become exceeding heavy.

USE.—Now for the use. Anyone who is thinking it shall be thus and thus, and whose time is taken up with these vexing thoughts of crosses, ye should live in a constant dependence upon God, and on bills of exchange. One cross shall furnish you with as much as will carry you on to another; and thus ye shall be carried still from one to another, if ye live by a constant dependence on God. This kind of life will keep His name great in your estimation. "God is our refuge and strength, and a very present help in trouble." I wish that the Lord's people, before they now go to His table, would resolve upon this, to live henceforth, as it were, on bills of exchange, and trust all unto God. Oh ! that all God's afflicted people would do this !

5. The fifth reason is, Ye will not yield to the cross, when it lays hold of you. Ye know when a beast frets and takes ill with the yoke, then the yoke becomes more grievous and irksome to it than it would be if it took well with it. So when He says you shall bear it, you say ye will not bear it. But you should say, "I see Thou art designed to cross me such and such ways; and now from henceforth I desire that I may receive strength to bear them." He allows you all means to hold off the cross ; but when it comes ye should resolve to bear it. For if ye say, that "at such a time crosses shall not come in my way ;" then they shall undoubtedly come in your way. As when the Lord sent a message to the Moabites, saying, "Let my people go through your land, and they shall take nothing from you." Say they, "They shall not get leave to pass through." "But," says the Lord, "they shall go through it, and to your cost too. Let my rod pass by you," says God; but ye say, ye will not have it come your way ; and when it comes, ye lay the blame on this person, and that person. But from henceforth never own the creature for thy party, but take

in the earth; neither have the inhabitants of the world fallen." There is a term, when their pain comes to a height, and they expect to be delivered; but their hopes are frustrated.

Doct. IV.—*That sometimes the troubles of the people and children of God come to a height; and then they presently expect an outgate, and they bring forth nothing but, as it were, wind.*

Now in this, it is Satan's way to make them hope on wrong grounds; for then he knows, that when they are thus beguiled, it is a hundred to one if they be not made to question all the work of God within them. Now we shall show you some of these false grounds, whereupon he makes you hope. And,

1. When ye see a sin which ye saw not before, oh ye think "Surely this has been the sin for which He hath contended with me. Now since He has let me see it, He will forthwith deliver me." And dost thou think He will deliver thee for that? Hath He not enough of reasons besides for contending with thee, although thou beholdest them not.

2. The second ground whereupon ye hope is, That He shall deliver you, because you have taken on a new duty, or engagement to duty.

3. The creature hopes for an outgate, when it seems to have attained to any measure of submission under the cross. But do not hope upon that ground; for that is but a weak ground or evidence for you to hope upon.

4. The fourth false ground is, that He makes them hope when they seem to have a promise of deliverance. But I say, take heed how ye understand the promise, for, I say, ye are not bound to believe any promise, but that which is necessary for salvation. But ye may believe in general, "that all his paths are mercy and truth unto you." Indeed, I grant that we may believe a promise for such a particular thing, if the Spirit of God so bear it in upon us, that we are engaged to believe it.

5. The fifth ground whereupon your hopes are wrong, is, that when ye come to such a height of distress, ye think, surely He will now either destroy or deliver you. But ye are mistaken; for He may bring you to the door, when ye think your troubles are at a height, and, as it were, let you get the air; and even put you back into your prison, and shut the door upon you again. Therefore, I say, limit not the grounds of your deliverance; for if ye lay down a ground, and hope upon that ground, and when it is frustrated, it is a thousand to one if ye do not question all your salvation to-morrow. Therefore lay down no such grounds; for

dead men shall live; together with my dead body shall they arise. Awake, and sing, ye that dwell in dust; for thy dew is as the dew of herbs, and the earth shall cast out the dead." And let all who are under trouble, apply unto themselves the two last verses of the chapter where my text lies; "Come, my people, enter thou into thy chambers, and shut thy doors about thee; hide thyself, as it were, for a little moment, until the indignation be overpast. For behold, the Lord cometh out of his place to punish the inhabitants of the earth for their iniquity: the earth also shall disclose her blood, and shall no more cover her slain."

But the words may be taken in another sense here. There is another conception that the daughters of Zion may have, and that is a conception of faith. And here,

I. We shall show you how there is such a conception.

II. How this conception comes to a height. And,

I. Of a false conception. Ye that have this false conception, we ask you these questions:—

1. The first is, how and when did ye conceive? Ye may say, that ye know the time; and yet by your conversation, I know ye have not conceived.

2. Thou sayest, thou hast conceived, and yet the evils of thy nature are still breaking out. Now when I see a man that says he hath conceived, and yet his evil nature is allowed in breaking out daily, I say, there is not so much as even a false conception in that person.

3. The third question we think pertinent to ask is, What fellowship or discourses have ye about the new birth? If thou hast no discourse about them that are regenerate, and the marks of regeneration; and if thou desirest not to be amongst those that are born again, it is but a false conception that thou hast, and not a true and genuine one.

4. The fourth question is, Hast thou any longing desires after this and that spiritual good? All that have conceived graciously, do still long for some new things; and they long "for the sincere milk of the word, that they may grow thereby."

5. Thou that sayest thou hast conceived, if thy conception have not stirrings, thou hast but a false conception. I think nothing of a man's having a stirring sometimes at a preaching. It is not a scriptural conception that hath not these marks. When there is a rich reward to be given to religion; as when there were gifts to be given to the Jews, many called themselves so that were not Jews. There was a stirring among them. So there is a stirring

they returned and enquired early after God."

And then there is a stirring, when there are great out-breakings. Then the man's conscience flies in his face, and he hath a great stir within him. Yet, I say, the man that hath but these, hath but a false conception, and shall bring forth wind. If thou trust to such a conception, thou wilt break thy neck by approaching unto these holy things in the sacramental ordinance, however thou prayest, think that thou bringest forth something.

II.—We come to the true conception; and we shall show you how it comes to a height, and thinks to be delivered; and yet brings forth the wind. Now,

1st, The first and great doubt thou hast is, that it was not a proper means that first set thee on foot. Thou sayest, "It was not the sight of my sin and transgression, and therefore I bring forth but wind." What was it then? "Why, it was a cross or affliction," say ye, "that first set me on work; therefore I bring forth but vanity." But that is bad reasoning. As if a man going about a base errand should find a purse of gold by the way; but he says, "I will not take the gold, because I came not to seek gold; but when I come to seek gold, then I will take it." Everyone sees the folly of such reasoning. Now that we speak of that which first set you on work, ye say it was a cross; we say, it is not the unsounder for that circumstance. With regard to most of those who came unto Christ in the days of His flesh, it was some outward trouble that made them come. Some came, as it were, to buy a needle. "But stay," said He, "I will tell you that there is not a whole shirt on your back." In this way He made many a bargain with poor fools. Some came there that did not so much as know that He was the true Messiah; and yet they were brought to say, "Rabbi, where dwellest thou?" And He says, "Come and see." And says He, "Ye shall bear testimony of me before the world. I shall give you enough." What is that to you? What set you on work, if ye be set on work? You believe the Master is speaking to you, and take it as from God, and hide your faces when ye hear this told you; but you need not do so; for it is a true conception, although ye have these doubts about it.

2ndly, A second question, or doubt, that ye may have about the soundness of your conception is, "I had no such pain as I conceive some have had in their conception; and therefore I think mine is not a true one." As for that that ye say, that ye have not been so damped with the works of the law as others, ye must know that the Lord is an absolute sovereign, and He works as He will. It is true that some that have the work of God within

ness, even in thy holy things, as made thee flee unto the Mediator and refuge set before thee. Then the Lord allows strong consolation to all those who flee unto the refuge set before them, or have fled for refuge to lay hold upon the hope set before them.

2. Whether or not didst thou see so much of the covenant of free grace as to make thee wonder at it, and say, "I see as much in free grace as can pardon the greatest sinner that ever was." Unto the new man all things are pure. Look if thou hast got such a view of justification as makes thee fear Him—"Blessed is the man that feareth the Lord." And thou art afraid to offend Him in anything. We use to say, "Burnt children dread the fire." Now this is all ye have to object against your conception. Ye say, "Seeing it is true, why then am I not established and delivered?" I say, for this reason, that ye walk upon false grounds. And,

(1.) The first false ground whereon ye walk is, That ye will not believe as long as ye see an outbreaking in yourselves, or as long as ye see an infirmity. So that if ye were once healed, ye would believe and come to Christ. But, I say, whether ye be healed or not, ye are bound to believe; and ye shall never get these evils mortified until you come to Christ.

(2.) A second false ground wherein ye walk is, that ye say "Such are some of the marks of the child of God; but I cannot believe that these are stirring in me, because I cannot get all the marks of the child of God. Therefore I am not of that number." "But shall the ear say, Because I am not the eye, therefore I am not of the body." When thou dost get nineteen promises that thou mayest lay hold upon, yet thou wilt not believe because thou canst not lay hold upon the twentieth; that is to give God the lie nineteen times.

(3.) The third false ground is, "Because," say ye, "I have not the condition of that promise, 'Come unto me, all ye that labour and are heavy laden, and I will give you rest,' therefore I will not come." But, if none should come but those who have the condition of that promise, of what use are all the promises in the Bible? For if none should come but those who have the condition of such a promise, there needed be no more promises in all the Bible. But because some have got the condition of one promise, and some that of another*—"Whosoever will, let him come and

* As the Lord has been graciously pleased to favour us with an absolutely free grant of Christ, and of eternal life in Him, so He has condescended to exhibit this grant in a wonderful variety of promises suitable to the variety of our cases. "And this is the record, that God hath given us eternal life;

it, then it stirs to be at the Mediator. At other times it will be silent. Sometimes, when it comes to a height, there is much of the power of God seen. When the person is walking through the sanctuary, then it begins to stir like John the Baptist, who as soon as he heard Mary's voice leaped in his mother's womb; so the true conception begins to stir when there is a day of Christ's presence in the sanctuary. Another time is when it receives a hurt—when there is some sin committed, then it strikes with hands and feet, and says, "Either take Christ now, or never." When threatenings come forth, then it resolves that it must set about believing. Another time is just before it be delivered. Now we may assign these three reasons as the causes that make persons bring forth the wind, and hinder them from being established in believing:— 1. There is somewhat in God's part, as an act of justice, that "because ye delighted not to believe, and to retain the knowledge of God in your hearts, therefore he hath given you up to strong delusions to believe a lie." 2. A second way in which it comes from God is, as it is an act of His wisdom. And 3. As it is an act of His absolute sovereignty. He would have the creature give up all claims to Him. As long as it will not believe, it shall never be established; otherwise, it comes from Satan's false way of reasoning with them.

1st, He reasons from wrong expounded Scriptures. But take no expositions but what agree with the analogy of faith and the grounds of religion.

2ndly, He reasons from sundry ways of providence. But I am not bound to these, for "no man knows love or hatred by all that is before him."

3rdly, He reasons from a part to the whole. "Thou canst not deny," says he, "that thou hast hypocrisy, then thou art altogether a hypocrite." But, Satan, this is groundless and foolish logic.

4thly, He reasons from one time to all times. Says he, "Ye dare not say that ever ye had love to God or to His people, therefore ye shall never have it." And then he reasons from breach of

and this life is in his Son. Whereby are given unto us exceeding great and precious promises; that by these you might be partakers of the divine nature, having escaped the corruption that is in the world through lust." Hence these words, "Some have got the condition of one promise, some that of another," must be understood agreeably to the nature of the gospel promise, as if it had been said, "The Lord has given us not one but many great and precious promises, so that though a person does not see one of them to be suitable to his case, he may see another to be so."

"But as far as the heavens are above the earth, so far are my thoughts above your thoughts, saith the Lord." And then he reasons from one saint to another—"Thou canst not find another saint in thy case." As Job's friend said unto him, "Unto which of the saints wilt thou turn?" But I am not bound to find another in my condition, if my condition be like a scriptural one. Then he will propose an objection, and because ye cannot answer it, therefore he says it is unanswerable. But he lies in this too. And then he reasons from what is done to what is to do. "Because," says he, "ye have not done such and such things, therefore ye shall never do it." I say this too is false reasoning.

But, upon the whole, take his reasons and throw them back upon himself. Go to Christ and desire Him to teach you how to answer them. But we add no more.

*"Let not them that wait on thee, O Lord God of Hosts, be ashamed
for my sake: let not those that seek thee be confounded for my
sake, O God of Israel."*—Psalm lxix. 6.

THERE are many mysteries in the world, amongst which these five
following are none of the least:—

1st, Who are those who are called "the Godly Party" in
the world? This is a great mystery.

2ndly, How comes it about that this party, called "the
Godly Party," cleaves so closely together? It is likewise a mystery
that they are so strongly united to one another.

3rdly, The variety of lots in this one party. Though they are
so closely united together, yet they are led to heaven in different
ways. Here is a great mystery.

4thly, What the exercises of that party are, when they are
at the worst, is likewise a mystery.

5thly, How they come to be guided and preserved in composure in their exercise, amidst all troubles, is another mystery.

Now these five things, I conceive, are contained in the text;
and I perceive that there are five doctrines that will natively arise
from them.

DOCT. I.—*The godly party are such as wait upon the Lord.*

Make of them what ye will, this is the true description of them.
They are so described, "Let integrity and uprightness preserve
me, for I wait on thee."

In this distinction of them, ye may take up these things following, that hold out clearly what they are:—

1. It says that their expectations terminate upon God; their
houghts are conversant about an invisible God. In Psalm xxxix.,
when David has told us that every man walks in a vain show, he
says (verse 7), "And now, Lord, what wait I for? my hope is in
thee."

2. It says that whatever that party be, their stock is in hope,
and not in their hand; they are but waiting; they are but just
looking for it; they have not as yet overtaken it. "For we walk
by faith, not by sight" or sense.

3. It says they are a party devoted unto the service and
attendance of the God of heaven; they are waiting upon God;
their eyes are fixed upon Him; and they look to what is His will,

---

* This sermon seems to have been preached immediately after the celebration of the Sacrament of the Lord's Supper.

events thereof, unto the God of ......

Him, and are content that their sentence should come forth from Him. " Let my sentence come forth from thy presence."

5. It implies an inclination to wait, and hope for good from God's hand. He only is a godly man who is actuated by the Spirit that inclines him to mercy's side of the question.

USE.—For use, try yourselves by these things, whether or not ye are waiting on God? Whether or not does your expectation terminate on God only? Whether or not are ye devoted unto His service? Do ye commit all events to God? Are ye content that your sentence come forth from before Him? Look if your heart inclines you to mercy's side of the question, and to look for good from God's hand? Can you say these things? There is no man in a natural state that can say so, or plead these things.

DOCT. II.—*There is a strange unity and communion among the godly.*

There is a strong bond of union amongst them. The Psalmist here supposes that all the godly will have their eye upon him, and he is afraid that he may carry not aright before them. " Jerusalem is builded as a city, that is compact together." But here I shall show you—

I. Some things wherein they are mostly united.

II. What makes them to be so closely united in one body.

III. What are the consequences that natively flow from these. Now,

I. For the first of these. They are,

1. A party that are one in heart. They have all one heart given them. It is a promise to all the godly, that they shall have one heart; that is, the new heart which is given to them all.

2. They are one as to their interest. Their first aim is, that the Lord Jesus Christ may reign and be great in the world, and that His kingdom may prosper; and then that they may be found in Him on that day, and in His righteousness. That is their interest, in which they are all one. If they were all asked, " What is your interest?" this would be their answer: " Let Christ reign, and be great; and let us be found in Him."

3. They are all one as to their design and endeavours. Their design is to be like unto Him, and to be conformed to His blessed will and command. This is the one way that is promised unto them all. " I will give them one heart, and one way, that they may fear thee for ever; for the good of them, and of their children after them."

4. They are all one as to their outward profession in the world

of the serpent. Whoever he be that is not in some cases a sufferer with them, he has reason to suspect his state, since it is the lot of all the seed of the woman to be persecuted by the seed of the serpent.

II. Now would ye know why they are all so completely united in everything.

1. They are all cast in one mould of the Divine decree, that is from everlasting.

2. They are all actuated by one spirit; therefore they must be one. This spirit is promised to them all to cause them to walk in His ways. They are all actuated by this one spirit. Hence the spirituality of their duties.

3. They are all designed for one end, that is, full conformity to God, and the immediate enjoyment of Him to all eternity, in so far as they are capable of enjoying Him. Since they are cast in one mould from everlasting, and actuated by one spirit, and designed for one end, then how can they but be one? Which brings me,

III. To what are the consequences that natively follow from this oneness of heart and mind. And,

1. A unity in exercises follows on it, amongst all the people of God. They are all exercised about some spiritual thing. They are all exercised about a corrupt heart, that is disobedient in the matters of God and will not abide in His way. They are all exercised about the threatenings of God in Scripture; such as that, "Cursed is he that doeth the work of the Lord deceitfully."

2. They are one as to temptation. One temptation they are all assaulted with is, whether or not there is a reality in religion and godliness; and whether there is a God above that rules all things on the earth below, since He lets all things go through one another in such a manner, and one man devours another, as the fishes of the sea. In this, and some other things, I would say, they have a oneness in respect of temptations. Satan loves to assault a man with that temptation whereby he prevails oftenest or most readily over him. But,

3. This follows on it:—They are one in respect of the same precious truths that they believe in and feed upon. They have the same *michtams*, or golden Scriptures. They have the same great and precious promises. Was not that a good word that you and many love well? "Although my house be not so with God; yet he hath made with me an everlasting covenant, well ordered in all things, and sure." Was not this a word ye loved well?

When one of them is glad, all of them rejoice; and they sorrow together. The wicked are not so. It is true, they are all one in evil. They are all one in the crucifying of Christ. Herod and Pilate were all one in this. They are all one about a visible God; but the other is all one about an invisible God. The one goes upward; the other goes downward.

USE.—Try yourselves by this, how it answers your condition. Can you say, ye are all one with the people of God in these things. If ye be one with them in these things; think it not strange if ye be one with them in persecution, and the cross of Christ also. If ye be not content to take that lot with them, then you want one special point of your character. Wherefore let me obtest all the godly to be more and more one. Let us be one, come of us what will. I would use these arguments with you, to make you study this oneness.

1. It is your strength.

2. I hope it has been your happiness. For some years past, we walked together in one profession. Therefore let us be one, seeing we have walked together as one these many years past. Therefore I would obtest and charge you to be still of one heart, and of one mind.

3. This feast that we have been at, says, that we are all one. We have all sealed it this day, and taken our sacrament on it. The unity of communicants is the report of the sacrament of the Lord's Supper.

4. I believe if ye were all posed on it, ye would own you had no great temptation to join with any other party in the world. What can be your temptation to be one with another party? Therefore be one amongst yourselves.

And I shall only add—I put this question home to everyone of you—Whether the Scriptures do not speak most favourably of the godly party? For as low as they are in the world, the Scripture speaks much to their commendation. You scarcely open your Bible, but you find it smile upon God's people, and frown upon their adversaries. Is it not of great advantage then, to be of the godly party?

DOCT. III.—*Although this party be most singularly knit together, yet it pleaseth their Master to exhibit some of them, as on a stage for Himself, more singularly than others.*

Thus it was with these men here. He does so ordinarily in one of these three cases.

1. He exhibits some of them singularly with regard to the temptations to sin they are assaulted with. Some of them have

their personal afflictions and sufferings. Justice is still pursuing your house or family, sometimes taking away the wife, sometimes the husband, and sometimes taking away the children. Job stands as a pattern for us of all this.

3. He uses to make spectacles of some of His people in their public trials, for the cause of Jesus Christ. He exhibits some of them singularly, in order to the trial of the cross of Christ. Paul was so; "Of the Jews five times received I forty stripes save one. Thrice was I beaten with rods, once was I stoned, thrice I suffered shipwreck, a night and a day have I been in the deep." The reasons of this dispensation are various. The Lord brings some of His people, as it were, on a theatre more than others.

(1.) Not because there is more sin in one, than in another.

(2.) Neither is it out of less respect to some, that He suffers devils to haunt and tempt them more than others. Nor,

(3.) Is it a greater stock of habitual grace that makes Him exhibit some as bearing the cross of Christ more singularly than others.

But the reason is, The absolute sovereignty of God, who will do with any of His people as He pleaseth; and that His wisdom and strength may the more illustriously appear in bearing them up under all their trials.

USE.—Let never one of you, great or small, dream that ye may not be exhibited, as on a theatre, in one or all of these three ways, and mistake not the reasons why it is so.

DOCT. IV.—*The thing that vexes the people of God, when at the worst, is, lest they should be a shame, or an affront to all the rest of the godly, by disowning the Lord's way.* "Let none that wait upon thee, O Lord God of hosts, be ashamed for my sake."

This says, that unless the carriage and deportment of the godly man redounds to the comfort of all the rest of the godly, through his being enabled honestly to bear up when he is any way called out to a public appearance for God, it some way tends to the discredit of all the godly. Since this is the case, when they slip aside or carry not aright, since they are all in hazard of doing so, it should be matter of affecting and afflicting exercise lest they do so. Fellow professors are ashamed of the person that carries not aright; they are ashamed that ever they should have been in company or fellowship with him; they are ashamed that ever such a person should have owned such a cause, and that ever such a thing should have befallen a professor of such a cause; and, besides, they are weakened by him in their hopes of through-bearing for themselves.

if they get not presently . . . . . .

USE.—All of you know how many ways ye are in hazard of being a discredit to the cause and to the rest of the godly, by yielding to temptations after this communion. And we will be ashamed of you if any of you fall into drunkenness and other vices after you have been at this communion. Oh, think on it, that ye are in hazard of being a disgrace to all the honest folk that know you, if ye fall so, and wrong the work and cause of God!

DOCT. V.—*The way to secure every one of God's people is, to improve and make use of God, as He has revealed Himself, according all the cases and conditions wherein they are in hazard of being a discredit to all the godly.*

And wouldst thou improve this art, thou who art dogged with some vile temptation? Hast thou reason to fear that thou mayest be a discredit to the godly? Then improve the Lord as He has held out Himself in a most answerable way to your case and condition. Dost thou fear that thou mayst wrong the cause of God and be a discredit to His people, thou art so weak and ready to fall? Then, look unto the Lord of hosts, who is able to bear weak ones through, even such as thou art. But when I bid you improve Him, then I allow you to look unto the glorious titles that He takes to Himself, that are most consonant and agreeable to your case and condition. Cleave unto Him; hang on Him for the performance of the promises by faith; wrestle with Him by prayer to make out these promises to you. " Let not those that seek thee be confounded for my sake, O God of Israel." This is the way to carry fair under every temptation; and may the Lord Himself help and enable you to do so. Amen.

'*Ho, every one that thirsteth, come ye to the waters, and he that hath no money; come ye, buy, and eat; yea, come, buy wine and milk without money and without price. Wherefore do ye spend money for that which is not bread? and your labour for that which satisfieth not? hearken diligently unto me, and eat ye that which is good, and let your soul delight itself in fatness.*"—Isa. lv. 1, 2.

THERE is in this chapter a proclaimed market, such as was never heard of, even the most pleasant, most substantial, and most glorious market that ever was; the most glorious wares; the most precious wares; the dearest bought and cheapest sold that ever any wares were. Here we have the most free and lawful invitation to all sorts of persons to come and have them. They shall get them and pay nothing for them. Now there is in this chapter

1st, An invitation to all persons in all places, to come and receive Jesus Christ, the King of kings, Lord of lords, and Prince of peace, who is even among our hands in the gospel, wherein He manifests Himself. Now that He offers Himself, take Him, and you are welcome to Him. Any person who hath anything ado with Him, come; for He is now seeking employment to be given Him. He hath balms for all wounds, salves for all sores, and cures for all sorts of diseases. And,

2ndly, There are some objections against this coming, and these He solves, and uses various motives and invitations to encourage souls to come unto Him and buy. Such are the following:—

1. The market is free. He is seeking nothing from you, but hath all glorious things to give you. Therefore, ye are fools if ye will not come and take when ye have nothing to give.

2. If ye will not come, your well-doing is over. Your doom is, Depart for ever;" and do what ye can, ye shall not prosper, nor get any soul-satisfaction any other way. And,

3. If ye will come, ye need not be afraid of wrath and justice. Ye shall not have that to say that ye dare not come for fear He execute justice upon you. The Father took Christ Jesus to be your Cautioner or Surety. Christ shall stand for you and manage in your room or stead. He will manage all that concerns you, both with regard to the guilt and the pollution of sin; for the

---

* This sermon seems to have been preached immediately before the celebration of the Sacrament of the Lord's Supper.

the like of you is allowed to come near Christ, instead of saying ye will not come unto Him. For God hath a mind to make Him unspeakably honourable in His kingdom, think ye of Him what ye will. For many shall come out of all kindreds, kingdoms, and nations, like flocks of sheep, and shall cast down their crowns at His footstool, even those that have never yet heard of Him; and what a shame will it be for you to be the last of all in paying your respects to Him?

5. If ye will not come and close with Him now in the offers of the gospel, wherein He is offered unto you, take care that ye sit not your time of the market; for there is but a set time of His offers, wherein He will be found of you.

But there are two formidable objections, which are these:—

Objection 1. We are so abominable, and have provoked God so often, that we think it cannot stand with His justice to accept of such traitors, though we should come. But God answers, "Away with such chat; for my thoughts are not like your thoughts, saith the Lord; they are as far above them as the heavens are above the earth."

Objection 2. Say some, "Ye may promise us fair words enough; but in the mean time, we get nothing in our hands, but bare words." "That is true," says God, "but I think My word effectual enough to perform anything I can promise; for I am both powerful enough, and willing enough to perform it. Besides My word must prove itself effectual, for it must be for a name, and for a praise unto Me in all generations." And then He hints at the deliverance of the people of the Jews from their bondage. So much for the meaning of this chapter. We now return, to make some improvement of it in the way of comparing it with the former chapter, in which ye heard many a precious promise made to the Church and her children. And now God will have them apply and bring home all these to their own souls, in closing with Christ; wherein we observe,

That whatever promise was made to the Church, all the members of it should believe, and apply them to themselves in the way of closing with Christ. And now we enter upon the words, wherein there are:—

I. The King's proclamation making way for our coming to the market, in the words, "Ho, every one."

II. A public intimation of the goods that are to be had at this market, and these are "water," "wine," and "milk."

III. The manner in which these goods are to be viewed.

ing unto Christ, and receiving Him as He offereth Himself in the gospel. I return,

I. To the first, which is the proclamation openly made for coming unto Christ. "Jesus stood, and cried, saying, If any man thirst, let him come unto me, and drink. He that believeth on me, as the Scripture hath said, out of his belly shall flow rivers of living water." Now Christ is crying this day, who will come unto Him? He is crying to deaf folk who never heard, "Will ye hear, and believe the word preached? I will make you see, ye blind folk, who are running upon imminent hazard. Ho! are there any folk who have wounds to heal? here is balm for you. Is there any man here who desires to be made clean? here is water to cleanse you. Is there any who have sores to heal? come, here is salve for you. Are there any fractured bones amongst you? here is healing for you. Are there any hard hearts amongst you? here is repentance for you. Are there any confused with darkness amongst you? come, here is light for you. Do any desire to be taught? here is teaching for you. Do you desire to be made friends with God? here is reconciliation for you. Would any be borne up under their crosses? here is strength for them. Is there any person who judges himself, though they suppose they are beguiling themselves? here is counsel for you. Come unto me and I will tell you where you are, and what ye are doing." But oh! what is the matter that we have to say unto you, that few of you will come to Christ, though ye know yourselves to be far from Him? The reason why a proclamation must be made before we come to this market, is,

1. That the King may declare publicly what goodwill He bears to the commonwealth of Israel. He would much rather have folk to be converted and live, than die and perish.

2. He makes it public, that He may evidence His power and sovereignty over all things.

3. He makes it public, that the mouth of all objectors to the contrary may be stopped.

4. That all his enemies may come to a rendezvous and see whether they are able to stop Him.

5. He proclaims it publicly, that all may know that the market has but a set time, wherein Jesus Christ is offered to souls; and therefore they should bestir themselves in the time of the market. Go not away, then, ere ye get the wares secured to yourselves, seeing the great God of heaven has made an open proclamation for all sorts of persons to come to Christ. Let no person be so foolish as to despise the King's proclamation.

such are to look upon themselves as the most vile and the maddest creatures that ever were known. They even savour of the earth. Any person that is truly acquainted with the exercises of closing with Christ, and dare say that they have Him for their portion, their countenance shall be made to shine in heavenly glory. As to any person who supposes he has any hatred of his sins, and yet, through a sense of guilt, dares not venture upon closing with Christ, I say, as long as he stands on this side of Christ, he shall have no true peace of mind.

Now we shall give you some motives that we think may put you upon a peremptory closing with Christ. And consider—

1. That these offers are threatened to be removed. God knows how long you may have them. Now, while you have your day of the Gospel, improve and make use of Christ for your salvation, by closing your interest with Him.

2. Though it should please Him to continue the same day of the standing of the Gospel, it will not stand long without a storm and many a winter blast blowing against it and its professors. Since the winter is approaching, ye have need to look that your clothes be provided for you, lest ye go with the storms and dint of the weather.

3. And is not God now plaguing all the land? We conceive it is for no other reason but because people will not flee from their idols, and cleave to Christ, and close with Him for their alone portion. But,

II. We come to the wares of this market, and these are of three sorts—(1) Water, (2) wine, (3) milk.

With regard to water, He is called "the water of life;" with regard to wine, the spouse compares Him to "flagons of wine;" and with regard to milk, He bids His people suck out the "sincere milk of the word (which is Himself), that they may grow thereby." The reasons will be taken from the properties of each of these, which we shall consider separately for your better understanding of the point. And,

Firstly, (1.) Water, ye know, is good for washing and cleaning away of all filthiness. (2.) Water is good for the softening of any hard thing. (3.) Water is good for refreshing, or quenching of thirst. (4.) Water is good for curing hot and fiery humours. All these properties are to be found in Christ. Art thou one of the most filthy creatures upon the earth? Then Christ is that fountain opened for washing away your sin and uncleanness. Is the wrath of God burning in thy conscience for thy sin and uncleanness?

mourn for sin that never mourned for it before. Is thy conscience galled for sin that thou canst get no rest? Christ is a Prince for that end, to make peace in a soul that is out of peace. Hast thou a desire after Christ, and are all things nothing to thee for want of Him? Then come and venture upon Christ, and thou shalt be satisfied and filled with Him in such a manner that out of "thy belly shall flow living waters;" that is, thou shalt have full satisfaction in Him. Is thy case one of the most strange and wonderful in the world? Then Christ's name is also the Wonderful, Counsellor. Art thou afraid of the removal of the gospel, which would oblige thee to flee to the mountains, where thy soul would be famished for want of this water? Christ can be a little sanctuary, and preach to thee there Himself. "But I fear," says one, "for all that, I shall fall into some error or other for want of instruction." I say, Christ will feed thee, lead thee, and teach thee. "But," say you, "what will I have there to live upon, on the top of a bare mountain!" Why? Christ can feed thee there, according to His prophetical office? "But," say ye, "what if the gospel be not totally removed, but is tainted with some mixture that will prove poison to me?" I say, Christ will "lead thee by the way that thou shouldst go," even up unto His own bosom, which is the ocean from which the whole gospel flows, where thou shalt drink pure and clear water without any mixture at all. And if thou thinkest thou canst not get Him served there, He can write His law in thy inward parts, circumcise thy heart, and cause thee to serve Him.

Secondly, As for wine, ye know it is good for comforting a weak and heavy spirit. It is also good for reviving one that falls into fainting fits. It is likewise good for fitting a man for more than ordinary pieces of work. All these properties, and more, are to be found in Christ. Then look what case thou hast to propose; there is still something in Christ to answer it. Is thy case a dead case? Then Christ revives the dead and dry bones of Zion. Art thou not only dead, but so very dead that thou art past hopes of recovery? Then Christ can say to these dry and withered bones, Live. Is thy strength quite gone? Then come to Christ, and He will be thy strength and portion for ever. Thinkest thou thyself one of the most needy creatures in the world? Then Christ is that noble plant of renown, that puts life, and holds life, in all His branches. Hast thou no strength to resist an enemy? Then say, "When I am weak, then am I strong in the Lord." Art thou oppressed and borne down with an enemy, and hast thou lost all strength to resist? Then they that wait upon the Lord shall

growth; hast thou such a ⸻
been taken upon thee thou hast never grown anything better
Then Christ is the choice builder who makes all the stones of the
house cement compactly together. Besides, He is that Sun of
righteousness who arises with healing under His wings for all
sorts of maladies and diseases, or kinds of diseases.

There are other reasons why Christ and all that believers have
in Him, are compared to water, wine, and milk. And Christ
represents Himself under these similitudes to hold out the variety
of cures that are in Him, suited to the variety of diseases in
His people.

Then, all polluted people, come away to Christ; He has cleansing
for you. All that are languishing under diseases, come away; He
has cleansing for you. Here is a cure for all your diseases;
strength for all your weaknesses; comfort under all your crosses
and trials; growth under all your backwardness. He takes away
the guilt of sin, and the filth of sin, and the punishment of it. He
makes the blind see, the deaf hear, and the lame walk and go
forward. He feeds the hungry with good things, binds up the
broken-hearted, and dandles them upon His knees, and tenderly
lays them in His bosom. We will say no more of that ocean of
fulness that is in Christ, but this, "that eye hath not seen, nor
ear heard it," nor is tongue able to express the bottomless fulness
that is to be had in Christ. Oh, that He were made use of and got
employment at our hands! How much more cheerful in this case
would many souls be than they are! There would not be so many
complaints amongst you; but we think all would be stirring up
one another to speak unto His commendation; and that would be
a sweet and comfortable life for you.

III. We come to the manner in which the party is desired to
come and accept of Christ in this market of free grace. And,

First, They are desired to come that are thirsty.

Secondly, Those that have no money. These are the only objects
of Christ's free offers. For thirsty folk, it is clear from the forecited text: "Jesus stood and cried, saying, If any man thirst, let
him come unto me and drink." And for those who have no
money: "Thou art wretched, and miserable, and poor, and blind,
and naked. I counsel thee to buy of me gold tried in the fire,
that thou mayest be rich; and white raiment, that thou mayest
be clothed." Now,

1st, For the first of these, viz., the thirsty. I shall speak to
so many sorts of them that are invited to come.

1. Some are afraid of hell, and thirst principally for heaven,

heaven's gates, if ever ye get there. Therefore close with Christ for salvation, and ye need not be afraid that ye will not get heaven; but without Him heaven ye shall never see.

2. There is a sort that thirst principally after Christ; and give them all the world, they count it but loss and dung if they get not Christ. Give them evidences of their interest in Him, it will make up all their other losses. I say, I wot well ye should come and close with Christ; for He cries unto all, who have any desire after Him to come, and He will fulfil and satisfy all their desires. "Come unto me all ye that are weary and heavy laden, and I will give you rest."

3. There is another sort that thirst after holiness; and these also are bidden come. But although this be good in itself, yet take care that ye thirst not more to be holy than to come unto Christ Himself, who must sanctify you, and make you holy by His Holy Spirit. And,

(1.) Beware of seeking holiness in order to make it a positive qualification, whereby ye may have it to say that ye have something in your hands to buy with, by which ye will spoil all the market; for the market is "without money, and without price."

(2.) I say, think ye ever to get the grace of holiness wrought within you until first ye venture your salvation on Christ, and take Him to be a righteousness unto you. Take Christ in the first place, and then seek holiness from Him. According to His own word, "Seek ye first the kingdom of God, and his righteousness, and all these things shall be added unto you." Seek first righteousness, and then holiness. Ye would think him a foolish man that would look for apples on a tree that is not yet planted. So people are foolish to think that ever Christ will make one grow in holiness as long as they dare not venture their salvation upon Him. How can ye believe He will make you holy, as long as ye cannot believe in Him, or trust your salvation unto Him. But,

(3.) In the third place, Think not that we discommend holiness, or those who are seeking after it. No, God forbid; "for without holiness, no man shall see God." Our meaning here is, that people should think nothing of their holiness. For anything that they can do is but as "an unclean thing," which needs mercy for the imperfection of it. However, they must be earnest in following after commanded duties, for fear of offending God; and the due honour of their Maker should be the reason of holy duties. And,

(4.) I say, if once ye were well interested in Christ for salvation, then He would put a principle of holiness within you that would not let you take a liberty to sin, and would make you so walk in

(5.) I say, every thought ....

as much as to say, ye will shift for yourselves without Him. I say, that is even the conflict betwixt Christ and souls: they would still have something in themselves; and Christ will have all flesh as grass, still abasing themselves as nothing, and seeing there is a daily need of Him, and a daily hazard without Him.

4. A fourth sort that have a thirst, that lets them have no rest, and yet they are so stupid that they cannot tell what it is. But oh how glad would they be to have some person's counsel, that could tell them the right way; and how ready would they be to do anything that would relieve them. I say, let such wait on Christ for counsel, and close with Him, according to that word, "He that hath no light, and walks in darkness, and sees himself to be in that case, let him stay himself upon God, and come to Christ, and he shall give him light." Seek light from Him who, I am certain, will not deceive you.

5. A fifth sort are those who have some desire after Christ, and yet spend their strength upon the world, and its vanities. I say, these may also come to Christ, and close with Him in the way of forsaking their idols. "Thou hast played the harlot with many lovers, yet return unto me, and I will have compassion upon thee, saith the Lord."

2ndly, The second sort of people invited to come to this market, are those who have no money. And,

1. Is there any man that has no money in his purse, and yet knows not where to get any, let him come to this market, and close with Christ.

2. Those who have nothing in their purses, and yet know where to get it, but dare not come to take it, I say, here is your warrant to come holden out to you, subscribed and sealed with the King's seal.

3. There are a sort of poor folk, poor indeed, while they know not that they are poor, but imagine that they are rich enough; they think that nothing is awanting to them. I say unto you, Atheists of this kind, if ye were once brought so far as to suspect yourselves, and were but afraid of beguiling yourselves, ye might make it an errand to come to Christ, and close with Him, that ye might get a better sight of yourselves, according to that third chapter of the Revelation before-cited. So that if thirsters, and those who have no money, are to be the only party at Christ's banquet this day, and the only persons who are to taste of these fat things, then anyone that sees his need, and has any desire of Christ and these things; and sees that he has nothing in himself

by some; but it will not be by those that are convinced they have no money. We know few that can boast of their duties or works at this time; we think all may be ashamed of their naughtiness. But we know of some that will say, that they are not of those who are thirsty, and therefore they should not come. Their objection will be this:—

(1.) A thirsty man is pained and troubled under his thirst; but this I am not. I have neither pain nor thirst.

(2.) We say that a thirsty man is not only troubled, but is impatient under his thirst; but this I am not; I have neither trouble nor pain for want of Christ; neither am I seeking after Him, or at pains to find Him.

(3.) A thirsty man is not only pained, and gets no rest under thirst; but even so much pained that he cannot forget it. But it is not so with me; I have no trouble for want of Christ; nor am I in pain to get Him; and besides, any thought or desire I have is soon forgotten. And how can any person in this case be said to thirst for Christ, and be among those that should close with Him this day?

1st, In answer to this:—Dare you say that Jesus Christ, in this text, excludes any person that has the least desire to be interested in Him? Here is a word for that. Boaz, who was a type of Christ, said to Ruth, " When thou art athirst, go unto the vessel and drink of that which the young men have drawn." So I say unto you, If ye have any desire after Christ, He is here offered unto you. Go, take Him, and close with Him. "And any man who will come, let him come, and drink of the water of life freely." But who dare put another qualification upon their closing with Christ, than what He has set down here in His word?

2ndly, I say, ye must consider that everyone gets not a like degree of thirst after Christ. To some the King measures with larger measure; and to some with less, according to His absolute sovereignty. How dare you be so bold as to make any qualification necessary that He has not set down Himself? Dost thou see any need of closing with Him? Seest thou any need of the pardon of sin, or any need of strength to be borne through, or any diseases thou hast to be cured? Seest thou that thou art not able to make any help to thyself? and that thou canst not remedy thy case? Seest thou any merit in Christ? Come then, and close with Him for salvation, in order to be freed from the punishment of sin, and to be cured of all your diseases, and to have strength for all your weakness. For, think ye ever to get a constant dependence on Him, adherence to Him, hunger after Him, and thirsting for

invited to it. But then ye would think that Christ is bound to ... you by your holiness, and ye would think salvation, so to speak, to be out of Christ's common. And,

Lastly, I say that the text excludes none living, whether they have any good desires or not. If they have any need of Him, let them come, be what they will. If ye be so self-witted that ye will not come, stand your hazard. If you can provide for yourselves without Him, never come near Him. If ye will not come till ye get something in your hands to put you out of His common, then ye shall not come unto Him, for that ye shall never get. And if ye remain as ignorant as stocks and stones of the knowledge of God, ye may not come unto His table; but if ye see your need of Christ, and are under the sense of sin, and behold anything in Him that will do you good, then ye may come forward to the table of the Lord, in the way of closing with Him as your Saviour, and receiving His wine and milk without money and without price.

*" Ho, every one that thirsteth, come ye to the waters, and he that hath no money ; come ye, buy and eat, yea, come, buy wine and milk without money and without price. Wherefore do ye spend your money for that which is not bread ? and your labour for that which satisfieth not ? Hearken diligently unto me, and eat ye that which is good, and let your soul delight itself in fatness."—Isaiah lv. 1, 2.*

WE spake, I. Of the proclamation making way for our coming to this gospel market in the words, " Ho, every one."

II. We spake of the intimation of the goods to be had in this market, which were " water," " wine," and " milk," which hold forth Christ and all that is in Him.

III. We spake of the party that were invited to come and close with Jesus Christ. Now we come to speak,

IV. Of the fourth particular in the method, which is to speak of our closing with Christ, which lies in these three things—(1.) Coming ; (2.) Buying ; and (3.) Eating.

All these hold forth people's closing with Christ, and their receiving and embracing of Him.

Observe, that the soul's right closing with Christ is a coming to Him, a buying and eating of Him, and an obeying of Him. Believing on Him is called coming. " Come unto me all ye that labour, and are heavy laden, and I will give you rest." " And him that cometh unto me, I will in no wise cast out." So that coming unto Him is a believing on Him, and a closing with Him for salvation. And so is buying of Christ, " I counsel thee to buy of me gold tried in the fire." And in like manner eating, "Whoso eateth my flesh, and drinketh my blood, hath eternal life. . . . For my flesh is meat indeed, and my blood is drink indeed."

The reason why a closing with Christ is compared to these things will be taken from the properties of them.

We will speak of the properties of each, and what each of them severally holds forth. And,

First, In a man's coming, ye know, there are three things.

1. He must come *from* such a place.

2. He must come *to* another place.

3. There must be some *certain way by which* he comes from the one place to another.

In like manner, in closing with Christ there must be,

---

* The second sermon on this text.

once they thought to win heaven by. They must come to the principles of their former walk and conversation. And they must come,

2. To a new King that they never had before. Their life must be a new life, wherein all things are new. So that it is a life hid with Christ in God, which is a mystery to the multitude of a dark world. They now see themselves blind fools that have need of daily teaching and direction, or else they would soon destroy themselves. They now see God to be infinitely wise in all He doth. They now see the principles of a vain world, by which they walked before, to be stark nought. They account any mercy they receive a free mercy, if it were but a drink of cold water. They see all the power of hell and wicked men as nothing in respect of the Lord. They see God in Christ to be a holy God, and one that heals all sin. They see that there is nothing in themselves that can make any help for their salvation, because of their insensibility; but they see God unchangeable in His love, though He correct them many times for their sins. They see all these things in a world as what are with us to-day, and away to-morrow; and therefore they make light of them, and are loosed from them in their affections. But they see that the counsel of the Lord stands to-day, yesterday, and for ever.

3. For the way that He brings on souls to close with Christ, I say, He may have many ways for converting them. For example, some may be brought in by some heavy rod of affliction laid upon them; some by great and horrible checks of conscience; others may get, at first, a calm view of the love of God, but God's ordinary way is by the preaching of the gospel. If any have got good by this, they have these marks following, to know or discern it by,

As first, The Spirit of God, by the authority of the word, hath circumcised their heart; and made them greedily attend on every word preached; so that as soon as ever the minister speaks a word, they will be waiting for the next word, and still as they get it they will apply it and make it their own. And,

1. The first thing that the word, accompanied with the authority of the Spirit, does to them, is to discover the man's sin and guilt to him, and upon that discovery to make him apply all the cures and threatenings of the law unto himself, as particularly as if there were no more than he, so that he is bound hand and foot, like one condemned to the gibbet. He condemns himself as liable to the wrath of God, and to all the threatenings against sin contained in the Scriptures.

whether or not they have got any benefit by the preaching of the gospel and by the free offers of Jesus Christ. I say, Was ever any of you determined greedily to take heed to the preaching of the word till it discovered to you your lost state and condition, and upon that made you apply every curse in the Bible as belonging to you in particular; so that ye were thereby bound hand and foot, not knowing of any help ye could make to yourselves, but on the contrary, obliged in everything to condemn yourselves? And after that, Was there any cautioner or surety discovered unto you? And were you made with gladness to embrace Jesus Christ in the offers of the gospel, according to Scripture promises?

Secondly, In buying, there is something that resembles a closing with Christ.

1. There must be in buying a sight of some valuable goods.

2. Ye must see that these goods are not your own.

3. Ye must see them to be such commodities as ye stand in need of, otherwise ye will not buy them at all.

4. Ye must commune with the merchant about the price of the goods, and agree with him the best way ye can, to get them out of his hand.

And, in like manner, I say, all these must be in a closing with Christ.

1. There must be an apprehension of the worth of Jesus Christ.

2. There must be also a conviction of your want of Christ, otherwise ye will never seek after Him.

3. You must also have a sense of your need of Him, otherwise ye will never receive Him. And,

4. There must be some exercise in the soul, in order to get a grip of Him. You must go about the clearest way that you can to get Him, and to get a union with Him, so that ye may have boldness to call Him, as the gospel warrants you to do, your Lord and Master.

Have you such a sense of your need of Him as makes you cry out, "What shall I do to be saved? I must have Thee; I cannot want Thee; nay, say what Thou wilt, I shall not want Thee. Bid me do what Thou wilt, I shall be content, provided I may find Thee; for it is by Thee alone that I must be saved; and what is the matter what become of me if I want salvation." Then try yourselves, whether or not there has been any transaction between you and Christ, about the matter of your closing with Him? Did ye never miss Christ? Saw you ever such a worth in Him as made you long to be in His company? Did you ever see that ye could not live without Him? And did it ever put you to your

1. There must be an appetite... [illegible]

2. There must be a judgment that the meat is good.

3. In eating there must be chewing of it in the mouth, to prepare it for the stomach.

4. In eating it must be swallowed, whereby its substance becomes incorporated with the body. So in closing with Christ there will be a sense of need, to excite in the soul an appetite or desire after Christ; or if they dare not say they have an appetite, yet there will be clear convictions in their judgments, that Christ is good for any person that dare make use of Him; and they say, that they are all blessed that dare call Him their own; and that they are all cursed that know nothing of Him. There is, too, a love in the soul, that is still acting in the way of trying to get Christ. Sometimes they see their sins, and have severe checks for them. Sometimes some beams of light calm their conscience again. They are sometimes essaying to grip at a promise; and sometimes they think that such a promise belongs not to them. At last they venture upon a way in which they may best get Him, and make Him their own; and in which they may feed upon Him, and have Him for their King and Lord, ruling, reigning, governing, and setting up laws within them, against all the powers of sin and Satan, that they are troubled with. And after they have closed with Christ, and made Him a King within them to subdue their corruptions, and regard Him as their own, both for sanctification and redemption; then they become one in an embodied communion with Him, so that they live no more, as it were, but Christ lives in them, and the life that they now live "is a life by faith upon the Son of God."

Now, the reasons why Christ useth these three words together to express one's closing with Him, are :—

1. Because He must let His people see, that there are different experiences in closing with Him. Some may get a sensible change from the power of darkness within them, and through the sense of sin occasioned by the great thunderings of the law-work upon them, may have a more piercing desire and lively appetite after communion with Him. Again, some may have got such a sight of the excellency of Christ, that they cannot think to have it said that they will want Him. No, the need of Him, and the value they see in Him, make them both supplicate and cry about Him, so that they can both name time and place when they met Him, and can relate what transactions passed betwixt Him and them ere they got Him laid hold of, so that they durst call Him their own Lord and Master.

there should be such exercise in His people that should not let them be satisfied about their closing with Him on slight grounds. And,

4. He uses all these words on purpose that folk may trace all their steps over again—both before and after their closing with Christ—and be convinced of their sin, and flee to Christ to intercede for the pardon of it.

Now for the clearing up of people's closing with Christ, let us mark out so many sorts of people as have been at this market of free grace yesterday.

First, There is one sort of natural folk that have been bold enough to come to Christ in His Supper, that, we daresay, have never yet known anything of closing with Him.

Secondly, There is another sort who dare boldly say that they have closed with Him, and are bold to tell of all the actions and motions of agreement that passed betwixt Him and them.

Thirdly, There is a sort that are halting betwixt these two, that dare neither say boldly that they have closed with Christ, nor dare they say boldly to the contrary. And,

1. For the first of these, we would say to you that are natural folk and atheists, and yet have made bold to meddle with these holy ordinances, I say unto you, acknowledge it, and mourn for your presumption in being so bold as to meddle with these holy things, and to profane this holy Sacrament; be ye assured that ye have drunk your own condemnation. But, I say, if it shall please God to make any of you sensible of that sin, we do not bid you call away your hope hereafter, as if ye had done that which could never be pardoned. Christ's market of His free offer is yet to be had for the salvation of any poor sinner who will have it. Oh, what a joyful sight would it be to see atheist ministers, atheist scholars, all the haughty and high-minded men in the land, gentlemen and commoners, only suspecting and judging themselves as a people living without God in the world and without Christ, then there would be some hopes; but as long as ye never want God, and think ye had Him, and believed in Him all your days, and never once missed your faith in Him, we say we have sufficient evidence, in that case, that ye never knew what Christ was nor what it was to believe in Him.

2. With regard to you that dare say ye have closed with Christ, and are sure of it, I say this unto you, For as sure as ye are, if ye have been so bold as to come to this ordinance without examination of your sin and guilt, and of your need of new pardon for it; and without any exercises of that kind, ye have done that which may

limiting to free grace any of your exercises. I say to you, though ye be sure, yet beware of being careless or secure. This feast, at such a time, says that God has some difficult work to put you upon—work that will try all your evidences of being in Christ; therefore dream not of ease, but prepare yourselves for trials of all sorts. And we think that though there were no more, it may even bind you to the diligent performance of duty that God has given you that feast in this place, before many other places that were longing for it, and has not left you disputing about that matter, like many a poor thing in the land.* I say, ye may bear the better with any piece of trial that it shall please God to tryste you with, and ye should stick closely to your duty, that ye may be examples to others of a stedfast adherence to Christ.

3. With regard to you who cannot tell whether ye have closed with Christ or not, we will—(1) Speak to some grounds of hope, that ye may have as to your closing with Christ; (2) speak also to some grounds of fear that may hinder your closing with Him, and are ready to kill you, when you would venture upon Christ. And,

(1.) For the ground of your hope, ye dare not deny but that ye have real conviction of sin, and of your guiltiness by sin, and that ye cannot help yourselves by anything that ye can do, although you should perish. Ye dare not deny but that ye have fled from any righteousness in yourselves. Ye dare not say but that ye see some difference betwixt our principles and the principles of the multitude, so that, for a world, ye dare not do many things that ye see them do. Ye dare not deny but that ye are fled from many of those principles ye once walked by, and now, for a thousand worlds, ye dare not do that which once ye thought it no sin to do. You dare not deny but that ye look for salvation from no other airth, but from Christ. Ye dare not deny but that ye hear the Gospel preached with another ear than ye were wont to do. You dare not deny but that ye think yourselves liable to the curses of the broken law, and apply these particularly to yourselves, and therefore ye would gladly be in hands with Christ. Ye dare not deny, though ye dare not say ye have really closed with Christ that ye would not for a thousand worlds give up your part of Him Ye dare not deny but that they are blessed folk in your esteem that have Christ and dare call Him their own, and that ye accour

---

* This sermon seems to have been preached soon after the restoration Charles II., when most of the faithful ministers were ejected.

of exercise with you; hence it is your good day when ye hear the most of these preached and cleared up. Ye dare not say (though ye get not all your idols brought down that are within you) but that at sometimes ye get such access to God that ye get liberty to curse your idols, and to hate them and to wage war against them. Ye dare not deny but that ye get some tastes and motions of light within you even such as ye would be at. Ye dare not deny that according to these motions ye apprehend some great worth to be in Christ, so that ye cannot think to want Him. Besides, if ye durst say that ye claim your interest in Christ, it would soon make up any other want; and though one should give you all the world, it would yield no contentment unto you as long as ye could not claim clearly your interest in Him. In fine, ye cannot say but that there is some exercise in your soul about finding Him, and that you essay in the appointed way to lay hold of Him.

Now, I say all these are evidences of your closing with Christ, and serve to keep the spark of life within you, and to preserve you from giving over your endeavour to close with Him, and are preludes to your further success in this matter. And,

(2.) For the grounds of that fear which hinders you from closing with Christ; (1.) Ye are afraid that you have never got such a deep sense of your sin and guiltiness as your closing with Christ requires. (2.) Ye fear that ye have never had such a lively spiritual exercise in you as the nature of closing with Christ requires. (3.) Ye cannot think that ye have closed with Him, because ye think that for all that is threatened against you, and for all that ye can do, there still remains some old predominate sin within you which ye think is still unkilled, and which you think inconsistent with the grace of faith. Now,

For answer to these doubts, consider,

1. That with respect to your sense of sin, God gives not every one a like measure of exercises for their sin that closes with Him. To some He gives more sense of sin, and to others less, according to the several employments He has to call them unto. Some He has to call to the work of the ministry, and these have need of a more deep exercise than others, for they have the charge of many souls to look to and to give account of; they have the doubts of the people to clear up to them, and they must be exercised in order to fit them for their calling.

2. Some, I say, have but small exercise about their sin on account of the company among whom their lot is cast. Were some exercised as deeply as others, the people who dwell with them would think them perfectly mad; they would never bear with

Have you been brought to loathe and abhor yourselves because of your filthiness? Have you been made to acknowledge that there is hardly a sin in all the world but what ye have been guilty of, at least that there is no sin but ye find the root of it to be in you, and that there has been nothing that kept sin in you from breaking out into the vilest of all outbreakings in the world but only the good hand of God that prevented it? And now thou art made to bless God that thou art not such a man and such a woman as many are this day. No thanks to thee that thou art not one of the vilest of outbreakers that ever lived, for such thou wouldst have been if God had given thee over to thyself as many are. Many professors were never brought this length of loathing themselves. The high heads of many, their shaking and tinkling bravery which they prance with, makes us fear that they have never known what it was to loathe themselves for sin. After that conviction of sin and loathing of thyself for it, did it work up thy heart to a high esteem of Jesus Christ; and wast thou made to yield to Him any way He pleased, provided He would be a King within thee, and subdue thy lust and corruptions? And now thou art made to esteem the holy law of God, and to account it holy, just, and good, yea, worthy to be observed; and thou now standest in awe to offend God, by breaking of His holy law.

I say, all these are evidences of a soul's closing with Christ:—

(1.) To be convinced that really by the breach of the law, you are guilty of sin, and so liable to be condemned unto the wrath of God. Then,

(2.) Fleeing from that unto Christ for a refuge. And,

(3.) After all, making the law a rule of your life, and whole conversation.

But now ye want the knowledge of that incorporating union with Him, which we spoke of as imported in the third word, "eating," when the soul comes to Christ, which is a making of Christ your own by a union with Him. And,

1st, The first way in which God gives them this privilege, is by the Spirit of discerning, whereby they can understand all the actions and motions within them, in order to their closing with Christ; while a divine command also holds out to them their warrant of closing with Christ. And,

2ndly, Some attain to the knowledge of this union with Christ, by the clearing up to themselves what marks of grace they find in life and vigour within them. Though the soul cannot clear up all the marks of grace as what are within them, yet they may not for that deny their interest in Christ; for if thou canst only evidence thou art proved to be one who is passed from death to life. However, we wish that people were clearing to themselves all the marks of grace in them.

3rdly, A third way by which souls may attain to the knowledge of their interest in Christ, and union with Him, and dare most confidently say that Christ is their God, is by the zeal and testimony of the Spirit bearing witness in and with and upon their spirits. Now the Spirit of God hath many ways of working. It is the Spirit that both convinceth folk of sin, and maketh them mourn for it, and bears testimony to the spirits of His people, that they are the children of God. And besides, He clears His people's judgment, so that He makes them know and discern what marks of grace they have within them that speak forth their union with Christ. And then He brings a promise to their hand that is suitable to their union with Him; and He Himself opens and unfolds that promise, and makes it look pleasant to them. He bears in the promise in a lively manner upon them, and will not let it admit of any objection. The Spirit rouses the soul, and makes it stir, and flutter, and run, and embrace the promise, and welcome it home. He makes them believe the truth of it, and apply it to themselves. On which marriage the soul is wrought up to a sort of heavenly and unspeakable joy; the greatest pitch of joy a soul can attain to on this side of time.

Now, to conclude, there are but few that can attain to such noble testimonies as these; and yet everyone that comes not that length may not deny his interest in Christ. I say, if thou canst discern any motions or acts in thy soul that lead thee to comply with the command to believe in Him, and if thou canst clear up to thyself any mark of grace which the Spirit of God calls a mark of grace, by which an union with Him is evidenced. As for your saying that ye cannot think there is any union between you and Christ, so long as your predominate sin is unmortified, I leave you with recommending to your consideration the apostle Paul, who got not all sin borne down within him; yet as it was his burthen, he was an enemy to it, and waged war against it, accordingly pleaded his integrity and interest in Jesus Christ; and so may you do. If that sin be your burthen, and if ye can say that ye are mourning for it, and using means against it, and daily representing it to the King to be taken order with; in this case, though it still remains as a strong fort within you, ye may both plead your integrity and interest in Jesus Christ.

But we add no more, but leave you to the Spirit of God alone, to whom it solely belongs, to confirm and establish you in all your

*N. B.*—Whether Mr. Guthrie's preaching on the Monday after the celebration of the Sacrament of the Lord's Supper, in his own parish, was owing to the paucity of the ministers, or the custom of the times, which is more probable, is not now certainly known. However, these sermons, with the most part of those which follow, seem to have been preached betwixt the year 1660, and 1665, in which all the rest of the Presbyterian ministers, except one or two, were cast out of their parishes.

*"Who loved me and gave himself for me."*—Galatians ii. 20.

IF we were in such a spiritual frame and temper of mind we should be in, and if our lamps were shining as they ought to be, we would wonder much at this text of Scripture. How would we admire that ever the eternal Son of God, the heir of heaven, should have made such poor and wretched creatures the objects of His love, and not only that He should have loved us, but that He should have given us such a testimony of His love as to be content not only to give Himself to be our Head and Husband, but to give Himself unto death for us, and that not an easy death, or an honourable death, but a most painful and shameful death, even the death of the cross.

Now, upon the Lord's day, ye were hearing* of the lover and of his death; and now we come to speak of the giver and of his gift. The lover and the giver are all one. "Behold, I lay in Zion, for a foundation, a stone; a tried stone; a precious corner-stone; a sure foundation: he that believeth shall not make haste." Now the lover and giver here, is the Mediator of the new covenant, God and man in one person. "He in whom it pleased the Father that all fulness should dwell;" and that "the fulness of the God-head should dwell in him bodily." This is He who is the lover, and the giver.

When we came to speak of this gift, we held out that our Lord Jesus Christ gave Himself to be a man, even to be accounted a sinful man. He knew no sin, and yet was content to set Himself up as a mark for justice to shoot at on account of sin. He knew not what it was to break a covenant; no, but He was content for the elect's sake, that their sin of breach of covenant should be laid upon Him, and that He should be charged with the breach of the covenant of works.

And next we came to speak of the persons for whom Christ gave Himself. The apostle says, that it was even for me. "Who loved me, and gave himself for me." In like manner, he says, "Even Christ also loved the church, and gave himself for it." John, the beloved disciple, signifies, that He gave Himself for them that were given Him of the Father, in that noble transaction betwixt the Father and the Son, from eternity. It was even for those that He gave Himself, who are both the fewest and the

---

* This sermon seems to have been preached about, or after the year 1662, either on the Fast-day, or Saturday, after the celebration of the Sacrament of the Lord's Supper.

'utmost parts of the earth, if they could get them. There would none of them have liberty to dwell in thir lands, but they shall not get all their designs in this. It was not for many nobles that Christ gave Himself unto the death of the cross. But as for poor believers, for whom Christ gave Himself, though the men of the world may count such worthy of prison, banishment, persecution, the scaffold, &c., yet let them do so; there is no great matter, for they are even the folk that Christ gave Himself for. Let them bind them in prisons and bonds as they will, yet they are Christ's free men. Christ hath paid all their debt; so that they are neither to be bound, imprisoned, nor banished, let the world think as they please.

Now I come to the third thing, and that is, to speak the fruits and effects that rebound to sinners by Christ's giving of Himself for them. But as it is said of the things that are treasured up for them that love Him, "that eye hath not seen, nor ear heard, nor hath it entered into the heart of man to conceive of it;" so it may be said of the great privileges that redound unto the soul of man, by the Lord's giving of Himself for it. But we must not stand here, but come to point out some of these benefits and privileges that redound to the soul by the death of Christ. And,

1st, There is peace made up between God and man. Ye know, Sirs, that God and man were at variance. The distances, you know, became so great that the Lord drove Adam out of the garden, and placed an angel there with a flaming sword in his hand, which turned every way, to keep man from the tree of life. There was an utter enmity, if we may so speak, between God and man. This is the benefit flowing from the death of Christ to us, that this variance is done away, and the poor believer, for whom Christ gave Himself, hath access unto the throne of grace, to make his suits known unto God. That vail is now done away, and we have now access to come "through that vail, consecrated for us, that is to say, the vail of His flesh."

2ndly, We have not only this advantage by Christ's giving of Himself for us; but also we are hereby redeemed from the slavery and bondage of sin and Satan, and from the power of darkness. "For ye were sometimes darkness, but now are ye light in the Lord; walk as children of light!" He gave Himself for us, and hath purchased life for us, that we might be freed from this bondage. He having satisfied justice, believers are set at liberty. "If the Son therefore make you free, ye shall be free indeed."

3rdly, Ye have this privilege by Christ's giving Himself for you, or whom Christ gave Himself; for, I am confident of this, that souls that know their need will think it no small privilege to have liberty of access unto a God in Christ, to make known to Him all their wants, and to speak to Him concerning those who injure and trouble them. This is one of the benefits we have by the Lord's giving of Himself for us; for if Christ had not given Himself, as ye were hearing, we had been so far from this liberty of access to God, that on the contrary, we would have run as fast from Him as ever Adam did to hide himself amongst the thick boughs, when he heard His voice walking in the garden.

4thly, Another privilege that redounds to souls through Christ's giving Himself for them, is, Nearness to God. By this the believer in Christ is advanced to be near of kin to God. There is, indeed, such a nearness between God and these souls for whom Christ died, that they cannot be separated. There is no union in the world so near as this union between Christ and His Church; for it hath the properties of all the closest unions among the creatures. It is their standing relation that God is their Father, and they are His sons. He is the Husband, and they the spouse. He is also called their elder Brother. Nay, He is all relations to them. A child can never go more familiarly to a father than they are allowed to come unto Him, and make known their requests to Him. Never wife could go more familiarly to her husband to ask anything, than the believer in Christ is allowed to go to the Lord for anything he wants. Sit up, Sirs, and sleep not; it may be, ye will get sleeping enough, for hearing of preaching, ere it be long.* Those for whom Christ gave Himself are advanced to be very noble folk. I assure you, though the men of this world think not very much of their honour, there are none in all the world that can lay claim to such nobility as believers in Christ can do. It is said of Caleb that he had another spirit with him, and "followed the Lord fully." Whenever souls begin to be made to act faith upon Christ, and the Lord begins by the effectual call of the gospel to call them unto Himself, then a change is wrought upon them; then they become men of other spirits, even of far more noble spirits, than they were of before. When they thus become men and women of other spirits, then they follow the Lord fully. Now, Sirs, that believers are advanced unto such a state of nobility by Christ's giving Himself for them, will more easily appear, if we consider,

---

* This was in a few years sadly accomplished, when all the faithful servants of Christ were thrust out from their flocks.

everlasting strength. And,

2. This will appear that these are men of nobler spirits than any other in all the world. If ye consider their food, it is not the food of the world, or the husks that the men and women of this world eat. No, that will not serve them. Their food is no less than the food that cometh from the Lord. It is no less than His flesh and His blood. As He Himself says, "Eat, O friends, drink, yea, drink abundantly, O beloved." Ye may see from this, that believers in Christ are men and women of noble spirits, for they cannot feed on common food and the husks of the world, sin and lusts. No less can prove satisfying food unto them than the flesh and blood of the eternal Son of God.

3. It will appear that they are the most noble folk in the world, if ye consider the language that they speak. They do not speak that broad blasphemous language that is spoken up and down the country. They do not speak that cursed language of Ashdod. What then is the language that they speak? Why, it is that noble speech and blessed language of Canaan: "Five cities in the land of Egypt shall speak the language of Canaan, and swear to the Lord of Hosts." Believers are a people of a pure language. That they are a noble people, then, appears from their parentage, and their food, and their language; no food will satisfy them but the food we have spoken of; no language pleases them but that blessed language of Canaan. But having spoken unto these points already we now come to a word of use.

USE 1.—Is it so, that Jesus Christ the eternal Son of God hath not only loved an elect world, but hath given Himself for them? Well, Sirs, you that find yourselves of that number ought to be much employed in praising God. I assure you, this duty of praise is most incumbent upon you all for whom Christ hath given Himself.

USE 2.—Is it so, that Jesus Christ hath loved you, and not only so but given Himself for you? Then Christ will withhold nothing from you. For if He would have withheld anything from you, would He ever have given Himself for you, and given Himself to be poor, and a man of sorrows, to suffer weariness and travail for you, and not only in His body, but in His soul. For you He endured travail in His soul and made Himself a whole burnt-offering. I say, He gave His soul as well as His body for you. "He shall see of the travail of his soul and be satisfied." Well, then, what will He withhold from you, believers? And what stand ye in need of but He will give it you? He that with-

He asks of you? He asks your heart, saying, "My son, give me thine heart." Well, Sirs, it is a great sin and shame for you to refuse Him your hearts, seeing that He gave Himself wholly for you. He insists that ye should follow Him and cleave closely unto Him through good and bad report, through affliction and persecution, even "through fire and water, unto a wealthy place." Well, then, be ashamed if ye refuse to do these things for Christ. He refused not to be scourged for you, buffeted for you, nay, crucified for you. If ye do not give yourselves to Him, embrace and close with Him, woe will be unto you for ever! But it may be some here will enquire, "If Christ is indeed making offer of Himself unto us, and hath given Himself for some, how shall we know whether we have got Him yet or not?" We may not stay here. But we shall point these few things whereby we may know this. And,

1st, If you have got or received Christ you will know that you have done so "by your following God fully," with Caleb. There is the disposition of a godly man, it is that "he followed the Lord fully." If you be souls that have closed with Christ, ye will be still following after Him; not desiring to run before, but to follow after Christ. You will always study to have Him in view, that so ye may follow Him. You will not be fools, taking a by-way. This will not serve your turn. If you be souls that have gotten Christ, you will be labouring all you can to follow His steps. And then,

2ndly, You will know it by your labouring hard after God, as children of light. "Walk as children of light." I say, If you be souls that have gotten Christ, ye will be labouring by all means to walk as children of the light; you will have fervent affection to God and to the people of God, as it becometh the people to have.

3rdly, If you have closed with Christ, you will walk habitually as in the sight of God. In Gen. xvii. 1, where the Lord is making the covenant with Abraham, He says to him, "I am God Almighty; walk before me, and be thou perfect." You that have gotten Christ, you will be always walking as in the presence of a holy God, and will be loath to do anything displeasing to Him.

4thly, If you have gotten Christ you will be making much room for Him in your hearts. Believers in Christ know that He is a great King, and must have much room in the heart. If you have got Him, there must not be a lust or idol left in all your bosom. No, you will be providing a large upper room for Him. You will put away all other things that you may solace yourselves in Him. You will be still saying with the Church in Hosea,

great room for Christ in your hearts? nay, I fear Christ gets not the least room in them, for they are full of something else. And,

5thly, If ye have gotten Christ, ye will have a longing desire of soul after Christ. For there was never one that enjoyed anything of Christ, but would still enjoy more of Him. I will tell you what these souls that have gotten Christ are like: They are like the horse-leech, that cries still, "Give, give;" or like unto the grave that is never full. The soul in this case will never be full of Christ till it is perfected in glory, till his soul be so filled with his beloved that he can hold no more. Will one kiss of His mouth satisfy that soul? No; "But let him kiss me with the kisses of his mouth." Let me seek salvation of Him with all my heart. "But I must have more of Him," says the spouse; "He must lie all night between my breasts. I must have continued communion and intercourse with Him. I must have Him fully and wholly, and that not for a day or an hour; but I must have Him and enjoy Him fully, not only in the day, but also in the night. He must lie all night between my breasts."

Lastly, If ye have gotten Christ ye will be much employed about the work of mortification and self-denial. When Jesus comes unto a soul, He works in that soul much self-loathing and self-abhorrence. The soul that hath gotten Christ will say with the apostle, "Those things that I counted gain, I now count loss for Christ."

This leads me to another point of doctrine, which is this: That the soul that is beloved of God, and for whom Christ hath given Himself, is much engaged in the exercise of self-denial. The apostle says not, "That the Lord loved me, and gave Himself for me, on account of anything that was in me;" but, "Christ loved me, and gave Himself for me, even me, who was a persecutor; for me, who was a blasphemer; for me, who was such and such." How much, then, was this minister, Paul, engaged in the exercise of self-denial?

Again, you may observe that the soul that is loved of God, and for whom Christ hath given Himself, will be much in the exercise of mortification; or it is a duty lying on all those who are loved of God, and for whom Christ hath given Himself, to be much engaged in this work of mortification and self-denial. Ye must not think that this is only the work of ministers and men in eminent stations, to deny themselves; no, you have Jesus Christ Himself saying, "If any man will come after me, let him deny himself, and take up his cross, and follow me." But that we may

Thirdly, Regenerated and renewed self.

1. Natural self is the man consisting of the soul and body united. This a man must deny comparatively, or when it comes in competition with the glory of God and your own soul's edification.

2. There is a sinful self, which is the old man, and unrenewed heart, with the affections and lusts. This sinful self we are to deny wholly and absolutely. We must not rest till we get all crucified and nailed to the cross of Christ. And,

3. There is a regenerate and renewed self—that is, the new man. This believers are to deny as to any merit in it. Indeed, believers should be seeking after more of the new man as their treasure; and they should make use of all means whereby they may be enabled so to hold it, that Satan and lust prevail not against it. There are some folk that deny the grace of the Spirit of God in this; but that which we press upon you hath these few things in it. And,

(1.) A knowledge of themselves. The man that would deny himself, must know himself. But,

(2.) As he must know himself, so he must loathe himself. And,

(3.) He sees vanity and emptiness in self. He sees that he is altogether insufficient of himself to do anything that is really good. The person that denies himself, as he is one who knows himself, and one who loathes himself, is a person that sees nothing in himself but emptiness, and has nothing in himself to trust unto in the matter of salvation. Therefore he must be denied to himself, and must lay the weight of his salvation upon another, even upon Christ. And there is this in self-denial, that as the man sees his own emptiness, so he is still emptying himself of all the old stuff. Old things must pass away, that all things may become new. So that if ye would know what self-denial is, it is even to throw all Satan's household stuff out at the door, and have no more to do with it.

(4.) As ye must labour to cast out Satan's stuff; so ye must labour to have these things of God's providing brought in. Ye must have furniture brought from a far country; and ye must have it from home. Think not, Sirs, that these souls are denying themselves aright, that are crying down all that they have; unless they be also seeking the graces of God's Spirit to replenish their souls.

In a word, to deny yourselves is to forsake all things in yourselves, when they come in competition with the glory of God; and to be still seeking furniture from above. That it is a duty incum-

follow me." This may be a sufficient reason for it, that it is Christ's will. If ye would not be rebels against Him, set about this work. Folk think it a great matter to be a rebel to an earthly king; but believe me, it is another matter to be a rebel to God. Well, then, ye see, Sirs, that self-denial is a duty lying upon one and all of you; and ye must set about it, if ye would not be found rebels against the God of heaven, and ye know rebellion against God, as the Scripture expresses it, "is as the sin of witchcraft."

2ndly, A second reason is this, that when ye look into yourselves, and consider what ye are by nature, you see nothing in yourselves but a heap of lusts, which rebel against God.

3rdly, Consider that Christ, who was the Heir of heaven, was content to be denied to all the pleasures of heaven for you. And think ye that it is too much for you to be denied to your sinful lusts and pleasures in the world for Him, who, though He was "the brightness of his Father's glory, and the express image of his person," thought nothing to be so far denied to Himself as to come into the world, and take on Him flesh, and be born of such mean parents as had nothing to offer up for Him, in the days of His nativity, but two turtle doves; who not only was contented to be denied to worldly riches and honours, but even to His own life. Have ye not good reason, then, to be denied to yourselves; since He was content to deny Himself to purchase salvation for you? And,

Lastly, To move you to this duty of self-denial, only consider the saints of God recorded in Scripture, and you will see that this has been their choice work. There are some in this age, too, that you would think have been much engaged in this duty, by their suffering for the cause and truths of God. But will ye look to these, that were contented to endure grievous deaths for Christ; that were sawn asunder, &c. I says, Sirs, consider the worthies mentioned in Scripture, that cloud of witnesses whom we are to imitate, and ye will see that this self-denial was a lesson that they were much in learning. But before we come to the application of this doctrine, we would speak to some few things that ye should not deny.

Whatever we have of conformity to the Lord should not be denied, but in point of merit or any worth, as if it might be any compensation to Christ for what He hath done, or any satisfaction to the justice of God, for our sins. And,

Take good heed, Sirs, that ye be persons loved of, and in covenant with, God. Seriously consider what ye should not deny. And;

2ndly, Deny not your profession; for there is much required of you that are loved of God. Encourage yourselves by "And they overcame by the blood of the Lamb, and by the word of their testimony;" that is, by adhering to their profession. They overcame that red dragon, who fought against Michael, and his angels, whose design was to drown the women with the man-child fleeing into the wilderness. Now, would ye overcome that red dragon, that is coming down into our land to destroy the woman with the man-child; to drive the Church of Christ out of her temple; and to make her flee away to the wilderness, to other cities, and to foreign lands—would ye overcome this red dragon that is likely to come amongst us now, that is likely to draw down the stars of heaven, and that is killing and banishing the people of God? then adhere to your profession which you must now overcome by. And,

3rdly, Beware of denying any of the truths of God. John has this in his commission to write to the church of Philadelphia. "Hold that fast which thou hast, that no man take thy crown." See, that ye consider well what is written in the Bible, and hold that which is there. For if ye degenerate from that, the vengeance and curse of God will be upon you; as we have it: "If any man shall add unto these things, God shall add unto him the plagues that are written in this book. And if any shall take away from the words of the book of this prophecy, God shall take away his part out of the book of life." Sirs, let the word of God be written in your heart. Through His strength, stick to your profession; and let the truths of Christ be so near and dear to you, that they may be as a girdle about your loins; that ye may part with your sweet life before you part with them. And,

4thly, Ye may not deny your covenant-engagements; ye may, by no means, deny the covenant you have solemnly sworn. For David gives it as a mark of the man that shall dwell on that high and holy hill; that he is a man that will not swear, nor forswear; he will not break his oath, though it should be to his hurt. So, ye must not deny your covenant, though it should be to your hurt; though it should be to the loss of houses, lands, goods, &c.; yea, and your own life also. It is said, "They like Adam have transgressed the covenant." Many a time the Lord charges this sin upon the people of Israel by the prophets. Now we must tell you in the name of the Lord this day, that ye should beware of breaking the covenant. In the name and by the authority of the Lord Jesus, we debar and excommunicate all such from the table of the Lord, as are not resolved to adhere to these covenants that the lands are under to the most high God. And,

know that the decree was established by the law of the Medes,
and Persians. But Daniel goes to his own house and, his window
being open towards Jerusalem, prays three times a day. In like
manner, ye must not deny your Christian duty and exercises, let
the great men of the world make all the acts and laws against
them that they please. Do not think, Sirs, that we preach
rebellion against any man. We are not pressing any man to rebel
against our rulers; but we would have you know, that we are
to follow their laws no farther than their laws are according to the
true word of God. Therefore, I say, ye must not deny the going
about of your Christian duties.

6thly, Ye must beware of denying your assistance to Zion, in
the time of her affliction. "If I forget thee, O Jerusalem, let my
right hand forget her cunning. How shall we sing the Lord's
song in a strange land?" Beware of denying your help to Zion.
I pray you, if you love your means so well, that ye will bestow
nothing upon the poor afflicted people of God that are imprisoned,
and banished up and down the world; will ye help them with your
prayers? I wot well, ye may say with a certain man, "That
many prayers of the people of God will do more for Zion, than
ten thousand men armed with the sword, will do against her."*
Therefore, beware that ye deny not Zion the help of your prayers,
in the time of trouble. "If I do not remember thee, let my
tongue cleave to the roof of my mouth." O Sirs, there were many
prayers put up for Zion in former times. She was well remembered. But, I trow, she is now like a poor stepchild put to the
door, whom the stepmother forgets to take in again; or like a poor
little one at night, that hath none to take care of it. So it is with
the Church, and poor banished people of God. There are few to
take care of them. You that are believers know, that if you
would not deny your duty, ye should not deny your help to Zion.
If any of you forget Zion, it is a clear mark that ye are none of
the people of God; for if ye were, ye would love God, and ye
would love His people; and if ye loved them, ye would evidence
it at such a time as this.

7thly, Ye must not be denied to the love of God. David would
not be denied to the love of God, whatever he was denied to. Says
he, "Many say, Who will show us any good?" and that is the
world's voice. They would have the fat things of the world. But

---

* It is said that Queen Mary said she was more afraid of John Knox's
prayers than ten thousand armed men, which may be here referred to.

are the things that ye should constantly adhere to. But let us press them upon you as we will, ye will not stand to them unless God Himself press you to stand to them. Whenever the temptation comes ye will go with it, swearing contrary to the covenant ye have sworn, unless grace prevents. I am afraid many folk will not hesitate much to do this.

But we come now to speak of those things that ye should deny, or be denied unto. And,

1st, Ye must be denied to all those things that are sinful, and contrary to the word of God. Such things you are to deny absolutely and wholly. And,

2ndly, Ye must here consider that there are some things that ye must deny comparatively, or when they come in competition with the glory of God; that is, ye must either deny these things or dishonour God, so far ye are to be denied to them; and I will mention three or four of these things. And,

1. Ye should be denied to your own life, when your life comes in competition with the glory of God. I will assure you, this is not an easy thing, but it is a thing you must resolve to do. Well, then, are there no Shadrachs, Meshachs, and Abednegos, who, if matters shall come to such a pass, that either their life must go, or they must worship the idol, will readily say, "Be it known to thee, O king, though it should be so, yet we will not worship the idol that thou hast set up?" I assure you there are many idols now going to be set up in the land; and we hope that many, ere they bow to them, will be denied even to their own life, and will, with Moses, "Refuse to be called the son of Pharaoh's daughter, rather choosing to suffer affliction with the people of God." They will rather choose to go to Barbadoes, France, or Holland; they will rather choose to take banishment than to worship these idols. But,

2. Ye must be denied to the world; for it is with many, as it was with Micah, who said, "They have taken away my gods: and what have I more?" Ay; but if thou refuse thy self-denial in this respect, thou canst not be Christ's disciple.

3. Ye must be denied to the wrongs and injuries ye receive in the world. Therefore ye have an example. When the Jews were stoning that holy man, Stephen, to death, he said, "Lord, lay not his sin to their charge." And that pattern of prayer, "Lord, forgive us our debts, as we forgive our debtors." And again, 'Father, forgive them, for they know not what they do." And,

Lastly, Ye must be denied to your gifts, your judgments, your duties, and even to your graces, such as faith, love, hope, and all

servants." I assure you, in the name of the Lord, if a soul were looking on the most special duties that ever he went about, he might see as much imperfection in them as might make him say of all duties that there is nothing in them all that deserves anything, so that he would see himself obliged to fly solely to the righteousness of Jesus Christ.

Now we come to another thing in the words, and that is, The way in which this godly man knew that Christ loved him, and gave Himself for him. Why, if ye would ask Paul this question how he attained this, he would have said, "Why, it was even in the way of being much in the duty of self-examination; it was by seeing these fruits and effects that the giver had wrought upon the soul." Hence

1st, We would have you consider that seeing it is a duty lying upon one and all to be much engaged in the work of self-examination, a duty never without difficulty, and yet a duty necessary at all times, yet the Lord calls for it at some times more especially. And,

1. When a church or particular person is under affliction or trouble. At such a time especially the Lord is calling for this. Believers should be much in examining themselves as to the reasons that they are thus afflicted and troubled. This ye see in the third and fourth chapters of the Lamentations. The Church was under very sad affliction, even as we are now. She is persecuted, and her worthy teachers removed to corners. Her ordinances are gone, and there are none frequenting her solemn feasts. What does she in that case? "Let us search and try our ways and turn again unto the Lord." Would you know your duty, in the day of Joseph's affliction, in the day of the Church's trouble? Then be much in self-examination to see what is in you that hath offended the Lord, and made Him deal with you; that so He is taking His farewell of these covenanted lands, and scarcely leaving a meat or drink-offering amongst us as a token for good. Go to the duty of self-examination, and see what injuries are in you that hath been a help in this.

2. A second special time when God calls for this duty, is when folk are under desertion, and death approaches: such was David's case. He goes to this work, and saw on what terms he stood with God. Therefore after self-examination he says, "Although my house be not so with God, yet he hath made with me an everlasting covenant, well-ordered in all things, and sure."

3. A third time when God especially calls for this duty, is

at your hands. "Let a man examine himself, and so let him eat of that bread, and drink of that cup." And I assure you, Sirs, in the name of the Lord, that there is good reason why a soul should be much in this exercise, before approaching unto the table of the Lord.

(1.) Because the Lord, the Master of the feast, comes in to visit the guests, and to see how they are all arrayed and prepared. Examine, then, and if any pin in your exercise be wrong, go away to Christ and say, "Thou must set this right, that I may come before Thee, having the preparation of the sanctuary." This is a reason why souls should examine themselves well before they come to the table of the Lord, for Christ will come through and visit them.

(2.) A second reason why folk should be much in this duty of self-examination before they approach the table of the Lord is, Because it is very requisite that they come to the great day of the King's coronation. It is requisite on such a day that they come with many requests. Communion days are the days of Christ's manifesting Himself as the Great King. Communion days have been sweet days in Scotland; but alas! Christ and they are gone! Alas! Christ is gone, and communion days are gone. We have all the blame of it ourselves. Many of us have, with the Gadarenes, bidden Christ depart out of our coasts. Why, rather than Christ should not go away many of us will abjure Him, and perjure ourselves that He may not abide amongst us. We will have Him away at any rate. But, I say, it is a great reason why folk should examine themselves when they come to these deal days, that then folk should present many requests. On such an occasion folk should know their need. Is it not by self-examination that you come to the knowledge of your many wants? For He "fills the hungry with good things; but the full soul goes empty away." We dare promise you in the name of the Lord that hungry souls that dare say their errand is to get Christ, and that they have much ado for Him when they get Him—we dare promise you in His name that ye shall either get Him, or a token from Him, or at least good news from Him as to your getting Him. He never sent away a poor soul from Him that had an errand without something.

(3.) Folk should be much in this exercise before they come to a communion, because it is very requisite that folk when they approach unto the table of the Lord should be self-condemned. Now, I say, that it is in the duty of self-examination, with the Lord's blessing, that ye come to get a particular view of the things for which ye are worthy to be condemned.

business of another concernment than the generality of mankind think it to be. Many a soul has got much good at a communion; and many a soul has got that loss which they have never repaired again. And though many have got over it afterwards, yet it hath cost them many a sad day's weeping and mourning. " For this cause, many amongst you are weak and sickly; and many sleep," saith the apostle.

2ndly, We would have you here consider that it is a duty incumbent upon one and all of you who do examine yourselves, not to rest satisfied with your own examination, but to be entreating the Lord that He would examine you. Therefore David says, " O Lord, thou hast searched me, and known me." As if he would say, " I have been at the work of self-examination, and I cannot be satisfied with my own examination, till Thou searchest and triest me." Nay, serious souls cannot be satisfied with their imagined examination. And no wonder that it is so, since they have often deceived themselves and made themselves think they were something, when they were just nothing. And then,

3rdly, That soul looks upon the enjoyment of God as of greater concern than to be ventured upon its own testimony, or upon the testimony of another, or upon any other than that of God Himself, who is "faithful and cannot lie." As Job says when his friends were labouring to persuade him that he was a hypocrite :—"I will not believe you; but if God say it, I will believe it." " Oh that I knew where I might find him! I would order my cause before him, and fill my mouth with arguments."

4thly, I would have you look to what is good in yourselves, as well as to what is evil; for there are many of the people of God that look only to what is evil in themselves, and hence they are poor melancholy creatures. O believer, thou mayst look to what is good in thee as well as to what is evil. If thou seest any good in thee, bless God for it, and acknowledge Him as Paul doth. "By the grace of God," says he, " I am what I am." But, on the other hand, the wicked still look upon what they think to be good; but Satan blindfolds them, so that they never see what is evil. They look always on that which is seemingly good; they think themselves something, when they are just nothing. But thou that art a believer in Christ, it is thy duty to look both upon that which is good and upon that which is evil. You may see the spouse doing so. "I sleep," says she; she looks on what is evil in herself; but she looks also to that which is good in herself. Says she, "But my heart waketh."

your strength and supply must come from another airth than from yourselves. Ye must have the candle of God coming down from heaven to enlighten you, before you can go through all the chambers of your own heart and soul. And,

2ndly, Ye must acquaint yourselves with the law of God, for how shall ye examine yourselves unless you know the rule you should be examined by? David says, "I have hid thy word in my heart, that I offend not thee. Thy word is a lamp unto my feet, and a light unto my path."

3rdly, If ye would go rightly about this work of self-examination, ye will be labouring to fit yourselves for the task in secret. Therefore when the Lord, in His word, calls folk to set about this duty, alluding to the eastern custom of girding themselves for work, He calls them to gird up their loins. Therefore, I say, ye should labour by all means to be fitted for this work. And,

(1.) I say, ye should call in all your thoughts and summon them all in the name of the great God at such a time to wait upon the diet of self-examination. And,

(2.) Ye should choose a place convenient for the purpose, for fear of being interrupted in the midst of it, before ye bring it to any considerable length or to a close.

(3.) You should set yourselves to deal as ingenuously with yourselves as you can. For a soul can never go about the duty of self-examination aright unless it set itself against itself. And,

(4.) Ye should, in the name of the great God of heaven, command all the affections and faculties of the soul to come, and be free and ingenuous with you. Let not your treacherous lusts rest in your bosoms; send them all out to answer for themselves. Do not cover any of them with the devil's mask; but seek to see them as they are.

(5.) Go about this work as in the sight and presence of God. I say that ye should labour to know that He with whom you have to do is the great and everlasting God. Ye should go about this work as in His sight, before whom ye must be answerable; and in going about this duty ye must condemn yourself, for "he that condemneth shall not be condemned." And,

Lastly, As ye must begin with prayer, so ye should end with prayer. When ye have, through God's help, found all these lusts, then pray to Him that He would subdue and kill all these iniquities in you; nor neglect to praise God for anything good ye find in yourselves in the exercise of self-examination.

But we may not stand now, time being so far spent, to tell you the things that might be further said concerning self-examination.

heart, and seen many traitors against God and His loving-kindness in Christ, so that he sees himself to be worthy of a thousand deaths, and there is never a word in the poor man's mouth but "Guilty, guilty." And,

Secondly, The soul that hath examined itself aright will cleave stedfastly to Christ and His finished work. "Indeed," he will say, "I have contracted much guilt; I am a rebel, and Thou mayest justly send me to hell; but, Lord, here am I come unto Thee, and I acknowledge myself guilty; yet, Lord, I beg Thy pardon; I am come unto Thee for mercy, and I shall never go to another; here I lie down at Thy door; here I take witness that I shall never die at another door; I confess I am guilty, and I am worthy of death; but if I fall into the hands of anyone, let me fall into the hands of the living God." But then,

Thirdly, Although ye be passing the sentence of condemnation upon yourselves, yet ye will be waiting to hear what "God the Lord will say." Ye will say, "Indeed I am condemned, and worthy to be condemned; but I would gladly hear what the sentence of free love and free mercy will be concerning me." Ye will be saying, "I am worthy of hell, and of excommunication from God, and from the glory of His power. I have nothing to say to the contrary, yet I will wait to see what free mercy and free love will be for me; I will hear what God the Lord will speak." Are there any such souls amongst you? Sirs, Christ is going away from amongst us, because He cannot find such souls amongst us—such as are condemning themselves, and likewise waiting to hear the sentence of free mercy towards them.

Now, there is another point from these words; but I shall only name it, and leave it to yourselves to enlarge upon.

It is this, that folk may attain to the assurance of it, that Christ hath loved them and given Himself for them. Ye see the example of the apostle who could say, "He loved me, and gave himself for me."

But I shall not stay upon it now, but desire you to think upon what ye have heard. And may the Lord bless it. Amen.

*But I said unto you that ye also have seen me, and believe not.
All that the Father giveth me shall come to me; and him that
cometh to me I will in no wise cast out.—John vi. 36, 37.*

ALL these things that we preach seem to show you whether ye be
in Christ or not. Now, all this is to clear it up whether ye
believe or not. It is needful, especially at such a time as this, to
know who is the believer and who is not.

Now these words speak somewhat unto believers or unbelievers.
There was a great number of people that followed Christ in the
days of His flesh; they were still proposing questions to Him, and
running here and there after Him, and yet were strangers unto
God, and knew nothing of Him. On this account Christ tells
them that their god was their belly. They gave royal titles to
Christ, and called him " Rabbi." When they heard of heaven,
they were bent on performing works to attain it. They sought
great things from Christ. When He was speaking of the bread
of life, they said, " Lord, evermore give us this bread." And yet
they knew no more what this bread signified than a child did.
Now Christ brings the charge home to their own bosoms, saying,
' Although ye have run after Me, and have heard and seen Me
do miracles, yet ye are as far from Me as ever ye were. Ye do
not believe. But if ye were included in the covenant of redemption, ye would come : ' For all that the Father hath given unto
me, shall come to me.'" He knew His people would say, " It
does not belong to us to know whether we be thus given or not."
But at leisure, says Christ, " I hold you upon this ground : ' He
that cometh unto me, I will in no wise cast out.'"

Now in the words there is a challenge given them that followed
Him. In the text says He, " Ye also have seen me, and believe
not." The reason is, " Because ye were not given me of the
Father;" for, " All that the Father giveth me, shall come unto
me." They did not understand how this could be the reason of
their unbelief. He expresses Himself somewhat darkly, yet His
own people are satisfied ; besides, He hath sent forth His ministers to clear up such things further unto the people.

Again, here is a large promise to support His people, and to
direct their attention to the revealed word of God : " And he that
cometh unto me, I will in no wise cast out." There is a word of
election, " They that are given me ;" and then the effects of it,
' They shall come." Then there is a word to believers, a large
promise for a ground of faith : " He that cometh unto me, I will

DOCT. I.—*There are many that run here and there after the Son of God, to see what He doth, and yet have nothing of God in them.*

And no doubt there are many of this sort of folk come unto this feast to-day.

Now for proof of this doctrine we think that all will grant that many do so that know nothing of God. And,

1. One sort is of those that professedly follow Him, though they believe nothing, and know nothing of God. These are they that follow Him with the half of the law in their hand. They will pray a while; they think that they may serve God well enough, and yet ban, curse, or swear twice as long for it. They will pray half an hour in their families, and then they will drink till it be day again. These strangers to God are spoken of: "They profess that they know God, but in works they deny him, being abominable, and disobedient, and unto every good work reprobate." They will profess and say that they have been serving God ever since they were born; but they cannot do any good thing, but are reprobate to every good work.

2. A second sort that run after Christ, and yet know nothing of God, are those that come to Him with the second table of the law in their hand, as that young man in the gospel did, saying, "Master, what shall I do to be saved?" Do not commit adultery; do not steal; bear not false witness. "Oh," says he, "All these have I kept from my youth." "Then," says Christ, "I will try you with one, and the first one: 'Sell all that you have,'" says Christ. But the young man understood not what that command signified—"Thou shalt have no other God but me." He loved the world better than Christ. Take heed to yourselves. Are there any that come with the second table of the law in their hands? They defy their neighbours to say an ill word of them, to lay any fault to their charge; and yet they know not where their thoughts are when they go a-whoring after the world. To such I say, You know not the first command, and therefore go home again and touch not these holy things.

3. A third sort that know nothing of God will one while seem to run with Christ, and then will run with His enemies another while. These are known enemies to Him. When they meet with the people of God, they will speak ill of the atheist: and when they meet with the atheist, they will speak ill of the people of God. They will go as the bush goes. Some of them will come into the company of the people of God, to see what liberty th

xactly in their heads, but they take it not home into their hearts, 1 order to make use of it. They are like seed sown by the way de, which the fowls come and pick up. Satan is like these fowls. uch persons sit, and hear the preaching with their ears; but their eart is never moved with it. They keep not His commandments. low we wish that these would go home again, and not approach 1e table of the Lord.

5. A fifth sort are they that run after Christ, to see what He m do; but they run with their idols in their hands—their idols hich they would not have mortified. Their heart is on these lols. These are they of whom it is said, " The word was to them s seed sown among thorns." There are some when they begin to >eak, that cannot speak three sentences, but their kine or their >rn is in the hinder-end of them.

6. A sixth sort run, and have not any ground on which they un. Many come here to the communion, yet to this day they ould never produce any ground wherefore they run. Such never ad their heart humbled before God under the sense of guilt. 'hey will be content to hear, and yet as soon as they are out of he church, other vain thoughts get their heart. Such hear the rord with joy for a season, and are compared to the seed sown on >cky ground. As soon as the storm blows in their faces, then heir religion is delivered to the wind. Now there are many folk ere that run as the tide runs; and think they are in no esteem, ow-a-days, that profess nothing of God. Therefore they will go s the most part go; and yet they have no ground whereupon hey were ever caused to come to the church; they were never ıade to believe.

7. A seventh sort that run, and know nothing of God, are such s have a ground; but it is a false ground. They make common rovidence a ground. " I think," says one of them, " to get good f Christ;" and why? " Because He has fed and clad me all my ays." But stay, friend, He has given that to His enemies, and to ?probates. I say, He will give all that to heathens that He gave > you. If ye have not another ground, take heed to that word, Friend, how camest thou thither, wanting the wedding-garment."

8. An eighth sort come, too, and come not aright, who are ever icking about the door; but they never come in. Come to them ow, and come to them three years afterwards, you will never now them an inch farther advanced in the knowledge of God. hey never grow more clear in anything. God is not in such. or where God is, there is light. " Strive to enter in at the strait ıte." Thus there are a great many that run to and fro after

Therefore we wish that ye would try yourselves. Provided ye have made no progress in anything that we have spoken of, hold off your hand. And yet if ye will come now and submit and yield yourselves to Christ, and fall down at His feet this day, and lay claim to Him, and believe in Him, we call upon you to come forward. Now,

1st, With regard to them that seek Him, there are many that seek the kingdom of heaven, but not the righteousness thereof. "Seek ye this kingdom of heaven, and the righteousness thereof also," says Christ.

2ndly, There are many that seek the kingdom of heaven and the righteousness thereof; but they do not seek it principally and chiefly.

3rdly, There are many that seem to seek the kingdom, and the righteousness thereof principally and chiefly, but they seek it not constantly. They seemingly begin to seek it chiefly at such times as this; before, or at communions, when they hear of damnation and salvation. At such times they make a kind of stirring; but it falls away again, and they forget all when they go home.

4thly, Others would seek the kingdom of heaven, and the righteousness thereof; and that chiefly and contentedly; but they do not seek it satisfactorily. Some appear contented with their condition, but yet they never seek so much of God as to satisfy them; they do not seek to get satisfaction in the ways of God.

5thly, There are some that appear to seek the kingdom of heaven and the righteousness thereof, first, principally, contentedly, and satisfyingly; but yet they do not seek it upon a right ground.

6thly, There are some that appear to seek the kingdom of heaven and the righteousness thereof, first, chiefly, principally, contentedly, and satisfyingly, and do it on some ground—I mean, they will give you a ground for their doing so,—yet they know nothing of God savingly. They will give you a ground out of the Scripture that will satisfy you well enough; but yet there is no real change in them at all. You know nothing truly of God, if there be not any change nor growth in you. You have not grace; hold off your hand. "But," say ye, "Who will come, then, if all these must keep away?" I answer, All that the Father has given to Christ, in the covenant of redemption, shall come. In regard that atheists are never satisfied—in regard they say that, if they be elected, they will get to heaven whether they do good or not, we must now speak a word about the covenant of redemption and election from the next verse of our present reading.

Son. Now, here stands election. The Lord speaks to two pieces of clay. To the one He says, "Thou shalt be with me in glory hereafter;" and to the other He says, "Thou shalt be a spectacle of my justice for ever."

Now, He does this as the absolute Lord God Omnipotent, having His being of Himself. "I will shew mercy on whom I will shew mercy," says He. He renders to no man a reason of His ways. He acts even as if one should take two stones out of a quarry, and say to the one, "Thou shalt have a conspicuous place in my window," and should take the other and place it as a stepping-stone in the mire. If we may exercise our freedom in this manner, far more He, who is the great Creator, do so. The Lord, as He is absolute, says to one, "Thou shall be employed in an honourable piece of service to me," and to the other, "Thou shalt be a reprobate, a stepping-stone to me." Upon the foreknowledge of man's folly, the Father bargained with the Son. Now, this bargain should be seriously thought on at this time, for now is the proclamation of it made to you. It is certain the elect were given. "Whether or not," say ye, "were they given freely?" No; they were not given freely; the Son paid for them. The truth is, the Father and the Son bargained for them; but, being fallen, they are not able to answer the law. Poor man can do nothing for himself. He cannot get a penny of the debt off his head; but in everything he does he still runs more and more into debt. Now the Father bargains with the Son, and He offers so many to Him if He would pay Him for them; and, says He, "These shall set forth the riches of the glory of my grace." Says Christ, "I will do it; I am well content. Behold, I come to do thy will; in the volume of thy book it is written of me." Then says the Father, "I will bear thee through, and defray thy expenses: wrath will enter upon you." Says the Son, "I am well content. Give me a body that I may be such a one as wrath may get hold of." And when He has got one, He says, "Behold I come to do thy will, as it is written; whatsoever they owe, I am content to pay; they shall be freed from death for ever; they shall be my children." And then He and the Father bargain when He has taken on their flesh and bone, and stands in their room. Then says Christ, "Let all their guilt fall on me." It falls on Him. Then says God, "Awake, O sword, against my shepherd, and against the man that is my fellow, saith the Lord; smite the shepherd, and the sheep shall be scattered." Stir up thyself, O wrath; thou shalt get one that will bear all thy wrestling. Now, the wrath of God never got full wrestling with any till it got it

said, " Take the rest out of my body;" ——— —— — —
hair from off His face. "He gave his back to the smiters, and
his cheeks to them that plucked off the hair." And then they got
a stone, and put it upon Him when He was dead, to hold Him in
the grave. But when the time came that He should rise, He
said, "O death, I will be thy death; where is thy sting? O grave,
where is thy victory?"

Now comes the intimation of this to a lost world. It is declared
to the disciples on the Mount of Transfiguration, where the Father
says, "This is my beloved Son, in whom I am well pleased; hear
ye him." This day there are messengers sent to declare that there
are so many given to the Son. This verse shows us that all whom
He has covenanted for will believe; and this may satisfy the minds
of the people of God. We have been proving that the Son has
bought them, and they are bought.

Notwithstanding all that the Son has given for them, yet He
counts them a gift, and this testifies that Christ is well pleased
with the bargain. Yes, He is well-pleased with it, notwithstanding
all the evil treatment that we gave Him; and He sets down this
in Scripture, to let us see that He counts all His people a gift,
notwithstanding all the price He has paid for them. "Thine they
were, and thou gavest them to me." This He does, that He may
put jealousy out of the breasts of His people. Look to His carriage towards His spouse, when she refused to lend Him a lift in
His greatest need. He never says an ill word to her. This is a
token that He loved them well. When He was in His greatest
need, He says, "Shall ye be offended this night because of me."
Says He, "I know that ye will be offended, and take ill with it.
Ye will not lend me a lift. But when the deed is done, I shall
remember you." This tells us He was well-pleased with the bargain. When an ill-natured woman would not give Him a drink
of water, yet He gives her not an ill word, but says that
it was His meat and His drink to do that same ill-natured woman's
soul good. And even to this day He is sending out His messengers
to tryst His bride and spouse. He is so well pleased that He
says, "Those who convert many shall shine as the stars in the
firmament." Now look on His carriage, and ye will see His will-
ingness. He says, "If ye will but grant that I have died for you,
and honour me by believing." But His bride will not do that.
She will not believe, though He pursues her in the time of her
backsliding, and says, "I shall never leave thee nor forsake thee."
Still she will not grant that He has bought her. But yet He will
not tell all the house what is between thee and Him. And is not

2ndly, He gives the Son, that is His dearly beloved, and is content to want His company a while to send Him to you.

3rdly, There is none that comes to the Son, but those whom the Father draws.

It is clear that the Father is content with the bargain. "Ask of me," says He, "and I will give thee the heathen for thine inheritance." Come then, be content to take Him, and believe in Him. Whatever ye have been, He will regard you as a gift. "But," say ye, "how shall we know whether we be one of these that are given or not?" The text answers, "All that are given shall come." If ye come and lay hold on the refuge set before you, then ye are given. "But whether or not is my name in the decree?" say you. We say, ye must first read your name in the promise, before ye read it in the decree. Inquire, then, whether or not are ye poor, and feel yourselves to have nothing? Then, "Blessed are the poor in spirit, for theirs is the kingdom of heaven." Or are you one that is hungering for righteousness? Then, "Blessed are they that hunger for righteousness, for they shall be filled." If these be your names, then they are written in the promises. Or is your name Sin-abounding? Then, "Grace doth much more abound." Or if you be one that wants repentance, and your name is a Wanter of repentance: then He is exalted to give repentance to Israel. "But that is still my question, What if I be not elected?" The Lord says to thee, "Come down; ye are too high when you would pry into the decree of God." He will have you go upon the ground of His revealed will. Try, in the first place, if ye be coming, or have come, and so ye shall know that ye are elected. But say ye, "Alas! I am in as great doubt as I was. I see some making a fashion of coming; but what wot I what is right coming?" "He that cometh to me, I will in no wise cast out." By "coming" here is meant believing, according to the 35th verse of this chapter. "He that cometh to me shall never hunger; and he that believeth on me shall never thirst." This is a promise to them that believe. Now we will lay down some reasons.

Coming imports a removal from one thing to another. Now,

1. If we would know who they are that come rightly; let us examine from whence, and to what place, and by what way they come. We are to enquire from whence, that is, whether or not he comes to Christ; and by what way, that is, whether or not he comes by the new covenant exhibited in the gospel. Now there are many that come wrong, that seem to come for a little, but stop short of Christ.

(1.) There are some that come from themselves in part, and come

their hearts they are saying, " I thank God that ... ... ... right in my doings." That is just to take a piece of new cloth, and put it upon an old garment; or to take a piece of Christ's righteousness, and set it on your own righteousness. "Good prayers will do no harm; they will help something," say most. I take Christ's righteousness for everything. "That is wrong," say they. But, I say, Thou must take Christ for everything thou dost, whether it be right or wrong. Ye must either take none of Him, or else ye must take Him wholly.

(2.) A second sort seem to come wholly from themselves in the matters of righteousness, and to venture themselves on the goodness of God. When they are challenged, they still say, "We are great sinners, but God's mercy is greater, and that will help us to heaven." But then they do not come wholly from themselves in the matter of wickedness; they love their sins as well as ever they did. Such may not touch this feast.

(3.) A third sort seem to come from themselves in the matters of righteousness and justification; and from themselves in the matters of wickedness, in part, but not wholly. Such a one was Herod. Herod would take Christ's righteousness to save him; he would seem to flee from himself wholly in justification, but not wholly from himself in the matters of wickedness. He refuses to let go some sin that was beloved of him. "Oh," say some folk, "such a sin sticks to me by nature." I say that and that nature shall go to hell together, except ye say with delight, "If I regard iniquity in my heart, the Lord will not hear my prayer." Hold off your hands, except ye resolve wholly to quit your iniquity and to regard none of it.

(4.) A fourth sort seemingly come from themselves wholly in wickedness, but not one bit from themselves in the matter of righteousness. Such were the Jews: they fled from themselves in the matter of wickedness; but they would abide by their own righteousness. Let not such approach the Lord's Table.

(5.) A fifth sort seem to flee from themselves wholly in the matters of righteousness and justification, and also in the matters of wickedness, as far as they can, yet their foot slips by many a time, and they continue not their course. When they commit any sin, then they resolve they shall never do the like again. And yet, perhaps, on the Monday evening, they slide again into the same sin. But such know no exercise of spirit, nor grief for sin. Hold ye off your hands here.

(6.) A sixth sort are such as flee wholly from themselves in the matters of righteousness and justification, and in the matters of

yet when they see this they are not stirred up to flee to Christ to get help and relief.

2. Now there are some that come aright, and can produce their grounds. Now for satisfaction to the minds of Christians, we shall speak something of the various degrees of them.

(1.) There is a sort, or rather a degree, that come in a confident manner. And then presently the Lord lays out large allowance to them and enables them to lay hold of it. When they are convinced of their iniquity and of their inability to be saved by their own righteousness, then they flee to Christ, and He so lets out of Himself to them that they are satisfied.

(2.) A second degree is, of those that come out of themselves wholly in the matters of righteousness and in the matters of wickedness; but for their life they dare not close with the offered relief, but stand and tremble. Now there is one word unto you. "Who is amongst you that feareth the Lord, that obeyeth the voice of his servant, that walketh in darkness, and hath no light? let him trust in the name of the Lord, and stay upon his God." This man feareth the Lord, and obeyeth the voice of His servant; he has fled from himself in the matters of righteousness, and the matters of wickedness; he is sitting in darkness, and he thinks he has no light. But the man we spoke of before, that comes from himself in the matters of righteousness and of wickedness, would not grant a possibility of his help. But this man is persuaded there is a possibility of his being helped. Let such a man trust in "the name of the Lord, and stay upon his God"; a man that has fled out of himself and is saying, "What shall I do to be saved?"

(3.) A third degree, is of those that come out of themselves in the matters of righteousness and the matters of wickedness, and yet they dare not boldly lay hold of Christ, because they see the iniquities of their practices. They dare not say they regard not iniquity in their heart, and yet they are content to yield to Him. They dare not say that they are come, but they are coming unto Him. All these we have spoken of are coming; and there is strong consolation allowed them that flee to the refuge set before them, as well as to them that are fled already. These folk are fleeing to lay hold of the refuge.

(4.) A fourth degree of those that have fled from themselves in the matters of righteousness and in the matters of wickedness, are such as have come and laid hold of the hope set before them, and yet they are fallen from close walking with Christ. Therefore, He says to such, "Strengthen the things that remain." They are

to Christ, to get that strengthened that remains, when thou art put to exercise about the course of thy life, and when thou seest much iniquity in it, and art afraid to go to God. "But if any man sin, we have an Advocate with the Father, Jesus Christ, the righteous."

(5.) A fifth degree, is of those that when they have fled from themselves in the matters of righteousness, and the matters of wickedness, and have closed with Christ, grow careless and inactive. As soon as they have gotten security of their salvation, down they sit and rest themselves there. There are many of the people of God in this case now-a-days. These are fallen from their first love. But ye must set to again and get God's loving countenance. You must work, and work over again; and fight, and fight over again, till ye be made to rejoice in His love. If ye do not this, ye shall want the fruit of this feast.

(6.) A sixth degree of those that come from themselves in the matters of self-righteousness, and the matters of wickedness, and close with Christ, are such as hold not on constantly in their motion. When they are convinced of this wrong, they do not renew the acts of their faith. They think shame, as it were, to trouble God so often with their sins and with their evil heart. O fool that thou art, He that bids us forgive our brother seventy times seven times in a day allows none to forgive so often or so much as He Himself will forgive.

(7.) A seventh sort or degree of those that are wholly come out of themselves in the matters of self-righteousness, and out of themselves in respect of wickedness, are such as continue their motion. As sin prevails, they renew their actings of faith and abide in Him. All these are real and true comers.

Now a word to clear a doubt in the way. How do they come to Him? There are sundry ways of the Lord's calling folks, and drawing them to come. But we shall speak of the ordinary way that He takes to bring in His people. When all the people are going one way, and everyone is thinking with himself he is like neighbours and others, some day something comes into his mind, and he thinks there is a possibility that he is wrong. Now this is the first stoop or goal he turns. And then he begins to think, "I trow I need something." Then says God, "Come, buy of me fine gold, tried in the fire, that thou mayest be rich; and white raiment, that ye may be clothed; and eye-salve, that ye may see." Now, when all this is done, the soul is but on the way to grace. The next stoop that he comes to he says, "Verily I think I shall

Lord, and he has no comfort, he has no hope in himself, and he is crying, "What shall I do to be saved?" And if one would ask him, "What think ye of your ways?" "Verily," says he, "I think they are most abominable. I will not be proud of my poverty; but I will flee to another, to get gold, that I may be rich." For now ye must understand, that folks that see themselves poor are not blessed folk; for there are some that see their poverty even on this side of time, that are proud of it, and they will despair. But blessed is the man who is not proud of his poverty; who ends his prayer with this, "Who knows but God will have mercy;" who thanks God that he is kept out of hell so long. But still he knows not whether to give God thanks for his creation, or not. He sees not as yet whether it had not been better for him to have been a beast than a man. At the next stoop he turns, he says, "I must have it from God; I wait and long for it;" then, "Blessed are they that hunger and thirst for righteousness, for they shall be filled." He sees that he wants much; but yet he sees not that the goodness of God can supply his needs. He next comes to this stoop, "I daresay," says he, "I am lost for all that myself can do; but He knows that the desire of my soul is, that He may reign in me, and that He may deliver my feet from falling." But what have ye resolved, friend, in the meantime? I have resolved to lie at his door, and die at it, for I know that there is help at Christ's door only; and nowhere else. I am not only content to live with Him hereafter, but I am also content to have Christ for my King. So the soul advances step by step till it close with Christ.

Now, I say, this is a way of coming that is approved of God.

There are many other ways of coming. According as our wise Lord thinks fit, so He will give them so many stoops or marks to run about. Any other way of coming that ye see in the Scripture, if your way has been like it, will prepare you for coming to this feast, and ye shall not be cast out.

Now, when times of trial are coming on, ye have need to make sure work of your coming. Amen.

*"And she said, Truth, Lord; yet the dogs eat of the crumbs which fall from their master's table."*—Matthew xv. 27.

It is a business of great importance that was prosecuted by this woman, in her depending on God, and in her address to Him through many difficulties. It was a discouragement that He was silent; but when He gives her an answer it was worse than silence. "It is not," says He, "meet to give the children's bread unto the dogs." But yet she had better skill of this answer than of His silence. From this she presseth her point. She gets some footing here. Christ tells her she was a dog. "I grant, Lord; I cannot deny it; yet I am such a dog as may expect a crumb. If I may have a relation to Thee, let it be what it will; it is good enough." She is content. He calls her so, and she says, "The dogs may eat of the crumbs." She grants all He has said, and yet she gains her point well enough.

The point of doctrine is,

DOCT.—*True humiliation doth not justle with Christ Jesus, but sweetly complies with Him.*

This poor woman did not justle with Christ. But when He calls her a dog, "Well, Lord, I grant I am a dog, and come of an evil kind, and evil of myself, and there are many much worthier to be set at the table than I; yet I will wait for a crumb, and that crumb is as effectual as a great piece of bread."

In speaking to this doctrine, we shall consider,

I. False humility, and in what cases it justles with Christ.

II. What is true humility, and in what cases it sweetly complies with God.

III. Some properties of true humility.

IV. The advantages of them that have it.

I. The first thing we are to speak of is false humility. This day we shall show what way false humility works. False humility is ever in one of these two extremities. It is either, 1st, over low, that is lower than God would have it; or, 2ndly, it is higher than God would have it—higher than can be tolerated before Him.

1st, False humility goes lower than God would have it in these following respects :—

---

\* The manuscript's title bears this to have been a Communion sermon at Fenwick, being the last Sacrament he had there, and so the last action sermon he ever preached.

whether to save or damn you. That is false humility; because He has declared His mind peremptorily to the contrary. People are still to press to get into heaven, until they be actually cast into hell. They will get no thanks from God for that kind of humility.

2. False humility leaves a latitude to God (where He leaves none) to save them whether they believe or not. "We know," say they, "that people should believe; but He may save us any way. He may bring folk to heaven as well without faith as with it." Do ye imagine that God will bring people to heaven except they believe? You are in a great mistake. "He that believeth not shall not see life. Without holiness no man shall see the Lord." This is a sufficient proof.

3. False humility puts a man lower than the reach of free grace. When a man takes such a look of his guilt that he thinks himself below the free grace of God; though he will not say that he has sinned the sin against the Holy Ghost, yet he thinks God cannot pardon him. It is a sin to think so, when He has said, "All manner of sin and blasphemy shall be forgiven." Thus false humility justles out the whole device of God in the covenant of free grace.

4. False humility is more tender of the glory of God than ever He was Himself. It is a strange sort of humility when one stands up and says, "I think it were an encroachment on the holiness of God to show mercy unto me. He may condescend to show mercy to whom He will; but He cannot condescend to pardon me." That is a strange thing. What is that to you, what encroachment it be on His holiness, since He has declared that He has found a ransom? And will ye be wiser than He? He will never account that humility. It is enough to us that He has made a declaration through the world; "This is my beloved Son, in whom I am well pleased; hear ye Him." I shall satisfy myself in myself. Trouble not your heads about that. I am satisfied.

5. The fifth case wherein false humility goes lower than God allows is, that it counts it indiscretion to put little things into God's hand. Many think it indiscretion for them at such a time as this, to bid God heal their sore head that incapacitates them to hear the preaching; to help your faint heart that hinders you to profit by the word. This is the devil's humility, for the Lord counts all the hairs of your head. Some think it a piece of indiscretion to seek a peck of meal from God, and a coat to put on their back at such a time as this; though He has commanded

told God often what you are. You have frequented many communions, and yet you are not the better. Ye have come often with one and the same thing, and ye blush to come to Him again. But in this ye are humble overmuch. I would have you ashamed that you have not come again and again about one and the same thing. Never account it indiscretion to come to Him, though the men of the world should think it so, while He has bid the brother forgive the brother, even to seventy times seven in a day. Oh, how much more will the great God of heaven forgive us in one day! So this humility is lower than ever God allowed it to be. Ye are ashamed to speak of your evil case over again, you have spoken of it so often. But truly ye must go again to Him with it, or else ye must do worse. For none of your ways are hid from Him. Ye think it would offend a saint to come so often to him about one and the same thing. But God will bear infinitely more with you than any saint will do. Although these things be marvellous in our eyes, yet they are not so in His eyes. You either grant that His mercy is like Himself, or else ye quite mistake Him. Now, these are cases wherein humility goes lower than ever God allowed it. And,

2nd, The next case is, wherein humility rises higher than ever God allowed it.

1. False humility goes higher than can be tolerated, in refusing to be in God's common. This is when people are still seeking for some qualification before they dare meddle with Christ in believing. They say they would not think much to go to Him, if they could get their hearts so and so broken—that is, if they could endure a penance for their sins. But this is to justle with God, for He is upon this string, to "come without money and without price." Oh, but there are many playing upon this string: "Had I such a measure of sorrow for my transgressions"—i.e., I have no will to venture on Him absolutely. But nothing shall ye have but God's curse or displeasure, if ye take not another way. Ye think it strange when people run still to Christ when they cannot do their own turn; but you may assure yourselves that it is the only way, for if ye stick at any qualification, ye spoil the market of free grace wholly.

2. A false humility has no will to be in Christ's common absolutely. It resolves to be but very little in it at all; though persons that have this kind of humility acknowledge they must be somewhat in His common, "For," say they, "He may show mercy to any other sinner, but not to such a one as I am.

But remember what distance is betwixt you, the creature, and God; and betwixt sin and free grace. The difficulty here is, to make God stoop to man, there being such an infinite distance betwixt them. But there is no such disproportion betwixt your sin, and the sin of any others, as there is betwixt God and the creature. But has free grace stooped to pardon the sin of any? Then the hazard is past, so that your humility is proud humility, because ye will not be absolutely in His common. Ye dare venture the pardon of one sin upon Him, if it were but an ill thought or so; but ye dare not venture the pardon of such a sin that is great. That is strange ignorance. Ye think, if ye were like unto me, ye would venture upon Him; but if ye know what I am, and if I knew what ye are, we would see there is no such disproportion betwixt our sins and those of others as there is between God and the least sin that ever man committed. But know that if God stoop to pardon any man's sin, then the hazard is past, for your sin is not so far beyond the sin of any other as God is distant from the creature. But since free grace has stooped to pardon any sin, then if ye have the heart to venture the pardon of one idle word upon Him, then ye may venture upon Him the pardon of drunkenness, breach of covenant, yea, of every sin. No sin can stand in the way, because the disproportion is betwixt sin and grace, and not betwixt grace and such a particular sin. Since God has stooped in this matter, the anger is past; His becoming Immanuel, God with us, is a greater difficulty.

3. This false humility justles with God about sin after conversion. At first it was content to be in His common absolutely; yet as to sin after conversion it hath no will to be in His common, or taking of new extracts of pardon or making special addresses to Him for the same. This is proud humility. There are many that think that, when they come first to close with Christ, they must resolve to take Him on His own terms, and to be absolutely in His common; but afterwards they think they cannot come, except they have such and such a stock of grace. "Would you have me going to God," say they, "in such a frame, before I get my heart humbled." But then, poor fools, ye may go any other way ye will. Are not all your repeated actings of faith, repentance, &c., from God, absolutely from God? And therefore ye must be in His common for repentance and a broken heart, as well as for the pardon of sin. It is not a time now-a-days to be prigging with Him as ye were wont to do. Ye must be absolutely in His common, as at your first closing with Him. It is true ye ought to have better framed spirits, yet ye must be ever in His common

4. This false humility will not acknowledge crumbs to be essential bread. Because persons meet not with special communication as others do, because there is something they have never gotten, because they never knew what sensible hearing of prayer and sensible presence was, therefore they cast at all they have experienced. Truly ye are very proud; ye think nothing of heart conviction while you have a broken state; but consider that a man may have a worse thing than that. Ye think it nothing that ye apprehend Christ to be a precious jewel; ye think nothing that your desire runs that way. But indeed I think very much of it. Ye think nothing of it that ye account all His commands to be right, and that ye have a respect to small and great of them. That is a miserable humility of yours, since the Scripture has said that they "shall never be ashamed who have respect to all his commandments." These crumbs are essential bread as well as big loaves. This was a prudent woman; she could be doing with little crumbs until she got more.

5. This humility that is over high will abate unto God some promise upon condition that He will perform other promises. But that is a cursed humility that would abate one promise, in order to obtain other promises that are of a greater concernment. I dare say there are many this day that would not seek health to their bodies all their days, nor the life of their wives or children, provided He would but save their souls and keep them from the troubles of this ill time. And is this fair, think ye, to set up such limits to the free bounty and holy majesty of God as not to deal liberally with Him according to His own Word? Doth He abate anything to thee? He is of a liberal heart, and allows His people to devise liberal things at His hand. Will He be in your common, so to speak, for giving Him down the performance of one promise for the out-making of another. Nay, He allows you to seek your salvation, your health, and the health of your children, with food and raiment to you and them, and every other thing that may be for your good. The people of God think it a singular virtue that they get all submitted to Him, except their salvation. I grant it is good if the Lord call for these things at your hand. In that case ye are to submit all to Him: but when He is not expressly putting you to it, ye are not to do it, but to put Him to His promise. Has He not promised, thou shalt have have bread, and thy water shall be sure? Ye may seek it from Him, for He can well spare it. He will never thank you for not asking a temporal benefit, though it were but the cure of a sore head, or sickly body.

arrant ye think that ye should never seek these things, but He ates the manner of a churl. It is still good to bode good, and get ood at God's hand. "The liberal man deviseth liberal things, nd by liberal things he shall stand."

II. Now we come, in the second place, to speak of true humility. nd,

1st, True humility complies with God in all the charges of sin. et God charge the man with what He will, true humility takes ith all. When He calls one a dog—"It is true, Lord; we are istly called so, being come of an ill kind; and we ourselves being ir worse, and like to grow no better. We are guilty of such and ach things." Thus true humility grants all, and yet is never a it the farther from its end; and this is the thing in which ye are o comply with Him this day. If there be anything in your way hen approaching to Him at His table, and ye cannot tell whether t be a sin or not, take with it as a sin, and never stand upon it.

2ndly, True humility complies with God in all the charges He rings of corruption. God says, "Ye have an evil heart." "I wot ell," say ye, "that is true." "You are not likely to amend, for ll the pains I have taken upon you." "I think so, Lord; I come ut little speed." "Your heart is as ready for an ill turn as ever t was." "Certainly that is a truth." "I think there was never n ill turn that fell out in the hand of any of thy people, but it is ike to fall out in yours." "True, Lord." "Your heart sways ome bad way at this time." "Indeed that is as true as any of hem all." Thus true humility takes with all the charges of cor-uption that are brought against the soul.

3rdly, True humility complies with God as to the remedy both or the pardon of sin and for help against the power of sin. True humility accounts it no pride to submit to the righteousness of God. True humility complies with God as to the remedy He has provided for the guilt of sin, and as to the remedy He has provided for the dominion of it. It grants that it is a slave to many a lust; yea, a very fool; but it will grant more—it will grant that Christ is "made wisdom, righteousness, sanctification, and complete redemp-tion." My heart faints and fails it is true, indeed, "But God is the strength of my heart, and portion for ever." That is true. If God say, "There is life in my Son," true humility is as ready to say, "That is true; I shall get life." If He say, "There is no way to destroy corruption but by abiding in Christ." "Well," says humility, "I will cleave to Him as the branches abide in the vine." "There is a fountain opened to the house of David for sin, and for uncleanness." "Well," says true humility, and it

He pleaseth. It is but pride to take God at His first word. This woman was an example of true humility: she was a pattern to copy after. "Thou art a dog." "I grant," says she, "I am a filthy one." "Thou art none of mine." "I grant," says she, "I was never worthy to be called one of Thine. That is true, Lord, but we must not part so. I will abide until I reach God's design;" which was to save sinners. All His hard sayings were never to put away a poor sinner; but to quicken their desires and bring them nearer to Himself. Thus true humility always complies with God in what He says. It will be grieving that it gets no more; but yet it still takes what it can have. Take good heed: this carriage of true humility lies much in these two things:—

1. It will be taking the essentials of life and peace, viz., Christ Himself: and yet will be still complaining of the want of these communications, these precious things He useth to distribute to His people. Yet it will solace itself in effectual grace when it finds itself under the condemnation for sin, through the conviction of heart. It sees Christ the essential treasure, worth all in the world. It will take up Him thankfully, as the essentials of life, and peace, and all the other graces. The awe of God being upon the heart, they that have this humility will make conscience of their way; but still there will be much sorrow at heart that they cannot get the love of God more abundantly shed abroad therein, with sensible presence and prayer taken off their hand. Ay, but these things are not meat; they are beautiful rings and jewels, but they cannot eat them. They are good and delightsome; but a man's life cannot be holden in by them. It is Himself that fills, and is all in all to them.

2. It will be taking what is essential, and yet it will know itself to want many things. It will be ever grieving or complaining for want of other essentials. True humility will be blessing God, and yet it will be loathing itself for what the person has done. It will be very low because it cannot get heart-breaking contrition, self-loathing, and self-judging for sin. It loatheth itself because it cannot love and take thankfully of God's hand, anything of love He bestows. It would gladly have more love. Though the person's heart be not so as he would and ought, yet he will take it thankfully off God's hand that He has brought him to this, to offer up the heart to Him, and also unto His whole law. But still it breaks his heart that he cannot attain to prac-

given him till he get more. Some will get leave to stand at the King's table, and some to dip their morsel in the platter with Him; while others are set at a bye-table with a piece of dry bread, and all are fed with the same substantial food—even he that gets the crumbs as well as he that sits at the table.

5thly, True humility takes things in the naked promise, and leaves the performance of them to God's own time. Give true humility a promise, and it will rest satisfied. It gives much glory to God, and is well pleasing in His sight, that we should hang all upon the promise. It is what God has designed, that we should all hang upon His word. True humility complies with God. If He will give me a word that will save me. Let Him do with me as seemeth Him good. Give me the promise that thou wilt break the dominion of such and such a lust, or idol; then I will leave it to thee to do it when thou wilt. Though I be impatient of its rule in me, yet I will not be so peremptory as to say that I will have it done at this communion or else never look for it more. Ye must not limit Him to such and such a time. Ye must not limit the Holy One of Israel. He hath said, "That it shall be well with the righteous." And "The foot of the wicked shall slide in due time." Then wait for it; it shall be accomplished, since He hath said that He will also do it.

6thly, True humility dares not help to bring about the performance of the promise in any way, but in the way He has allowed. If the Lord commands a peremptory duty, it dares not dispute with God about the event, whatever cross or difficulty may follow thereon. It deals more with Christ for the removal of the wrath than of the stroke in the cross. It closes with Him as the only remedy; whereas false humility would shake off the cross and take some nearer way. But true humility will wait on a while, for it still expects good at God's hand. If He command me to go to such a communion, though I want a frame for it I must go there. And then I am to apprehend Himself, and exercise the faith of adherence, till I get more. Though I be not in a good frame, I am not to stay away from the communion; for where is a good frame to be had if not in His way? True humility dares not take any sinful way to bring about God's promise, neither dares it venture upon anything not commanded of God.

7thly, True humility complies with God in this, that it still makes more bold with its own things than with the matters of God. Hence, when its own interest and God's come in competition, it stands to God's and lets its own fall. For example, there is a thing the doing of which is a sin, or I shall be made to suffer.

sin. Suppose my suffering to be sin consequently; yet — —— —
called to venture upon what is manifest guilt, because my suffering
may be sin consequently. True humility will venture more upon
the body than upon the soul ; and in this it complies with God, for
God regards the soul most. Take this example for a proof : God
cut down Job's children and all his worldly substance ; yea, all he
had, that he might get a little more grace. Oh, but God will
squeeze a man strongly in his body, interests, and goods, to increase
his grace.

III. The third thing to be spoken to, is : The properties of true
humility. And,

1st, Although it is most condescending and complying, yet it is
most sagacious and wise to take up all that God says or does to
His people. It discerns that God thereby designs to save and not
destroy His people. It takes up all that God does, as what is in
order to bring them to Himself, and not to chase them away from
Him.

2ndly, True humility is wise to distinguish between spiritual
truths and those called canonical. Every word of Scripture taken
by itself is not canonical, as, "I will deliver you no more,"
whereas He delivered them many a time after that. And, "I am not
sent but to the lost sheep of the house of Israel." Can these liter-
ally be called canonical ? Then they must agree with other Scriptures, and with the analogy of faith. Every place of Scripture,
taken by itself, could not be called canonical, except it were compared with other Scriptures and the analogy of faith.

3rdly, True humility is most wise and sagacious to take up sin
as the worst thing in the world ; and then it is most charitable towards God in all His procedure, but most uncharitable to itself in
all the cases we have spoken to. True humility puts a good con-
struction on all God does or says. If it cannot extricate or falsify
itself by one particular truth, it will run to another that relates to
the sovereignty of God. It still deviseth liberally of God. What
if I cannot see a consistency between such a promise, and what He
seems to say in such or such a particular ; or how such or such a
particular work shall be brought about—well, in this case,
humility runs to some particular truth that is absolute, as, "Marvellous in our eyes ;" yet it is not so with Him. Let Him do
what pleases Him ; for it is in His power. Then true humility
has still true faith going along with it. It dares not question
whether He will condescend to all these things, even to whatever
He has said in His word. He says, "That in all the afflictions of
his people, he is afflicted." And yet all the world cannot tell how

place of dragons, and they see the wicked "flourish as a green bay-tree."

4thly, True humility is most legal, and dares not dispute any of His commands whose will is a law, a prerogative that belongs to no sovereign power on earth. True humility dares not dispute His commands; but if He charge and command in His own name that any who sees his need should believe in His Son, and that he should turn the grace of God into wantonness, he must do it. He commands the man who brings his idols this day to be slain by the death of Christ, to take his communion as a seal of the pardon of them, and a seal of all the promises that ever He hath spoken. They know it belongs to them to perform duties, and not to debate commanded duty. Then true humility will weather out many blasts, and ward off many assaults. It sees a reason why it gets not such a thing it would have at such and such a time; and why He deals this and that way, and not another way, with His people. It sees a reason for all these things. Then true humility will not be wiser than God; for it knows He sees a way to glorify Himself more in pardoning and saving the person, by believing, than by letting him die or rot in the prison of sin through unbelief. He will never have so much glory in that way; for He is more glorified by believing in Christ, than He would be if ye should burn in hell to eternity.

IV. Therefore ye see the advantages of true humility, that whoever has it, their condition is most promising for growth in grace; for He "giveth grace unto the humble." He giveth more grace to the man that will not strive with Him, but is still taking and waiting for more. If the Lord is dealing anything to His people, such a one is the most likely to get something. He is the man that gets the quickest despatches from heaven of any. For He hears the desire of the humble; yea, if it be but come to a desire, it will be answered, and that is a great advantage; and if he happen to fall or make a slip, such a man or woman has a promise to be raised, or made up again. "To this man will I look, that is of a humble or contrite heart." Then this humble frame has a great advantage in this respect, that God will let such as have it know what way to go in a dark and cloudy day sooner than any other; yea, and to keep the way when many others run wrong. Here it is, "The meek will he guide in judgment, and the meek will he teach his way." Nay, though he be otherwise a fool, he is assured (which is much worth in an evil day) that nothing will offend him.

Use.—Let me then exhort you to beware of false humility at-way for you to go or to get your case helped.  Never cast at crumbs, but remember that in true humility lies your best frame of spirit and most sure outgate.  Take with all your sins, and with all that God charges you with as to sin and corruption, and yet cleave closely to Him; and any bit that falls to your share take it, and be still weeping and seeking for more.

*"And she said, Truth, Lord; yet the dogs eat of the crumbs which fall from their master's table."*—Matthew xv. 27.

The DOCTRINE is this:—*Although there be gradual differences in many things in God's house, yet there is no essential difference amongst these things.*

This woman acknowledges that there was a feast at the table, that people might partake of, as also crumbs not essentially different from the great loaves. There are some that sit at His elbow at the table; and there are others that have a true interest in Him, and yet are but dogs in their own esteem in respect of others; and these creep in among the children and eat the crumbs that fall from the table; and yet these crumbs are essential bread as well as the great loaves are.

Now, in speaking to this subject, we shall,

I. Show what are these things or matters of God, wherein there is such a gradual difference, and wherein this doth appear.

II. Show you that, though there be such gradual differences, yet there is no essential difference.

III. Show you why the Lord hath resolved to keep such a difference amongst the receipts in the various administrations to His people, that often we think it would be much better if we had the managing of the business; and that all should be equal and of one size in this respect.

I. The first thing then, is, to show wherein this difference does most appear. And it appears,

1. In this, that there is a gradual difference among people's transgressions; and therefore there is a gradual difference amongst them in the law-work which they undergo. There are some that have such strong convictions of their sins that they can scarcely say they have any impressions of them upon their hearts. And again, there are some others that are kept many a day under the spirit of bondage. Yea, upon some they have been so heavy that they have been ready to kill themselves; and others put almost stone-blind with terror of conscience. But it is the mercy of some that they are not put upon that extremity.

2. There is a difference in the Lord's outletting of His saving grace. To some He has given but a little measure of grace, but yet so great that they still take up God to be God, and sin to be

---

* This, the second sermon on this text, was preached upon the Monday after the last Sacrament Mr. Guthrie had in Fenwick.

of quarrelling; so it is in all the graces;—some get strength to stand in a tentation, and there are some that dare not venture on sufferings as others do. And,

3. There is a gradual difference in the special manifestation of His favour, and in the shedding abroad of the light of His countenance, which ye call sensible presence, or the shedding abroad of His love upon a man's heart. There are some that have but tasted of these things, so that, even though they had them, yet they would scarcely have the confidence to affect that they have anything at all. Others have been feasted with apples and wine " well refined on the lees for many days." And yet there is no ground of quarrelling with Him where there is a gradual difference amongst His people in this respect. There are some called babes, being weak; some called young men, being strong; and some are called fathers, because of experience.

Lastly, There is a gradual difference in the promises relating to all these fore-mentioned sizes, the Lord having made one or other of the promises answerable to each person's case, size, and condition. There is a promise made to him that hungereth and thirsteth, to him that is called and to him that wills, to them that can but look to Him, to them that open their mouth, and to them that are far off. All these promises are moulded differently by Him to answer the case of each particular person.

II. The second thing we would speak unto is, to let you see that there is no essential difference amongst them. This will appear, if we consider the true nature of the things themselves that we have spoken of; for to partake of them in the meanest degree has in it no essential difference from partaking of them in the very highest degree spoken of in the Scriptures. For,

1st, As to the law-work, which makes way through people's souls for Christ, some have got but little of it; and yet they have walked afterwards, so that they durst not say but that they had the grace of God, as well as those who had more of it, for in both cases there has been a real belief of the wrath and curse of God, due to them for sin and transgression.

2ndly, There hath been a proportion of the curse of the law directly to themselves for sin; and then the party, from an apprehension of misery, flees from himself, being now past hope of any relief from himself, feeling his utter inability to help himself. Christ has thus made room for Himself to come in, and has discovered sin in such a light as has excited in them a hatred against it, even the most earnest beloved sin as the worst thing

never call it faith ; and there are others that have strong faith, and yet, I say, there is no essential difference. It is called " the like precious faith," and not the like strong faith. For is there not in the former persons the denial of self-righteousness, or anything that could help to fit them for appearing before God. This is to be found in both parties. And have not both had the faith of Christ's fulness; they believe that there is a fulness in Him to satisfy and satiate the soul. But all the matter is, how to get it? However, there is real faith in both parties. Both consent that there is a fulness in Him suitable to their case. In the weakest faith there is a desire and an endeavour to have it implanted in the heart. Herein stands the true essence of faith ; when the creature applies Christ in the promise to itself and its own case, although it knows not if it shall come speed. If so, then, what need ye make such a noise that ye have not so much faith as others have?

4thly, Then there is a gradual difference in the grace of love. There are some that durst never say that they have love to Christ; and yet are loathing themselves that they could never love Him. Again, there are others that find the passion of love so carrying them out toward Him, that they are made to disdain all other things besides Him. Oh, but there is a great difference here, and yet no effectual difference! For is there not that operating love to Him, that sets Him above all other creatures in their esteem? There is an invincible respect to Christ which sets Him beyond and above all creatures, "so that many waters cannot quench it, nor can the floods drown it."

Yea, I may say, many ill turns done you will not quench it, nor will many waters of afflictions alienate your affections from Him. If the dearest friend you have in the world had done the hundredth part of that which you did to Him, ye would never be reconciled unto him; they would never have got your hearts again. Then, is there not respect to Him that turns to jealousy, and that jealousy burns like a fire? If ye have true grounds of jealousy of His love and respect to you, is there anything in the world that can quench it? As ye could not readily fall upon that thing in the world that could satisfy you, as to the jealousy that He loves you not. Again, if there are jealousies that ye have not a regard to God's commands, upon which the Spirit of God has terminated that love, although ye have not yet overcoming assurance or dare affirm that there is effectual obedience to His commands, yet I hope by this ye may find yourselves to have the essentials of true love. Again, that it is not the least degree of patience that they have; for they have given away their souls to Christ, and have respect to His commands, and that must fix the character of the party: for patience will not do where that is awanting. If ye grant that, then ye must grant this also, that all the graces of God are there in the habit. And then the exercise of this grace of patience appears in their self-judging and acknowledging that they have justly procured these things that they have met with. It looks like patience when they judge themselves worthy of much more punishment than ever He laid upon them. It looks like true patience, as I think, when there is a cordial justifying of God in what He does to them, and a deliberate submission to Him in cold blood; and when their heart will not go with them, then they appeal to God to make it submit. And herein, I say, lies the nature of true patience. By this ye may apprehend that there is no essential difference in the work of grace amongst the hearts of His people; because the promises are equally directed to all the several degrees even to the meanest of His people. This says they agree with others essentially. Whatever promises are made to the man that receives Him with open arms are also made to him that but looks toward Christ, and cannot tell if he shall get Him; the promises are made equally sure to both. And this will make it out that there are many a time as good accounts had of the meanest of gracious recipients, and of the meanest sizes, in difficult cases in the day of suffering and testifying for Christ's interest in the world, as there are of them that are of a greater size and capacity; by which we may discern there is no essential difference. It has been often found that some who durst never claim an interest in Christ, nor had the confidence to do so, yet have been as bold for the interest of Christ, when it came to the bit, as those who were of a greater size both for gifts and graces. And many a time the man that could never think to bear an ill word from his neighbour has suffered cheerfully to be dragged to a prison and hanged for the cause of Christ without ever opening his mouth. Many a time the weakest, that ye never made any account of, have, at their death, made a better confession of Christ than the greatest professor in all the country. And the reason is, Christ has got His pennyworth, so to speak, of the man that has been a professor for years past, and was known to be such through all the country before his death. But there is a poor man, or woman, that was never known to have anything before he was taken by death, is seen glorifying God and His free ends. And that says that there is no difference essentially, although there be different manifestations and administrations. It is unity with Him, and conformity to Him that all these administrations drive on; that is the great end of the whole.

III. The third thing is, Wherefore doth the Lord keep or make these gradual differences in His way of dealing to His people? Ye would think it much better for God to give a great stock of faith, love, patience, &c., to all His people, and that it would be more comfortable to them than when they are kept at such a great distance, and with such a scanty measure of gifts and graces. It is true we think so.; but He is much wiser than we. For·

1st, He does it because He has resolved to give out divers administrations to the body whereof He Himself is the Head. He will have different members of His body, and different qualifications with which he will be served. He will have in the body eyes, hands, feet, &c. And yet they are but one complete body, and communion of saints; which could not be if they were all alike. "Ye know more than I do," says one, "and have greater understanding in the matters of God." "Well," says another, "but I love more than ye do. Ye think ye would do more for Christ than I would do, but it may be if there were ought to do for the cause of Christ I would fight better than ye would do for all that."

2ndly, By this gradual manner of His administration, the Lord keeps the ransom still in request, and the intercession of Christ in heaven still in request. For if we had gotten it in our own hand, Christ would soon have been out of request with us, and we would soon lose respect to the ransom. But now when infirmities appear from day to day it keeps the ransom still precious to the soul. Oh, but Christ is precious to the soul when it thinks upon this, "I have gotten much from Him, but I want much, and I must have more from Him."

3rdly, The Lord is pleased to continue this diversity of administrations of grace because the earth could not bear grace in its perfection. Therefore hath the Lord given it out in a small measure. For the Lord hath determined to transplant all the trees of grace into Immanuel's land, where only there is the full and uninterrupted breathing of the Holy Ghost. The creature while here cannot bear perfection. And then

4thly, The Lord is pleased to do so because He intends there shall be a clear difference betwixt earth and heaven. And oh, how sweet will heaven and Christ be, and the fulness of joy that is at His right hand to the poor creature that never could be satisfied with Him here on earth! If folk could get a satisfying

day by day; and many a sigh they heaved and many a groan for their redemption while on earth. Oh, but heaven and glory will be sweet unto them! since the hopes of it are sometimes so sweet and comfortable even now in this militant state.

USE.—Now for use let me farther obtest you that since there is such difference in the administration of these graces, you do not mistake Him, nor go away with an evil report of Him, though ye find not these things in yourselves that others have.

1st, I obtest you that ye always account these crumbs essential bread and cast not at them though ye get no more at present. As for the being and true nature of grace, never cease till it have an existence within you. Make sure of this, and then have a respect to all His commands. Acknowledge God in this, and thank Him for it, although ye cannot attain unto a greater degree of grace.

2ndly, Although I would have you covet the best things, yet I would have you be thankful for the least things ye have received. Be thankful, although ye have not attained unto such a frame of heart as you would have desired at this time. And,

3rdly, I pray all of you that ye judge not others because they are not of your own size. It is a miserable evil in these times, that a dreadful spirit of jealousy prevails one of another, of their falling in with the snares of the time; because below them in understanding in the matters of God that are now in debate. And yet when it comes to the point, these may be as particular in their confession of the truth as ye will be, and perhaps may abide better by it. Neither on the other hand are ye to think that those who can speak better in these things than ye can do are under a delusion. And,

4thly, Make this use of it, that if it is so, that gracious recipients under many degrees suffer many foils by corruptions, then what will grace suffer in them that have but a third degree but turn it over again? If he that has but a third degree of grace resist a temptation and comes honourably through, how much is your sin and shame that are soiled and snared by corruption, though you have received grace in the sixth degree? But be it known unto you that it is not the degrees of grace that hold out against corruption and enable to debate with it and to resist temptations, but the sovereignty of grace; otherwise how comes it that he that is in the lively exercise of grace is almost overcome and foiled by temptations when he that is out of frame, and grace much under with him, is not so much undone with corruption? Truly no man can give a reason for it but this, that He hath set a bound

...en usually receive in the administration of it; for many times those from whom least is expected prove most forthcoming for the glory of God. Who would have expected this of this Canaanitish woman? And oh but she proves a frugal and wise woman!

But let us then, Sirs, for farther use of this doctrine, observe,

1st, That the gradual degrees of grace and parts is not from the disagreement of natural properties; for many a time those persons that have but little promising-like, and are but like striplings, will get as well through as those who are of a greater stature; shrubs will sometimes stand, yea, even small plants in God's garden, when the most tall cedars will split, fall, or break in pieces before the wind of temptation.

2ndly, It is most consonant to the nature of grace that where least is expected most should come forth to the praise of God. Because grace runs in that channel, "Not many wise, not many noble, not many mighty are called; but God hath chosen the foolish things of this world to confound the wise; and God hath chosen the weak things of the world, to confound the things which are mighty."

3rdly, This is most congruous to Christ's prophecy: "Many that are first, shall be last; and the last shall be first." And,

4thly, This is disagreeable to the experience of the people of God. In all ages it was still so, that there was most good found at the hands where little was expected. What then are these things that make us expect little at some people's hands?

1. They are come of an evil kind and of an ill education. But is a small matter with God to make such profitable. For such as this woman. She was come of an ill kind, and of a bad education; and yet she was as wise a woman as was in all that country.

2. Where there is an unfruitful soil, and want of the means of instruction, it is a circumstance that makes little be expected at their hand. But that will not tell; for there is many an open-hearted Christian in the world that no person can tell where he got his knowledge, for in the bounds allotted him there is not one ill meal to be gotten; but they have been obliged to break over into some other soil for sustenance.

3. Little profession of the party makes us suspect them and look for little good from them. They were never much heard of. But this is nothing; for truly ye will not know them. And,

4. They have fallen into some temptation so easily, that ye ever look for more good at their hand. But what would ye have thought of Peter, that a simple girl put so shamefully out? Yea, but Peter will be hanged for the same cause afterwards for all that.

knowledge and parts will make a foul slip and disappear, then others who never knew the tenth part of these things that they knew will stand it out to the utmost. It was so when a deluge of error came through the land. There were some poor folk that kept their feet better than those who had ten times more knowledge. It will be so yet in these times of trial that approach.

(2.) There will be forthcoming in many likewise, in respect of faith and of pure gospel ordinances, where little is expected. When there is no opposition, we use to say it is easy calling in the court when there is none calling again. So it is easy professing the truth and a work of reformation as long as none are called to an account for it. But stay a little till the trial come as to the faith of the gospel ordinances, and then ye will see one who durst never profess much confidence in these things cleave fast to pure gospel ordinances, when many that now profess much will draw back and fall behind in the truth.

(3.) In point of charity there will be much forthcoming where little was expected. There is much talking of religion; but will ye evidence your religion by works of charity to the banished ministers and others of God's people who are in straits for Him. There are many who have no great profession, but they are liberal in love and kindness to the people of God. And I assure you that is no small piece of religion; true love to His friends in their straits for His sake is not one of the least parts of religion. And,

(4.) Such people as there will be little expected of in point of patient suffering for Christ may yet be as free and frank as can be; nay, go beyond others that more might have been expected of.

But then ye will say, "What makes our Lord Jesus Christ take that away, that in those of whom least was expected there should be most forthcoming for Him and His cause?" The reasons may be :—

1. That God loves to take a way of His own with all His works; as we see ordinarily that whenever we pitch upon any way we think most fit, suitable, and convenient for carrying on any matter, it is a hundred to one if ever God take that way but another way with it.

2. He does so because where there is much, people are ready to idolize that stock of grace they have and trust much to it; but where there is but little on hand, there is much or more relying on God by faith in duty.

Then for another USE of improving this. If there be much forthcoming in those from whom little is to be expected, then

pected of you; if you come short of it, the more will be the loss
d disadvantage to the cause of God and to yourselves also.
isgiving in you will be more shameful than in many others.
e that are great professors in the country side, I pray you, take
ed how ye desire the day of trial; for people will say they will
this, and that, and the other thing, and what not, when they
e not put to it; but away with such foolish romances. Ye will
id a trial in suffering for truth another thing than ye think.
 me think they will do and suffer because of what they have
ceived, and because of their former engagements and great
irts, which thought is but a trusting to their own strength.
ut truly if ye look for standing in that way, it is a hundred to
ie if ye fall not, and that shamefully. Ye must never reckon
on your stedfastness in one trial, or your resolutions and
igagements, or upon this, that other folk think much of you;
it think ye still the less of yourselves. For ordinary in the day
' trial God uses to stain the glory of all flesh. If others think
uch of you think little of yourselves, otherwise ye shall perhaps
ll into some scrape, ere all be done, that shall make all the
untry think little of you. Then, if ye would keep your feet in
day of trial, keep up a constant trade with heaven for fresh
ipplies from God, for that will do it. Be content to be amongst
ie meanest in respect; for we always hope that the Master shall
ive most praise from many people's faithfulness and honesty,
iat have least help or hope in themselves. Then pray for them
' whom we have little expectation, for their standing may be
uch for the Master's praise. Do not think it strange that you
iar that some people that ye would have expected little from
ive given such testimony and not joined with the times,
itwithstanding their little or no profession; for it has pleased
ie "Father to reveal these things to babes and sucklings," and
de them from the wise and prudent, even so it hath pleased
im to do.
And moreover, I would gladly engage some of you who are
intlemen, great folk and professors, to bear testimony for the
uth. I would have you not to think it foolishness to be engaged
the matters of God. There are many of you gentlemen, and
untry men, that think we look for little at your hand as to your
iiding by the truth and being valiant for it. Well, then, will ye
guile us? Indeed we think much of you, and we hope there is
good turn in some of your hands yet for the cause of God. I
ould not have you over busy to comply with the folk in the
ast. Since we look for your hand if there be ought ado, then
ill ye be commending the controverted truths to your families

for you, and pray for you, and say "I have resolved to quit my estate as well as others, before I sin. I shall bear witness that I shall be as denied to it as others that may be promising more, and it may be I shall go to prison as well as others, before I deny the work of God and break the Covenants."

And then we would have you beware of giving way to despondency. But leave room to the promises when the matter is come to this push, for God will bear your charges and give out the expenses.

Lastly, We shall speak a word to you who are great professors. Oh, but ye have need to study to be much to the Master's praise both in word and deed; to be particular in faith, in doctrine, in temperance, and holy walking with God, and generally to make it your study how to be for His glory, for He has taken much pains with you and for your encouragement. The Master's glory is much concerned in your being faithful, and His glory and your standing are twisted together, and that connection is of much value. And further, your standing in these evil times is an accomplishment of the great Gospel promise in the word for your comfort. And further, ye have the very flower of all the people of God's prayers in the three nations with you for your consolation. There is many a beautiful cloud of prayers going up in the three kingdoms in behalf of them that keep honest as they are engaged in the truths of God. And truly if we were not more beholden to others' prayers than our own, it would not be well with us; for though ye be not still at prayer yourselves, yet there is some still at prayer for you. Then behave yourselves honestly. God has given a good account of those gone off the stage for the truth already. God has given us a good break in them that have suffered and are banished. These have given the cross of Christ a noble testimony,* a circumstance that speaks much good to us who are to follow after. Then, Sirs, take up your ground and state yourselves. Has God given you Christ? "How much more will He give you with him every good and perfect gift?"

Now have ye gotten Christ? Truly, then, all other things will be but little to that; any other thing is but like a pin in your clothes. This will be your victory, even your faith. Faith is accounted the more precious that it endureth temptations—faith that dares cleave to Him in all opposition gets still the quickest

---

* By these gone off the stage here, no doubt, is meant Christ's cause in Mr. James Guthrie, the Marquis of Argyle, and Lord Warriston; and by the banished, those seven eminent ministers who were in the years 1662 and 1663 banished to Holland.

ry hour."

*"Then answered Jesus, and said unto her, O woman, great is thy faith: be it unto thee as thou wilt."*—Matthew xv. 28.*

THESE words, as we have heard before, contain the result and conclusion of the business that passed between Christ and this woman. He commends her faith and grants her her errand to the full, and gives her the word she was waiting for. Ye have heard from these words that the more and greater difficulties that faith honestly wrestles through, the more it is esteemed by the Lord, and well pleasing in His sight. Her faith is called great upon this account, that she wrestled honestly through great difficulties. Ye have heard also that sometimes the Lord bears testimony to grace in His people. Here ye see He gives testimony to this woman's faith: "O woman, great is thy faith."

I proposed lastly, this third DOCTRINE, *That of all the graces in God's people, faith still proves most victorious, and attains its errand best.*

Faith is still victorious with regard to what it is depending upon God for. It is upon this account that He calls this woman's faith a great faith, because she had so absolutely hung upon Him till she obtained it.

In prosecuting this doctrine, we told you what this faith was: that it was a resolute depending upon God for necessary mercies in His own way, and that this faith was joined with prayer, with diligence, with patience, and with courage, in and under occurring difficulties, and with hope in God in and beyond all these; and what it was this faith overcame; and how it overcomes these things by setting prayer on foot, by engaging the glory of God in the business; by setting former experiences of His thankfulness and kindness against new threatenings; by engaging Christ in the business; by aiming at glorious ends, and so making the mercy that they got redound to the glory of God, and by turning all disadvantages into encouragement. It cannot be other than victorious when it keeps this way and method. The last thing that we left off at in the doctrine was this, the time when it attains and carries its errand, or is victorious. How it is victorious we have already spoken unto; and that it prevails with omnipotency and how it prevails has been shown you. But though that be true that it overcomes and carries its errand, yet ye must understand that it

---

* There are other two sermons (in manuscript) preached before on this text, and also some following which could not now be published.

orks faith in a soul, it is a good instrument for doing such things as you have heard, and which ye may hear of afterwards. But I say, it doth not carry its errand until the time of the decree. But now ye may be all ready to think with yourselves, "Since faith carries not its errand till the time of the decree, truly we will never wait on it. It may be a long term day." For preventing this, I would put you in mind of these two or three things :—

1. Everything is beautiful in its season, as saith the Scripture. And I hope ye will not think that the Lord moves unjustly and imprudently in His purposes. He who had all time in His own hand could not fail to take that time which would be the most proper time. Never think that the time of the decree is an unfit time, since God has made everything beautiful in its season. He has pitched upon the right season of everything, and of the out-letting of every mercy. Ye cannot think otherwise of God, unless we think dishonestly of Him. He who was before all time, and had all times in His eye and option, saw what would be the most fit time and season for the outletting of every mercy. Our time and the timing of our mercies are in His hand, where they are better than in the hands of any other. There would have been a sad work amongst the saints ere now, if their time and the timing of their mercies had been in their own hand. I hope ye will give credit to God in the works He has done, that they are all beautiful, according to that word, "God will help her, and that right early." This is still a good word at all times, and in all places, "The Lord will help, and that right early." If He let out His mercies right early, then they will still come in season to His people. The mercy will be with you in as good a time as if ye had been watching all night for it. It will be with you ere ye get on your clothes, so to speak. It will be at your hand ere ever ye be ready. So I say, faith carries still its errand in the time of God's decree. All things are "beautiful in their season." "The Lord will be an helper, and that right early." And,

2. When things appear to be for the glory of God, then faith carries its errand. Faith does not carry its errand at every time. No, nor till the thing appears to the praise of God, as Peter expresses it, "That the trial of your faith being much more precious than of gold that perisheth, though it be tried with fire, might be found unto praise, and honour, and glory at the appearing of Jesus Christ." This woman got an answer, but when was it? Not until she had buckled a while with the trial: not until she came into this with it, "Be what I will, I shall have that mercy." Then

"Send her away," said the disciples, "she will annoy us all, if she get not somewhat." Then was the time for faith to carry its errand; for then it appeared to the praise of Him who gave it. Ye have been wrestling for the Church these two or three years past, and ye cannot get a good answer; but ye must wrestle better yet ere a delivery come. If once it were for the praise of God then it will come. Ye must once come to this with it, that if God should drag us through hell, so to speak, we will be at Him; whatever difficulties occur in the way we will be at Him, then readily it will be for His praise to answer your petition. There is a

3. Third thing that speaks forth the time, and that is, patience. "Let patience have its perfect work," and then readily faith will carry its errand. Indeed, I must confess, some folk have been right well-exercised this good while, still waiting some chance of it. But patience must come to a perfect work. Folk must resolve to be made what He pleases; and then they will be made something of by God. But truly there are not many of us at this with it. Yet truly the most part of us are but, as it were, binding and lowing with it, yet in somethings; but this must be laid by before faith have its perfect work. Faith's work is to be content to be made anything He will. This woman was content to be made anything He would, provided she could gain her errand. When the person is content He should do anything He will with it; that He should try better try; that He should afflict more afflict—then the person has resolved if all should go to all, still to hang upon Him for the mercy, and is ready to receive every impression but the wrong impression, that he will by no means receive. Faith is content to receive any impression He will; but a refusal of the mercy it will not admit of. There are many things the Lord has upon the wheels yet to be done; and if all these things were done and ready, then faith would carry its errand for the Church of God in her delivery. Ye must not think it long till the number of your brethren have suffered, and several things be done that God hath to do, then faith will carry its business. Ye must let God alone. I mean ye must not peremptorily limit Him to any time for working what He has to do. Ye know not how much He has to do yet ere He deliver the Church. Ye see not all the irons He hath in the fire, so to speak; for truly if ye saw them all ye would not speak as sometimes ye do. Though He be coming for the deliverance of the Church, yet there are many things withstanding Him in the way. The prince of Persia must stand in the way till Michael come. The work of God may be retarded for many

tand the work of the kingdom of God for many days. Would ye
ake patience till these days be over, the prince of the kingdom of
Persia must withstand the work of God till Michael your prince
ome. But ye shall be no losers by this, for he will come at the
et time; and ye shall see good reason to bless God that He chose
out the time for the Church's deliverance.

Now for USE of this doctrine: It is no wonder that many folk
ie in the mire with regard to many things that they have depend-
ng before God. Why, they never set faith on foot to help them.
Faith is a victorious grace. "Be it unto thee even as thou wilt;"
" All things are possible to him that believeth ;" "And they could
not enter in because of their unbelief." I say, it is no marvel
many folk's business lies low, because they do not set faith on foot
o carry its errand. Would ye have anything that ye have to do
with God to come good speed with you, then set faith on foot and
make it move in the business. Now, I know as soon as I speak
his, it will raise this objection in many (for I know it is the
thought of many of your hearts) that the thing that ye have
lepending on God is what ye cannot get faith acted about. Ye
annot make faith move, nor yourselves believe it. I am pressing
ou to set faith on work for doing anything that ye have to do.
Now ye object to this that ye cannot get faith acted anent anything
e have ado. Now that I may speak to this, there are several
things that I shall tell you of that hinder faith from going out,
rom acting and moving as to such and such a business. Now ye
must either remove these, or else ye will never believe anything
hat ye have depending upon God, so as faith may move, act, and
arry its errand in the business. And,

1st, The first thing that ye would remove out of the way is,
our delight in known iniquity; for wherever there is any regard
o any known iniquity, faith cannot move. "If I regard iniquity
n my heart, the Lord will not hear me." Whenever a man is
condemned in his own heart for cleaving to any known iniquity,
aith, so to speak, will never go out at that man's door for the
ringing of anything from God to him, for it never expects to see
im more. Remove this then ere you send out faith. Ye that
re still saying that ye cannot act faith as to such and such a

* If we apply this to the Revolution and what followed upon it, it may be
onsidered as respecting the coming of the Prince of Orange from Holland,
nd the accession of the Prince of Hanover, one of the principalities of
ermany, to the British throne; or perhaps it may apply to the present
ommotions in Britain, France, Germany, and America—commotions which
ay perhaps bring about much good to the Church of Christ.

2ndly, Ye should understand this, that unless a necessity be both pressed and received, ye do not act faith as to any business. Faith moves best on a clear ground. Faith is such a grace as cannot move but upon serious and necessary things. That which this woman has to do here is serious and necessary business. Faith always moves best when it is distressed with wants. The children of Israel, ye know, were under distresses and want, and their faith moves (Judges x.). So if ye would have faith move anent anything ye have dependent on God, ye must remove indifference anent that matter out of the way, for faith moves not but in serious and necessary business.

3rdly, Faith moves only when folk are diligent in duty. It is but a fancy to think that faith will move without diligence in duty and uprightness in your walk. Faith has still hopes of meeting God, when the person is diligent in duty; but so to speak, faith has neither hand nor heart to move in matters that it has dependent upon God, unless there be diligence in duty, for "the hand of the diligent maketh rich." Faith is made to move, and look for good, when the soul is diligent in duty, working righteousness, and walking uprightly before God. And,

4thly, Faith has no skill in moving, when it cannot say that the thing that it would have shall someway redound to the praise of God. Says James, "Ye ask, and receive not, because ye ask amiss, that ye may consume it upon your lusts." Faith moves always best, and can believe most, when it can say, "If God give such a thing, it shall redound to His praise." This is an argument the Psalmist makes use of for the Lord to arise and deliver His Church. "The kings of Tarshish and of the isles shall bring presents; the kings of Sheba and Seba shall offer gifts." And that a generation unknown should serve Him. In this case, the thing redounds to the Lord's glory. "Spare me, and I shall shew forth thy loving-kindness to this generation." Therefore, it were still best to send out faith with a vow in its right hand; for faith never moves well but when it has a vow in its right hand. When such a particular receipt of mercy shall be in such a particular way for God's glory, then faith moves well. And I tell you ye should put some argument in faith's hand, for it is not good enough for us to hold at generals. No, truly, we are not well known by generals; we must come to particulars with it, or else faith will never move when God gives you such a mercy as ye are interceding for. Then say that such a particular mercy shall redound to the Lord's praise. Lay on the vow, and say that it shall be for the glory of God. Promise that at such a time ye will do such for the glory of God. Once come to particulars with it this way, and then faith will move. Think ye that Scripture useless, "Thy vows are upon me, O God"? And ye know that when Jacob went to Padanaram, and left his own country, says he, "If thou wilt be with me, and keep me in the way that I go, then shall the Lord be my God, and of all that thou shalt give me, I shall surely give the tenth unto thee." So, I say, faith moves always best when it has a particular aim and a vow in its right hand, and that particular aim must be to the glory of God. Ye remember that which I spake to you not long ago: "If I deliver you," says Jephthah, "then shall I be your head." If Christ shall deliver us, He shall be our head; He shall be the Head of the Church Himself; there shall not be a rival that shall get a part of it. It is true He shall be our head whether He delivers us or not. But I would have you to come to some particulars with it, that if He shall help you through this evil time, ye shall do such a particular thing that shall be for His glory. The last thing I would say is this, that faith never loves but to go upon known grounds. The thing I mean is this, faith would still know what to say; it would still have its mouth filled with arguments when it has anything to do, and then it will move and go boldly on. I am persuaded the great reason why our faith in this generation never gets out fairly for anything we have to do with the Lord is, that we are never at the pains to fill its mouth with arguments. I grant that true faith is the evidence of things not seen, yet it is as true it desires not to go upon unknown grounds; for ye must understand faith is no fancy; it doth not move without some grounds, therefore ye should fill its mouth with arguments that ye may move the more boldly. For all that we are intending is this, to see if we can get faith to carry its errand for matters that it has depending upon God (as ye heard the last day), so that it may prove victorious at last.

And there are only these three cases I would condescend upon; and I believe a great part of you would gladly have faith moving as to all the three, in bringing you a good answer from the Lord concerning them all. I believe ye will think them cases of importance and conscience. And faith is to be waited on and employed in all these three cases. But unless ye fill faith's mouth with arguments, it will not move nor bring you a good answer from the Lord as to any of these; therefore we shall endeavour to let you see what arguments will be fit to put in its mouth, so that it may the more confidently move and bring you a good answer anent them all. The

we shall tell you what arguments you should put in faith's hands, that faith may bring you a good answer as to your souls.

2. Another case is as to your through-bearing in this evil time. I warrant there are some of you would gladly know if they shall be carried honestly through in this evil time. Ye cannot make faith take footing well in this business. Well, we shall tell you what arguments ye should put in faith's mouth that it may take footing, and move on these arguments if it move at all. The

3. Case is anent the Church of God. I am sure some of you would gladly have a good answer from the Lord for His poor Church; therefore we shall tell you what arguments ye should put in faith's hand for this, that we may expect some good thing from the Lord's hand to the poor Church, notwithstanding all these sad things that our eyes do behold. I think these three comprehend the substance of the great work that now we have to do concerning ecclesiastical affairs and matters of religion. Now, these three are the most important cases under the sun. Well, then, if ye would have faith moving and bringing you a good answer from the Lord, as we have said, there is a necessity of filling its mouth with arguments. Let us then see what arguments are proper, that we may the more confidently believe and look for good from God concerning all these three things.

I now return to the first of these—the case of your souls. Ye would gladly have that perfected which concerns your souls. It may be ye have been labouring to set faith on foot; but it would never move that way yet. Well, we would now press you to take trial of faith further. There are very many arguments that we would have you to put in faith's hand as to this. If faith move not with these arguments, truly, if we may so speak, faith is far in the wrong to you. And on the other hand, if ye have bidden faith move and have not put these arguments in faith's hand, truly ye are far in the wrong to faith. And if ye cannot appropriate these to yourselves when ye hear me pronounce them, I have the worse notion of you, and so may continue to have this twelvemonth for anything I know. Now the

1st Argument I would have you to put in faith's hand is this, "I have even been one of those to whom the Lord hath discovered his lost condition." Have ye this to say, "I wot well, I saw myself lost upon a thousand accounts? I have seen myself verily guilty and liable to wrath." I am sure that must be a good argument for you, since "the Son of man came to seek and to save that which was lost." It is likely ye may think little of this argument, but truly I'll tell you, you will put many arguments in faith's

lition, and mourn for it and the causes of it as one mourneth for his first born." In a word, this has come nearer your heart than anything ye ever met with in the world. Have ye this to say, that you have been made to mourn over your lost condition, as one for an only son; and that it has gone nearer your heart than anything that ever you met with in the world? This indeed is a great argument when ye dare take the Lord to witness, that now and then, though seldom, this business has gone nearer your heart than anything ye ever met with. Indeed if ye can say so, ye look like one of those to whom that promise of washing is made by that fountain "that is opened to the house of David, and to the inhabitants of Jerusalem, for sin and for uncleanness." It was opened for them that mourn for this, as "one mourns for his first born, or an only child."

3rdly, Have ye any more to say? Yes, I have this to say, "I have lost all hope of relief in myself." Well ye are then like those folk that have no confidence in the flesh, whose rejoicing is in Jesus Christ. I would not wish for a better argument than that; take heed to these arguments, and remember them, and gather, and keep them well together:—you are one of them to whom God has discovered their lost condition; and when ye were made to see it, it went so near your heart, that ye never found anything go so near it before. Ye saw there was nothing in yourself. Ye might well make the plea worse, but ye could never make it better, and therefore you cast off all hope in yourself. Very well said indeed, these three agree very well together. But,

4thly, A fourth argument, Have ye any more to say? Can ye say this further? that your eyes have been thus far opened, though ye wot not well how, that you now see where your help lies, so that ye are not afraid to say this, "I wot well, my help is in Christ if I could attain it; I would seek no other thing from God, as miserable as I am, but what that ransom Christ paid did procure. I will have no more, and I will have no less. I will tell you more, if I had a thousand souls in one, I would venture them all that way upon that purchase. I would not venture one of them upon another way." A very good argument, truly! I cannot see ye can be well refused. Ye see ye want help in yourself, and ye see where your help lies if you could have it; and ye will not go another way for it. Ye grant God has made you see where your help lies both suitably and satisfyingly for your state and condition. Ye say ye dare venture upon it for all need, both for the present and for the time to come. Indeed it is very likely ye hear of something promising-like concerning your soul. For "he that

5thly, A fifth argument, What more can ye say? Can ye say any more to faith ere it go? Yes, I can say this farther: That he is happy that gets this though he were burnt at a stake; I have such an esteem of it, that I think if God would uphold me I would be content to be burnt at once myself for it. Truly that is very well said. Indeed Christ is the pearl of great price, and that treasure hid in the field to you. And I think you are the merchant that would sell all he hath to make that your own. I will assure you that is a valid argument if ye hold on. Such faith could not be long till it brought you a good answer, believe it, if ye follow on in that way. And,

6thly, But have ye any more for faith to say before a throne of grace? Yes, I have this to say, that in such a way as I could get it done, I closed with Christ with complacency and satisfaction, my heart bended towards Him, and acquiesced in Him, and rested on Him, so that I thought I was content to close with Him as my Prophet, Priest, and King. I was content as I thought to have Him with all the crosses that follow Him. Truly that says more yet, and is a very strong argument. Indeed, there is much strength in it. I warrant you, if ye hold on, such faith would betake itself to its feet very soon. I dare not well say that I have the thing you call closing with Christ; but I wot well in the way I thought I was to close with Christ I closed with Him. I wot well I thought my heart was content to take Him in all His offices, as well as King to rule me, as Prophet to teach me, and Priest to intercede for me.

7thly, Have ye any more to say, or add to these? Yes, I have this to say more, that of all these my heart condemns me not for the contrary. I wot well for ought I know I closed with Him this way; and my heart condemns me not for the contrary. Oh, good argument indeed! For if ye have not a mind to beguile yourselves, God will not beguile you. And what more have ye to say? Are we parted? Have ye any more to say that ye think will do any good in this case?

8thly, Yes; I have this to say, that from that time forth, I know not how it was, the fear of God fell upon my heart; from that time forth, I have felt it otherways than ever before, and ever since, I have had a respect to all His commandments. Indeed that is a very good argument for a poor man or woman that has not many high school terms. But have ye any more to say to faith, that it may go the better about this business?

9thly, Yes; I have this to say, that in all the business that I

ust and a faithful God, He would not only prevent a poor thing
from beguiling itself, but that He would let me know whether I
was right or wrong. I appealed unto Him and bade Him try me,
and let me know whether I was in the right or wrong way. Well
said; truly there is much good in that argument. I assure you,
there is as much in it as in other two. Light draws still to light
and darkness to darkness. The wicked with their evil deeds draw
still to darkness. Oh but I love this well! It is always promising-
like, when man dare appeal to the God of heaven, that He would
'search and try them, and see if there be any wicked way in them."
There is good hope in that, when folk have cordially and seriously
appealed to God that He would let them know whether they are
right or wrong. Then ye can say this, that ye appealed to God
the Lord and desired Him as He was faithful and just, and delighted not in the death of sinners, not to suffer a poor creature to
deceive itself unwittingly and unwillingly. Have you this to say
further, that the answer that came back from His word to you
came as an answer of peace, at some solemn and supplicating time
when ye have put it upon God to give you a return, you found the
return come from His word though by the mouth of a stranger ye
knew not? But there came an answer of peace to you, and it came
in such a strain and on such a Scripture ground that ye knew well
from whence it came. A good argument indeed! Ye put yourself into the hand of the Lord, and having appealed to Him in the
thing, the answer from Him to you was peace, and ye thought
yourselves more happy than ye were wise. But,

10thly, Have ye any more, for in my mind ye that have that
have more to say? Yes, I have this to say to prove that this
answer took effect on my heart, when it came; I mean, as I said
before, in all this my heart condemns me not. Indeed that is far
said. I marvel, then, if ye have not confidence in God; if it were
not for your ignorance I wot well ye would have it. If it were
not for your ignorance I assure you ye would not be without it.
But indeed ignorance will mar this; for if there be any challenge
or sin in the conscience, it will not be; for there are many folk who
take challenges off the conscience for heart-condemning. But of a
truth I take it not so. But when ye have this to say, "My heart
doth not condemn me"—that is, "I hold not nor allow myself in
any known iniquity, nor do I desire or allow myself to omit or
shift any known duty competent to me in my place and station."
Oh, but that be a strong argument to put in faith's hand! That
is not the question. I may be free of heart-condemning in that case,
for heart-condemning is when my heart condemns me for allowing

hear him. Think ye that the greatest rebel against God at this time will condemn a man upon suspicion that he is a rebel, because he went under the name of a fanatic, while they could not instance wherein he was treasonable, but only because he was called a "Remonstrator." Well, shall I be condemned of my own heart while it cannot instance or inform myself of a particular wherein I am dealing deceitfully before God. This were the greatest ignorance in the world. I would not be condemned of my own heart unless it can instance some particular for which it condemns me, as I said before. Ye ought not to receive from your own heart a sentence of this kind; but when ye know a particular sin ye are given to and ye will not have deliverance from it, or some known duty that ye slight and do not go about it, in that case I am heart-condemned; but I am not so if my heart cannot charge me with a particular that I am guilty of as to any known sin, or slighting known duty. It is a strong argument if ye can truly say ye allow yourself in no known sin, nor shift any known duty.

11th, Have ye any more to say? Ye have said right well since ye began; but have ye any more to say? Yes; I have this to say, that the business I have been speaking of is not a new start got up with me, but I have been labouring on therein this long time. Indeed, that is a very good token too. Ye have not been hypocritical. Job's friend thought very wisely, that a hypocrite will not always call upon God; indeed it is well said, and I would that many had this to say. But,

12th, Can ye say any more? Why, I have this to say, that I have been labouring or drawing at this business a long season—seven years and more—and I dare even say another word too, to conclude all with. Truly I would love you much worse for all you said, if you would not say this; and it is even this, and see if ye can say it: "I dare say that God has determined my heart at this time to join with Him, and to continue on His side, and to win and lose with Christ and His people." Dare ye say that God has at this time, determined thy heart with Moses, to choose affliction with the people of God? Have ye this to say, that ye have looked through all the business with deliberation, and closed with Christ and His cross? Indeed this is a very good closing argument, that these long seven years or more ye have been following religion, and have had these blessed transactions fore-mentioned as signs betwixt God and you; and now ye have even this word to close all with, ye will choose affliction with the people of God. I daresay that there is many a soul of you here that has

make use of at this time to prove that it will be made perfect that concerns your souls. If ye cannot make use of one of these I have told you of, I wot well ye are far in the wrong; for I have told of a considerable number of arguments that the people of God have to make use of, and they are all very significant, full and clear in their exercise. Now judge with your own hearts whether or not ye have done your duty to faith, and have bidden it move and fetch you a good answer from the Lord concerning your souls when ye could not put this into faith's hands. I believe this is a thing ye have been looking to these many years past, what would become of your souls? Now, if ye would have that made perfect which concerns your souls, put these arguments in faith's hand, and see what answer faith will bring you back from the Lord.

Now dare ye hold by them all? Can ye say that God has made you see your lost condition, and has brought it so near your heart that He has made it bitter to you, and made you mourn for it as one mourns for his first-born? Has He emptied you of all hope of helping yourselves, and made you see where suitable help lies, even in the blessed Jesus, whose name was as ointment poured forth unto you? Did He deal with you in such a way that ye ended your course towards Christ, and closed with that help that is in Him and was well content with it and all the inconveniences that follow it? And in all this does not your heart condemn you? From that time forth did the fear of God so fall upon you as made you have a respect to all His commandments? Again, after that time, and in all this business were ye afraid that ye had been deceived? Ye appeal to Him that He would make you know whether ye were in the right or wrong way; and did you get a good answer and a return back from the Lord? Does your heart not condemn you for any known sin you have committed, or any known duty that ye have omitted? Have you been following on these long seven years after religion? and to conclude, Have you now chosen affliction with the people of God, and resolved to win and lose with them, to stay at home or be banished with them, being contented to take your lot with them? If they should never rise again, are you content never to have a joyful day in this world again? Truly there is a good stock of all these, each of them speaking much good, and much more when they are all together. Now, I am sure, if ye have put this furniture in faith's hand, faith will run and bring you a good answer concerning your souls.

The second case I promised to speak to was this: If ye would have faith going to bring some good tidings concerning your being

the other, that if ye would put them in faith's hand that he
should be made perfect as to what concerns your souls. But I
cannot give you such sure grounds for this. But I shall give or
advise you to put arguments in faith's hands, that if it move at
all and bring you a good answer, it will be upon these grounds or
arguments, and I think, faith being your friend, ye may come to
receive that good from God amongst the rest. Then that bodes
good yet; therefore put some good argument in faith's hand, and
see what it can do in order to your being honestly borne through
in this evil time. If it move at all it will be upon arguments.
And as we said of the other, look if ye can say this from the
bottom of your heart.

(1.) And first have you this to say that the Lord has called you
by His name? that is, "I am a professor of godliness; His glory
and my good name are interwoven together." Ye are content to
give out yourself for one of His; and ye cannot, will not, dare
not deny this; though I confess folk should not make too much
noise about this. For it is a great disadvantage to that man that
has had such a name, if he hath not been real, or if he lose his
feet in a day of trial. But it is a great advantage to him and to
others that look on, if he has not been dealing deceitfully with
God, but has been professing God in reality and has had the
inward coming up to his outward profession. Oh, but he has a
great plea in law when he has this to say, "I am one of those who
professed thy name." This was an argument that the servant of
the Lord, David, had. "Put not away thy servant in anger;
thou hast been my help, leave me not, neither forsake me, O God
of my salvation." Wherefore that? why they will say, there is
one who would still be called the servant of God go where he
would; but see how he owns Him now and look and see if thou
wilt have much credit by it; if you are likely to lose a step in
the day of trial when there are so many on-lookers; put in this
word in faith's mouth, His name and your name go together, His
glory and your glory go together; and His credit and honour
will suffer with yours. Make this go, and ye will get the belief
of this; "for to the pure He will show himself pure." He will
deal faithfully when He finds honesty. But,

(2.) In the next place have ye this to say, "I have no confidence in the flesh?" Truly, if ye be not come this length I fear
very much that you give but a foul testimony. But if ye are got
this length ye are far forward. Ye have left Peter a step behind
you already. It is true, indeed, it is very good to resolve well,
"If I should die with thee I will not deny thee;" a good resolu-

irgument, and my mind is, that ye that think so your confidence s upon surer grounds than ye imagine.

(3.) Well, can ye say any more? Have ye this argument also? That ye are losing every weight that presses you downward? Truly ye will sail the better for that if you are going to Barbadoes.* Truly if ye be for this ye must be loosing the ties betwixt wife and children, houses and land, and whatever more re may have, putting your affairs in order. But if you have not these ties loosed, but your heart and eye will be in them (for it is even that which they would have, and if they cannot get a hair in rour neck, as we commonly say, they will even do it for your means), I say if ye loose not yourselves from these, ye will come foul off some way or other; therefore loose yourselves from these things that tie you to them. If you do not I am persuaded there vill be a rack amongst you. Lay aside every weight that presses rou downward. Either you must have that argument to use, that your heart is fully loosed from these things, or ye will get no answer about your being honestly carried through in this evil time. You must loose your hearts from your estates and farms, otherwise, there will be news of it. The house and the land have been long called by one name, and ye are loath that it should go out of that. No, truly, you must loose that weight and let it go. Now have ye that argument to use, that every reight that ye know that presses you downward ye are laying aside and ye are loosing the ties where ye find them fastest? This is a good argument indeed, as good as some two that I know, o that if ye would have faith moving as I said, then ye would

(4.) In the fourth place have this to say, that there is nothing now that ye are afraid of at this day of trial; but what to do and rhat to say ye know not if Christ help you not. This is no bad argument; ye are not vexed what will become of this and the other thing; what will become of wife, children, house, and estate, portion, and all the rest of it. But this is your anxiety: "What rill I do or say, for a subtle enemy will accuse me; and if I, a poor ignorant creature, speak a wrong word they will take occasion from that to reproach religion and the name of God, and much more." If I am even vexed what to do or say, lest His name or religion be injured by me, this is a good argument; and I think ye will get an answer for good with that same argument.

* Here it is to be remarked that in this instance Mr. Guthrie seemed to be a true prophet in regard that several years afterward a number of his hearers were banished to Barbadoes for the cause of Christ, although there was no appearance at this time of their being exposed to such hardships.

take no thought now or what ye shall speak, ... ... ... ...
you in that same hour what ye shall speak." I trow that promise
is made for your mouth; for truly that promise is made for that
party who is careful for nothing, but what to do and what to say
for the glory of God and religion. To such it shall be given in
that hour what they shall do and say lest they should wrong the
glory of God and deny His truth. They are careful for nothing
but that they get not a word to say for the glorious name of Jesus
Christ. They are only careful how to debate the cause for the
glory of God, and how to do answerably to what they say. For
such, says Christ, I pass my royal word upon it that it shall be
given them in that hour what to speak or say. And,

(5.) Then ye would have this argument to make use of, if ye
would have the faith of being honestly carried through in this evil
time, that all the hope and expectation of your soul is only upon
the account of free grace in Christ—not because ye have done
this or that, not because ye have cast away every weight that
presses you downward—I look not to be carried honestly through
because of that, but I look only and solely to free grace in Christ
Jesus.

(6.) And then ye would have this further to say, if ye would
have a good answer from the Lord concerning this, that as far as
ye can ye are dealing faithfully in the little that God is putting
into your hand. That is also a good argument; better than two
friends up at court yonder. It is better than the favour of a
Lord of the Seal up at Edinburgh. It is good to be still faithful
as to anything God hath put into your hand. It is very likely
that when ye are faithful in the little that God has put in your
hand, that God will make you faithful in that which is much also.
But let me tell you, if ye keep to the last with those that still
defer, saying, "We will keep our testimony to the last and great
shock," I fear ye may come foul off; for if ye be not faithful in
little, I am afraid ye will never be faithful in much.

(7.) Have ye any more to say? Can ye make use of this
argument, that as you are able you are helping them that are
foremost in giving a testimony for Christ? Help is good in all
places, and "with what measure ye mete, it shall be meted unto you
again." It is no small matter to have so many thousand honest
folks' prayers to light at your door, so to express it, for your
good every day. This is no small business indeed.

Now, these are the arguments ye are to put into faith's hands.
If ye can make use of them, it is well—though I cannot say these
are infallible grounds for faith to move on, for bringing you a

1. It is a great thing to have it to say, "My name and thy glory are interwoven together."

2. "I have no confidence in my flesh, nor anything that I have received, but only in Christ."

3. "I am loosing all weights that press downward, and letting them go."

4. "The great matter that vexes me is not these things I have let go; but the thing that troubles me is, what to do and what to say."

5. "The hope I have as to the business is, even free grace in Jesus Christ."

6. "As I can, so as I am called, so I resolve to give a testimony even in little things."

7. "As I am able to lend them a lift that are called to give a greater testimony than I am yet called to give."

But I go no further. If ye dwell much upon these things, I am assured that very soon faith will bring you an answer of good from the Lord, that ye shall be honestly carried through in these evil times.

*N.B.*—There is another sermon upon this text, wherein Mr. Guthrie begins upon the third particular here not spoken to, viz., church deliverance.

*"I wait upon the Lord, that hideth his face from the house of Jacob, and I will look for him. Behold, I and the children whom the Lord hath given me are for signs and for wonders in Israel from the Lord of Hosts, which dwelleth in Mount Zion."*—Isaiah viii. 17, 18.

THE prophet, in the former part of this chapter, has been threatening the adversaries of Zion with an overthrow; then he comes to threaten sad judgments on the married bands, which they should not be able to resist or escape; and withal he inhibits the Lord's people from joining with those who decline in an evil time. In order to prevent their destruction, he exhorts them to "sanctify the Lord of hosts, and to make Him only their fear," and to cleave close unto Him, who promises to be a sanctuary unto them; but all that join with decliners in an evil time he threatens with utter destruction. Yet the prophet, thinking these words would not have weight enough, except with a very few, further says, "Bind up the testimony, seal the law among my disciples." Here he hints at the duty of the godly in an evil time, which is to wait on the Lord. While he speaks for himself, he likewise speaks in the name of all the godly. Truly he speaks what will be the case and condition of those who resolve to be waiting, namely, that they shall be for signs and wonders in Israel.

Here he hints not only at the lot of the children of God, begotten by his ministry, who should be made signs and wonders amongst the profane and ungodly, but also those children who, by their abiding faithful, though reduced, should signify good to the Church. Then he warns them against charmers—not to make application to these dead dogs, in seeking the living amongst the dead, but to cleave to the true God, to the law and to the testimony. To encourage them to go to God, and keep them from going to these charmers, he denounces dreadful judgments upon those who make application to them; such as, that they "shall curse their King, and their God, and look upward." They shall receive comfort from none of those whom they have followed. Now in the text there is,

1st, The sad lot of the Church of God held out in these words: "That hideth His face from the house of Israel."

2ndly, Ye have the ordinary lot of the Church of God in that case, that they are made signs and wonders in Israel, to be mocked and gazed at; but there is a mystery in it, in regard that it is

om before Him; until He plead their cause, and execute judgment for them. Many a time it falls out to be the lot of the children of God, that He hides His face from them. "Verily thou art a God that hidest thyself, O God of Israel the Saviour." And this is often the complaint of God's people in Scripture.

Now for clearing of these, I shall speak a little unto these things.

I. What is signified by the Lord's hiding of His face.

II. What are the causes why the Lord does so.

III. I shall speak of the duty of the Lord's people when He thus hides His face from them.

I. Then what is signified by the Lord's hiding of His face? And for answer to this :—

1. By the hiding of His face is meant: The Lord's seeming to and aloof from noticing the cause of His people. Hence the Psalmist complains, "Why standest thou afar off, O Lord, why hidest thou thyself in times of trouble?"

2. By the Lord's hiding of His face is meant, or understood: the refraining of His Spirit on the ordinances, or withholding His influences therefrom, so that the Word of the Lord has not that kindly effect, and operative power upon the heart as it has had formerly. But your hearts are hardened from His fear. Hence the prophet complains, "Why hast thou hardened our hearts from thy fear?" A complaint put in beside these words, and where is the sounding of thy bowels.*

3. By the Lord's hiding of His face must be understood: The Lord's refraining of the Spirit of prayer. "We all do fade as a leaf, and our iniquities like the wind have carried us away." There is none that calleth upon thy name; that stirreth up himself to take hold of thee." We have not an heart to pray; and he gives the reason for it, "Thou hidest thy face from us, and hast consumed us, because of our iniquities."

4. By the Lord's hiding of His face is meant: The Lord's keeping of His mind from His people. The Lord is doing strange things; but His people have no open vision. Hence they complain, We see not our signs; there are no more prophets; neither is there any amongst us that knoweth how long!" Job likewise complains that the Lord passed by on his right and left hand, that he could not perceive Him, or what He was doing. I confess then the Lord wraps up His mind in the public ordinances, it is the saddest of all these ways mentioned of the Lord's hiding of His face from His people.

* See Sermon V. upon this text.

Lord may hide His face from particular persons for the trial of their faith; but He will not readily do it from a whole land, but for the punishment of their sins; and that, because there is no land so clean and upright, but that He may have many things to charge against it. But the reasons I shall specify why it is that the Lord hides His face from His people, are:—

1st, Sin. Sin separates many a time betwixt God and us. Many gross and grievous transgressions have filled this land, and defiled it so that the Lord has no more honour or credit by His people therein.

2ndly, The Lord hides His face in the public ordinances for the deceit of the people in their approaches unto God. There is hypocrisy and deceit in our frequenting of ordinances. Few come with a design or resolution to improve what they hear. "Is the Spirit of the Lord straitened?" Do not my words do good to those that walk uprightly? That is, if ye deal not deceitfully with God; and thence I give this reason as particularly relating to the former cause of the hidings of God's face from His people. But,

III. What is the duty of the Lord's people in that case when He hides His face from them? And,

1. His people should search and try their ways, and turn unto the Lord. This is thought a common truth, yet it is a good old truth. Many look for vain things to be done as their duty; but I will assure you, till the land, especially the godly in it, search and try what is the evil of their own ways and doings, and turn from them, ye need never expect peace from God or that He will be at peace with you again. For this was the way His people took of old, "Let us search and try our ways, and turn again unto the Lord." Therefore acknowledge your sins, and the evil of your own ways, or you shall not soon have a comfortable visit of God again. Yea, and more, if ye do not search and try your ways His vengeance shall be upon these lands.

2. When God hides His face, it is the duty of His people to justify Him in all that He does, and to judge themselves to be guilty. Lay aside then your ornaments, and lie in the dust. It is not a time now to dress up yourselves in a gaudy manner. No, ye should sit in sackcloth if ye would expect manifestations of favour from God. Be humble before Him. Many of you are ready to say, "The king, the nobles, and ministers have all the blame of what is now upon the land." But no man says, What have I done? But till everyone look what himself hath done, I

me of the Lord. You are ready now to make light of this
word. But it shall find you out and witness against you one
y or other yet.

3. When the Lord hides His face, it is the duty of His people
strengthen what remains. Is there anything left! Go, I pray
u, and strengthen that, "and take unto you words, and return
to the Lord." Is there no more left but words, make use of
ese; and speak the oftener to one another.* Is prayer left? I
ay you, ply it well. Can ye pray better with others than by
urself alone? then improve social prayer well. Whatever duty
come best speed in, ye should make it your care to go about
at duty. Whatever remains, ye should strengthen that. It is
e will of God you should do so. If ye do not, ye know what is
reatened. "Be watchful, strengthen that which remains, which
ready to die; for I have not found thy works perfect before
od." And then He threatens to come upon them as a thief
expectedly and suddenly.

4. When the Lord hides His face, it is the duty of all His
ople, who are doing these three things mentioned, to wait on the
ord and expect good from Him, both unto themselves and to the
hurch. "Let Israel wait upon the Lord, from this time forth,
d for ever. Wait upon the Lord, and be of good courage; and
e shall strengthen thine heart; wait, I say, upon the Lord."
eflect again upon the ground of hope ye had long since, and see
hat more grounds ye had then than ye have now. Had ye the
ope of the Lord's work thriving then when it was very low
efore? Then what ground of hope want ye now that ye had
ien? Are armies gone? the spirit of prayer gone? Shall the
ope of Israel depend on these things—on a few men in arms,
nd on the blowing of the spirit? Is this all our hope, that we
ave armies in the field whose rottenness is too visible this day;
r shall the ground of your hope and expectation be founded upon
he breathings of the spirit of prayer, which proceed more from
he prosperity and success of arms than from any other thing?
r did not many of you say, betwixt God and you, after Mr.
Iacdonald's † days, that ye would no more be ashamed of your

---

* I suppose he here means society or fellowship meetings, a duty
istituted in Scripture, and however much neglected and flouted at, yet
ʳas much practised in our land when religion flourished.
† This Macdonald rose with Montrose, and fought with the Covenanters,
nd killed 30,000 of them.

face from His people at this time. There are, no doubt, some who think these are the best days ever they saw. But dreadful is the case of such. "Let not my soul enter into their secret." There are some that say the ark is returned out of the land of the Philistines. I shall say no more for confuting the opinion of such but this: I fear ye shall, ere all be done, miss in that ark these two principal things :—

1. The two tables of the law written by the finger of God Himself. And

2. Aaron's rod blossoming. But when our covenanted God hides His face, then turn unto Him and take with the evil of your ways. Be serious in all the parts of God's worship, and diligent in them all. Wait upon Him and expect good from Him in the use of all these means.

DOCT. I.—*When God hides His face, then faithful ministers and their converts are for signs and wonders in Israel.*

So much says the text, "Behold I and the children which thou hast given me are for signs and wonders." David says, "I am a wonder to many."

Now, in speaking to this doctrine, I shall notice these things—

I. It supposeth that faithful and honest ministers have some children begotten by them in the work of the Gospel.

II. Those children are the gift of God.

III. There is a mutual interest between these two, viz., the minister as the parent, and the converts as the children being converted by his ministry. And,

IV. It is ordinary for faithful men or ministers to be put first upon the brunt of the trial. And,

V. Let the minister and his converts suffer what they will, it is ordinary that they are both one, especially in being made signs and wonders in Israel in an evil time.

1st, For the first of these, it supposeth that faithful ministers have converts; and,

1. For ordinary, when the Lord lights a candle there is a great light; so when the Lord plants an honest and faithful ministry, there is some work there, though they are often but few in number.

2. These converts for ordinary are hid from the minister himself.

---

\* Duke Hamilton went to England with an army to assist Charles I., A.D. 1648.

† By the English I suppose he means the invasion under Oliver Cromwell.

R

and therefore hath little to glory in or boast of, so that people have no ministers to thank for their conversion. And yet it is their duty who are ministers to labour as it were in birth, to see if they can be instrumental in forming Christ in any of those over whom they have the charge and oversight in the ministry.

3rdly, There is a mutual interest between the minister and his converts. And that is,

1. In regard of spiritual things, "They have one Lord, one faith, and one baptism;" and that which edifies the people may be edifying to the minister himself.

2. In regard of sympathy, what troubles the one affects the other also; what makes the one sad makes the other sad also, and when the one rejoices, the other is glad and rejoices also.

3. As to giving and receiving, there is a mutual communication even of things temporal. All things are, as it were, common—if the one have, the other will not be in want.

4thly, It is most ordinary for ministers that are most faithful to be first put upon suffering in an evil time, and the reasons are:—

1. Because they are for ordinary most free in the discharge of their duty in an evil time, a circumstance which lays them open to the malice of the adversary.

2. It then comes to pass that those children begotten by their ministry are discovered, and made appear, who were in some measure latent and obscure before.

3. It is because those that are good have in providence a thorn in the flesh given them, that they should not be exalted above measure. This serves to keep them humble for all that the Lord hath made them forthcoming for to Him. He exposes them to straits and difficulties; and then it were good for all to judge of them as the Lord doth. There is a time when the Lord appears in the Church openly, and shines upon them, and then they are honourable. Again, there is a time when He hides His face from them, and they are troubled and despicable. They are then for signs and for wonders in Israel.

5thly, The last thing in this doctrine is, that ofttimes ministers and their converts share in one and the same lot, especially in being for signs and wonders in Israel. And,

1. They are noticed and taken for strangers and singular persons who are the troublers of Israel.

2. They are signs and wonders in Israel, as they become and are made the common talk or discourse of the country side and the times they live in. And,

4. Again, they are for signs and wonders as to their carriage or deportment. This is a clear proof that may be expected or looked for of the choice that His people make of God for their party in an evil time. Ye should consider—

(1.) That nothing falls out to the people of God but what is according to His determinate purpose. There cannot an hair of their head fall to the ground without His providential hand or disposal, hence it is said of Christ, "Him being delivered by the determinate counsel and foreknowledge of God, ye have taken, and by wicked hands have crucified and slain." No more than this they could do.

(2.) Again, He hath thoughts of peace towards His people, come what will. "I know the thought that I think towards you, saith the Lord, thoughts of peace, and not of evil, to give you an expected end." And seeing that the Lord hath thoughts of peace towards His people, it says that He doth not always afflict them, and therefore they are to search out the causes of their affliction. And,

(3.) Although the thing falls out according to the purpose of God, yet instruments are not the less culpable or guilty, nor shall they escape His judgments for their wickedness in due time. It, however, concerns all the people of God to take Him for their party, and to study to have Him upon their side as their second; for this is the great work the people of God have to do upon such an occasion.

Use 1.—This should quell and compose the hearts of God's people very much, that nothing more nor less can be done or fall out towards them but by His determinate counsel.

Use 2.—Let the faith of this be fixed in your hearts that He hath still thoughts of peace toward you. Let me see the man or woman that hath chosen Him as their God and treasure, even that treasure hid in the field, and hath accounted Him the pearl of great price, valued at the highest rate. Such may wait for peace, according to His word, "He shall sit and rule upon his throne, and the counsel of peace shall be between them both." What two? The offices of Christ as king and priest, that are so fixed, and the peace of His people as settled between them; so that as He can no more remove these two offices of Christ, so neither can the peace or safety of His people be removed, for they are equally fixed and made sure.

Use 3.—Lay aside all passion and rancour, then, at men; go and secure your interest with God in Christ. Get Him on your

in Mount Zion. He hath His abode there. Wherefore ye should remember—

1. That the Lord dwells not in His Church as One who is not affected with her case and condition. No; He is mindful of her concerns, and those who touch His people touch as it were "the apple of his eye," thus He is concerned in whatever, either good or evil, befalls His children and people.

2. As long as God dwells amongst His people, He hath always some work to work amongst them. He is not there without a cause as an indifferent spectator.

3. Although it be true that He is in the Church, yet He is not confined unto any particular Church in the world since the days of Israel. He engaged Himself unto His people of Israel until the Messiah came; and He hath engaged Himself to return again unto them when the fulness of the Gentiles is brought in.

4. Although it be so, that He is not engaged unto any particular Church, yet there are some Churches have more ground to expect His abode with them than what other Churches have. And I take Britain and Ireland to be of that number, for the following reasons:—

(1.) I take Great Britain and Ireland to be a part of the ends of the earth that are given to Christ. "Ask of me, and I will give thee the heathen for thine inheritance, and the utmost parts of the earth for thy possession." Besides it is the very parcel or plot of ground that He intended for that end or use; for the Lord did take possession of these lands beyond any other land since the apostolic age.

(2.) These lands have sworn away themselves unto the Lord most solemnly, singularly, and frequently. Seven times hath Scotland been sworn away unto the Lord, in little more than the space of an hundred years.* I grant indeed, that these covenants

---

* According to Knox, Spotswood, Calderwood, Petrie, Defoe, Stevenson, Crookshanks, and others, what they called the first Covenant was entered into at Edinburgh in December, 1557; the second at Perth, in May, 1559; the third at Edinburgh, 1560. What is called the National Covenant was entered into in 1581 and again subscribed in 1590; again renewed by the Assembly in 1596; and afterwards sworn with great solemnity by all ranks through the land in 1638. The Solemn League and Covenant was sworn in October, 1641. These Covenants were again taken by the king and others in 1650, and were renewed by the handful of witnesses at Lanark, November 20, 1666. What a sad reproach it is to the present generation that they seek to cast off the obligations that our forefathers came under to the Lord! There are many in our day who not only slight and neglect the

party in the land who adhere to these covenants, and have given
a testimony for them, and that party is and will be accounted to
the Lord for a generation, or the holy seed and substance of the
land; since this is the case, God and these witnesses will not part
yet if they shall abide by and adhere to these covenants.

3. A ground of hope that God will not quit His interest in Scotland, England, and Ireland is, that there was no land or nation
wherein the Lord's work was carried to such a pitch, such a high
pitch, as it hath been in them, since the days of the apostles.
And do ye think that the Lord will eradicate and utterly overthrow that work? I think He will not.

The last ground I observe is this, that according to the text
the Lord is in His Church in Britain and Ireland. And it is
good token that He is yet amongst us and that "God will help
her, and that right early."

USE 1.—We are then a people and a part of the Church of God,
seeing there is so much of the true ordinance of God to be yet
found amongst us.

USE 2.—Seeing God is in the Church, He is not far off if ye will
seek Him. Seek Him therefore seriously; for He is most willing
to be found of you.

USE 3.—Although God be not absolutely bound or engaged
to any one particular Church, since the days of Israel of old, yet
from the foresaid grounds we are not left without hope that the
Lord will yet dwell amongst us, "and the God of Jacob will be
our refuge, Selah."

DOCT. IV.—*That when a people are shaken out of all self-
confidence it is their duty then to wait upon God.*

We are to do so

1. Because we are commanded. "Wait on the Lord" is often
commanded in Scripture.

2. We should wait on the Lord because of the promise that is
annexed unto this exercise. "Those that wait upon the Lord
shall never be ashamed."

3. To wait upon the Lord is the most quiescent and composed
posture one can possibly be in. In an evil time "it is good to
hope, and quietly wait for the salvation of the Lord."

4. Wait upon the Lord, for it hath been the work and practice

duty of covenanting, but deny the warrantableness of it, though we have
manifold Scripture examples of covenanting (Josh. xxiv. 25, Nehem. ix. 38,
2 Cor. viii. 5). We have prophecies of it, as what would take place in New
Testament days (Isa. xix. 18, 20). We have precious promises of it (Isa.
xliv. 5). We have precepts for it (Psa. lxxvi. 11, Mat. v. 33).

our God, we have waited for him, we will rejoice in him."

But that you may the better know, when it is your duty to wait upon the Lord, I shall in the next place, show you, (1.) What proceeds, or goes before waiting upon the Lord. (2.) What it is to wait, or what this waiting doth import. And (3.) What follows upon a right waiting upon the Lord. And,

1. The thing that goes before waiting upon the Lord, is,

(1.) The duty itself is fully holden forth in this chapter. "Say not a confederacy with them to whom this people shall say a confederacy;" that is, Let not their words make you afraid. "But only sanctify the Lord in your hearts;" that is, be only afraid of offending Him.

(2.) Consider that there is a promise held out to those who make Him their fear, "He shall be for a sanctuary unto them."

(3.) There is a threatening pronounced against the common multitude who decline and join with the times. "He will be for a stone of stumbling unto them." It is but a promise held out to those who walk aright; while it is a threatening against those who go wrong and comply in an evil time. And then there follows a wrapping up of the law and ordinances amongst the disciples or people of God, for a time.

2. There is the duty of waiting, which imports,

(1.) The termination of the heart, with an expectation fixed only upon God for help, and upon none else. "My soul, wait thou only upon God: for my expectation is from him." That is, Wait upon God, and upon no other. Similar is that word, "Help us, Lord, for vain is the help of man."

(2.) To wait upon God imports this also, that their expectation is more on God Himself than on any created means. God can give you means; but if you get not Himself no matter what ye get. He may send back your means for a plague unto you and not for your good; therefore plead with Him, and be positive with Him, and say, "Go with us, Lord, or else carry us not up hence." So I say, ye should plead more for God's presence than any other means under heaven.

(3.) To wait on God imports a submitting to the seasons of the outgate from your present condition, and the ordering of it and all that concerns you, while under the trial.

(4.) To wait upon God imports a resolution to abide at the duty of waiting, until He show you what else ye should do. For waiting on God is still your duty while ye are in the dark, and can use no other means for your relief.

3. These things follow after waiting, and are clear from the text.

(2.) A great many temptations follow a waiting upon God.

(3.) There will be few left to preach the gospel or to consult with in that dark time. He says, "Go to the law, and to the testimony." Ye must then make use of your Bibles instead of your ministers. But,

(4.) The manifest vengeance of God shall be upon those who turn aside. That shall be their lot who oppose the work and people of God.

Use 1.—Have ye your work and duty in a dark time? Then go to God and do not pretend ignorance, and say, "What shall we do?" I say, "Wait upon the Lord," and judge yourselves happy, that the thing which is your duty men cannot take from you though they may take your life from you.

Use 2.—Lay your account with temptation, under that lot to cause you to turn aside. Therefore study to be clear in your judgments, as to the honesty and justness of the cause, and for that end be well acquainted with the Scripture, and there see what is your duty.

And to conclude, believe this, that God's wrath abides on those that turn aside from Him; and all which they before took pleasure in shall forsake them, or shall be embittered to them in that day, when the waiters shall enjoy what they waited for.